Dedicated to
Homer Ainsworth, Joe Albritton, and Waller King

Three young men went to Korea
Two came home
One survived

CONTENTS

MILITARY UNITS

corps—two or more divisions totaling 30,000 men

division—up to 15,000 men (often only 12,000 in Korea)

brigade—a unit larger than a regiment that includes support battalions, tanks, artillery, etc.

regiment—three battalions led by a colonel and totaling up to 4,000 men

battalion—four companies led by a lieutenant colonel and totaling between 700 and 800 men

company—four platoons led by a captain and totaling between 175 and 240 men

platoon—45 or more men led by a lieutenant

squad—10 or more men led by a staff sergeant

UNITED NATIONS SUPPORT IN KOREA

Australia—2 infantry battalions, naval forces, 1 fighter squadron
Belgium—1 infantry battalion
Canada—1 infantry brigade, naval forces, 1 squadron of transport aircraft
Colombia—1 infantry battalion, 1 naval frigate
Ethiopia—1 infantry battalion
France—1 infantry battalion
Great Britain—2 infantry brigades, 1 armored regiment, 1½ artillery regiments, 1½ combat engineer regiments, the Far Eastern fleet, two squadrons of carrier-based aircraft
Greece—1 infantry battalion, transport aircraft
Luxembourg—1 infantry company
The Netherlands—1 infantry battalion, naval forces
New Zealand—1 artillery regiment
The Philippines—1 infantry battalion, 1 company of tanks
South Africa—1 fighter squadron
Thailand—1 infantry battalion, naval forces, air and naval transports
Turkey—1 infantry brigade
Denmark, India, Italy, Norway, Sweden—medical aid

LIST OF MAPS

FALLEN COMRADE

INTRODUCTION

There is an old military dictum that a war is not over until the last veteran has died. The Korean War is a distant memory, starting more than seventy years ago in an obscure country on the other side of the world. There are veterans of that war still alive who have stories to tell. *Fallen Comrade* is one such story of three Marine reservists who were called to active duty.

Korea was the first hot spot in the Cold War between the United States and the Soviet Union. In contrast to World War II, a global conflict, the Korean War was fought on a small peninsula, about 300 miles in length and 150 miles at its widest.

Historians have grappled with the question of why a war occurred in Korea. Interpretations range from regional warfare—the Soviet Union encouraging the North Koreans to attack the South, hoping the United States would intervene and find itself in a land war with China—to civil war between North and South Korea after the South's suppression of the guerrilla war waged by the North. North Koreans called the conflict the Fatherland Liberation War.

Korea was not a conventional military conflict, fought between professional armies in large-scale battles. It was a hybrid struggle combining massive firepower with guerrilla warfare. The specter of the atomic bomb loomed over the armies fighting on the peninsula, but the United States wisely refrained from using that weapon. The war didn't end properly. It simply stopped.

Korea has been called a happenstance war. Chance circumstances led the Soviet Union to encourage and support North Korea to attack the

South. The US decision to intervene was a reversal of President Harry S. Truman's policy excluding Korea from the US defensive perimeter in Asia. The president wanted UN support in defending South Korea, and because the Soviet Union was boycotting the UN Security Council over its refusal to seat Communist China, Truman gained UN assistance. A series of unexpected circumstances culminated in war.

Americans supported the Korean War in the early months but wavered when casualties began to mount. When General of the Army Omar Bradley used the phrase "the wrong war, at the wrong place, at the wrong time, and with the wrong enemy," Americans believed that his words applied to Korea, not to Bradley's true subject—China. Bradley thus summed up American perception of the Korean War: it should never have happened and was best forgotten.

Korea was the first limited US war, fought to protect US interests without upsetting the international order. Korea was ill-suited for the type of war it turned out to be. It was difficult to fight a war without trying to win it in the traditional sense of the word.

Korea has also been called America's "forgotten war." Just five years after the end of World War II, the Korean conflict interrupted the postwar peace. The war was never popular with the American people, and with the Vietnam War and its social and political conflicts in the next decade, the war in Korea was forgotten.

Korea was an infantry war. Airplanes and helicopters flew, tanks and artillery tore up the landscape, and naval vessels fired on targets from offshore, but the war's burden rested disproportionately on the back and feet of the foot soldier. On both sides, infantrymen carried the battle, living in the dirt and fighting with rifles, hand grenades, mortars, machine guns, and in some cases fists and shovels.

Korea was another playing field for the military rivalry between the US Army and the Marine Corps, a contest that started during World War I and continued unabated in the Pacific theater during World War II. Army leaders tried unsuccessfully to reduce the Marines to a ceremonial role during the US military reorganization after 1945. When war broke out in Korea, the Marines were initially denied a role. But General Douglas MacArthur, commander of allied forces in Korea, saw a need for the Marines.

Army generals commanded the Marines in Korea, making all high-level strategic and tactical decisions. Marine generals had a voice in shaping operations only at the division level. Conflicts between Army and Marine generals were many, with Marine leaders often ignoring or circumventing orders from their Army counterparts. This book attempts to present an accurate picture of all military forces in the Korean War, but the Marines are discussed in greater detail because the volume tells the story of three young men from Clinton, Mississippi, who served with the Marines. Modern names of countries are used when appropriate, but old-style spellings of Korean place-names have been retained.

More than 1,000,000 Americans—among them several thousand Mississippians—served in the war, with 92,134 wounded and 8,176 reported missing. A total of 36,940 Americans died on Korean soil, a number that included 376 from Mississippi, 23 from Hinds County, and 1 from the town of Clinton.

When the war ended in 1953, America wanted to forget the terrible ordeal. Some states and communities raised memorials to honor those who served, but no national monument to the Korean War was erected until 1995.

On Veterans' Day 2012, the people of Clinton, Mississippi, dedicated a monument honoring all of the town's war veterans from the war against Mexico in 1845 to military action in Afghanistan and Iraq in the early twenty-first century. The monument, *Fallen Comrade*, depicts a Marine carrying the body of his friend from a Korean War battlefield. This volume tells the story of those two young men from Clinton as well as a third.

Chapter 1

THE BACKSTORY

There was something in the very atmosphere of a small town in the
Deep South, something spooked-up and romantic, which did extravagant
things to the imagination of its bright and resourceful boys.
—**Willie Morris,** *North toward Home*

Among young boys, there always is the question of who you were named
for. George Waller King was named for his grandfather George Riley.
Waller was his grandmother's maiden name. Joe Burson Albritton was
just Joe, and his middle name was his mother's maiden name. Homer Roy
Ainsworth was named for his father.

Waller, Joe, and Homer were childhood friends in the small Mississippi town of Clinton. Born during the Great Depression, they came of
age after World War II and wondered if they would ever be called on to
fight for their country. Like many of their generation, they knew that
there was something going on called the Cold War and that the Soviet
Union was the enemy.

The Clinton of their childhood was the quintessential small Mississippi
town—population 916 according to the 1940 census, an increase of 4 from
the 1930 tally. In 1945, the town marshal estimated that 1,500 people were
living in Clinton, including 125 Blacks. Like virtually all southern towns,
Clinton was rigidly segregated.[1]

Though small, Clinton was no hick town. It had Mississippi College,
which dominated the town's religious, cultural, social, and political life.

The mayor, a chemistry professor first elected in 1931, had run unopposed since 1937. Professors dominated the five-member board of aldermen. They kept taxes low and voters satisfied. The mayor and aldermen believed that children should work during the summer months, so the town offered no recreational programs.

Mississippi College shared its facilities with the townspeople, offering what little summer activity was available. The college had a nine-hole golf course, tennis courts, and an indoor swimming pool as well as twenty-acre Lake Wilson for fishing and swimming. Clinton High School's team played on the college football field. As long as parents didn't expect too much, college facilities sufficed. Town and gown seemed to live together comfortably.

Waller King's family had deep roots in Clinton. His maternal grandfather was a Baptist preacher who had served as president of two small Baptist colleges in Kentucky before moving to Clinton around the turn of the century. Waller's grandmother, Lily Waller Riley, served as principal of the preparatory school at Hillman College, the Baptist female school in Clinton. His aunt, Susan Riley, taught at Hillman. The King family had been traveling west in a covered wagon in the late nineteenth century, when one of their oxen died and they stopped in Mississippi's Itawamba County, bought some land, and began farming. Waller's father, John, became an accomplished baseball player and was skilled at removing stumps from fields.

John King came to Clinton to play baseball at Mississippi College in 1915. He was put to work clearing trees and stumps on college property, and his size drew the attention of Dana Bible, the college football coach. After persuading King to play football, Bible saw the newcomer in uniform and called out to the trainer, "Get that baby bigger pants!" King was "Baby John" thereafter, and became a local football and baseball legend.

After the United States entered World War I, the Mississippi College president invited the National Guard to establish a military company on campus. Organized in 1917, an artillery battery trained on the college's farm. John King enlisted and went to France when the battery was activated the following year. He had the rank of lieutenant when he returned to Clinton in 1919.

Baby John King subsequently married Mary Belle Riley, a Clinton girl, and they moved to Brookhaven, where John became the high school football coach and later the namesake of the football stadium. The Kings had two sons born in Brookhaven: John Jr. and George Waller. In 1938 King took a job with the American Red Cross in Jackson, and the family moved to Clinton. During World War II, he served the Red Cross as a field director in the North Africa, Italy, and China-Burma-India theaters.

Joe Albritton's family also had strong ties to the college. His father, Jackson native Baylus Richard Albritton, enrolled at the college in 1917 and joined the artillery battery when it was organized. He too went to France in 1918 and later returned to Clinton and the college to complete his studies. Dick met and married Martha Burson, a Hillman College graduate from Calhoun City, and went into the banking business. The Albrittons moved to Clarksdale, where their sons Baylus Richard Jr. and Joe Burson were born. Dick Albritton accepted the position of bursar at Mississippi College in 1932 and moved his family to Clinton.

Homer Ainsworth's parents had no ties to the college. His father, also named Homer, was a mechanic who did some preaching on the side. Rev. Ainsworth and his wife, Mary Lee Tullos Ainsworth, lived in Magee when their son was born. Two daughters came later. The family moved to Clinton sometime during the 1930s, and the senior Ainsworth took a job at a service station on College Street, living with his family in a rented house behind a café. Rev. Ainsworth considered studying at the college but never enrolled. He supplied pulpits when called and preached an occasional revival. Ainsworth coached football part-time at the high school during World War II.

The King and Albritton families were considered middle class by educational and economic standards of that time, while the Ainsworths were working class. These distinctions meant nothing to the friendship of Waller, Joe, and Homer. They lived in the same neighborhood and attended Clinton's schools and the Baptist church together. In 1940, when Homer and Joe were in the third grade and Waller in the second, they saw a harbinger of the future when a convoy of Mississippi National Guard jeeps, trucks, and carriers passed through Clinton along College Street (Highway 80) over four days on its way to Louisiana maneuvers that constituted the largest peacetime military operation in the country's history.[2]

After the Japanese attack on Pearl Harbor in December 1941, Waller, Joe, and Homer experienced the war like other Mississippi youth. They relived battles at movie theaters in Jackson, watching Movietone newsreels of airplanes spiraling down to earth, Marines raising their rifles above the surf as they waded ashore, and artillery weapons firing at distant enemies. The boys saw misery and death on the movie screen and were curious and disturbed, like all boys that age. John Wayne was their favorite actor.

War came closer to home in 1943 when the government built Camp Clinton, a German prisoner-of-war camp south of town, and Mississippi College gained a Navy V-12 program. Dutch and American pilots training at an Army Air Corps airfield in nearby Jackson, completed the military presence. Pilots filled the skies with their acrobatics and daredevil flying, enlivening the imaginations of the boys in their own dogfights against German Messerschmitt and Japanese Zero fighters.

The Navy V-12 program brought midshipmen to the campus and forced the college to loosen some of its Baptist mores. Navy personnel held dances in Jennings Hall and published a weekly newsletter, *The Watch*, that featured a column written by Hillman female students. The V-12 program brought needed money to the college, so the president overlooked the violations of Baptist teachings.

The Sharps were one of the families that moved to the area to work at Camp Clinton during the war. They lived in a garage apartment on Capital Street, about halfway between Homer and Waller's houses. The father was a guard at Camp Clinton and worked at Ratliff Motors as a mechanic after the war. The family included two sons, George, who was several years ahead of Joe and Homer in school, and Joe, who was in Waller's class.

Clinton residents were plagued by constant rumors of escapees from the POW camp. In 1944, when German POWs were reported to have climbed the town water tank one night and poisoned the water supply, the town marshal climbed the tank, inspected the seals, and assured onlookers everything was secure. Townsfolk later said that two Clinton boys had actually climbed the tower, and many locals suspected that Joe Albritton had been one of the miscreants—he had been known to climb the tank many times as a teenager.

When they were old enough, Homer, Joe, and Waller joined the Baptist church's Boy Scout Troop 12. Joe quickly lost interest and dropped out, but Waller advanced to the rank of first class. Scouting also appealed to Homer, who remained active through his senior year in high school when he received the Eagle badge.

When the war ended in the summer of 1945, Waller, Joe, and Homer's world changed. They were teenagers now, about to start high school.

Homer, the preacher's son, was quiet, serious, a follower of rules. During the summers, he worked as a youth counselor at Camp Garaywa south of town and gave swimming lessons at the college pool. Friends described Waller as bright and well-behaved, a good athlete. Joe was different. He was fearless in everything he did, always courting danger. One friend later recalled that "Joe lived in a state of anarchy." He was the leader of the trio.

What is known about Waller, Joe, and Homer's early years comes from the memories of their friends and family. Though they may not constitute the most reliable sources, these memories have preserved what might otherwise have been lost.

Waller, Joe, and Homer became fixated on automobiles when they reached driving age. George Sharp owned a 1926 Packard roadster with three rows of seats and a cigarette lighter attached to a cable that could reach the back seats, a feature that amazed Waller, Joe, and Homer. Sharp worked with his father at Ratliff Motors in town and gave the neighborhood boys rides in his car, increasing their interest.

By this time, Joe was becoming more adventurous, and his adventures were a problem to his parents. Hoping to keep Joe occupied and out of trouble, Dick Albritton purchased a surplus B-26 bomber engine and set it up in his garage/barn. Joe and his friends spent hours on that engine, breaking it down and putting it back together. Getting the engine to start was another matter. Working alone late one night, Joe started the engine. The roar woke up half the town. Joe became skilled with motors and in short time could hot-wire his parents' car.[3]

Waller, Joe, and Homer had other friends, but the three were almost inseparable. They had cousins in distant towns, but none in Clinton with lives to share and stories to tell. This probably drew them closer together. Joe had cousins living in Calhoun City, his mother's hometown, and traveled there for Burson family reunions a couple of times each year. Joe's cousin, Henry Lackey, remembered Joe's escapades.

On one occasion, Joe's older brother, Dick Jr., drove the family car to his future wife's home on a date. He parked the car and went inside. When the couple came out, the car was gone, replaced by Joe's bicycle. Joe also took flying lessons without his parents' knowledge, buzzing their home several times and did a touch-and-go on the roof of the college girls' dormitory that became legendary in Clinton.

Lackey, four years younger than Joe, saw him as the leader among his cousins in Calhoun City and his friends in Clinton. Recalled Lackey, "I don't think Joe understood the word or emotion of fear." Joe was a mechanical genius, "always tinkering with some type of motor or vehicle. Joe wasn't a mean person. He was just mischievous and cunning."[4]

Other friends remembered Joe's driving, particularly the speed with which he drove his parents' 1938 Plymouth. According to Tom McMahon, Joe hit the railroad tracks on Monroe Street and became airborne, scattering gravel when he landed. After one ride with Joe, Waller swore never again to get into a car with Joe at the wheel. Betty Jo Connolly made Joe let her out of his car near the Camp Clinton grounds and walked the two miles back to town. His friends wondered how Joe survived his teen years.[5]

Connolly and Bettye Shores lived in the neighborhood and were in the same grade as Homer and Joe, and the four kids often walked to school together, with Homer's mother offering them encouraging talks before they left on the final leg of their journey. Joe's German shepherd would escort the children to school, wait on the school grounds while the children were in class, and then walk the children home. Waller King remembered wrestling playfully with Joe's dog. Connolly equaled the boys in strength and daring during their childhood years. Shores "was sweet" on Joe during their childhood years.[6]

The lineup of boys and girls in the neighborhood changed in 1947 when Plautus Iberius Lipsey Jr.; his wife, Sue; and their three daughters returned to Clinton, adding spice to the small town. P. I. Lipsey had grown up in Clinton, graduated from Mississippi College, and served in World War I, before embarking on a career as a journalist with the Associated Press, serving as bureau chief in London and Geneva, where he covered the League of Nations during the interwar years. Sue Lipsey, a former Hillman College professor, accepted a position in the English department at Mississippi College.[7]

The chamber of commerce asked Lipsey to start a weekly newspaper, something Clinton had not had since 1918. Lipsey's *Clinton Parade* featured international news and stories on world leaders and the new atomic age. His daughters Jeannie and Ann wrote local stories. After two years the *Parade* gave way to the *Clinton News*, which focused on civic and garden club happenings, birthday parties, and a popular column, "Bea's Buzzzz," written by Bea Quisenberry. A transplant from Memphis,

Quisenberry had moved to Clinton, hometown of her husband, William Young Quisenberry Jr., in 1940. Bea's father-in-law, William Young Quisenberry Sr., was a Baptist missionary who used Clinton as his home base. Rosa Quisenberry, Bea's mother-in-law, was the longtime librarian at the college. Bea's column kept readers informed about visitors to town, locals' illnesses, and even who had gone fishing and where. Bea's column was popular among the *News* readers, who had little interest in stories about the wider world.

After the *Clinton Parade*'s demise, P. I. Lipsey joined his wife on the college faculty. Their middle daughter, Ann, was friends with Betty Jo Connolly and Bettye Shores. Ann was a year older than Joe and Homer and two years older than Waller. She had no interest in the boys, and they kept their distance.

While in his teens, Joe developed an interest in photography and bought a 35mm camera. He also took a part-time job operating the projector at the Hilltop Theater, about half a block from his home. Joe would open the theater early on Saturday mornings and let his friends in to watch movies with the sound turned down.[8]

Joe played quarterback (at the time a blocking back position) on the high school football team, becoming a three-year letterman. Despite his short stature, slight build (he never weighed more than 130 pounds), and on-field aggression, he never suffered a serious injury.

In 1947–48, Joe was elected vice president of the junior class. Class president Elwood Ratliff shared a special bond with Joe: both had been born on May 4, 1932. Ratliff lived in the Tinnin community north of Clinton and had attended school with Joe since first grade. Dick Albritton took the birthday boys to lunch at a Jackson restaurant each year. Like Joe's other friends, Ratliff marveled at Joe's dangerous behavior and his uncanny ability to escape harm and punishment.[9]

Homer Ainsworth had fallen back a year in school for health reasons but rejoined Joe for their senior year. The 1948–49 Clinton High School yearbook, *The Arrow*, said Homer was "known to all for his pleasant disposition." Homer did not play sports but was active in the Future Farmers of America. Joe Albritton, by contrast, was "a fellow you can't fail to notice. He played first string quarterback on the football team and is sergeant-at-arms of the 'C' Club. He is also credited with plenty of ability to repair cars." Given Joe's reputation, some may have been amused that he was selected to keep order at club meetings. One photo montage showed Joe with a camera in hand. The yearbook also had a photograph of Peggy Cain, a sophomore who lived in the Clinton Boulevard zone between Clinton and Jackson. A popular student known as a school "beauty," she and Joe had a secret courtship going by the time of Joe's graduation.

The family of another of Joe and Homer's classmates, Bobby Hannah, also included a foster child, Ralph Marston, who graduated in 1948 and was a good friend of Homer's. Marston was popular, played football and basketball, and drove a school bus to earn extra money. He enlisted in the Air Force after high school.

Joe Albritton, Bobby Hannah, Betty Jo Connolly, Bettye Shores, and eleven of their Clinton High classmates enrolled at Mississippi College in the fall of 1949. Homer Ainsworth went to Hinds Junior College in Raymond. Elwood Ratliff chose Mississippi State College. Waller King's older brother, John Jr., was a sophomore at Mississippi College, while Joe's older brother, Dick Albritton Jr., graduated from the school that spring and began teaching at Gulf Coast Military Academy outside Gulfport. Peggy Cain started her junior year and Waller King his senior year at Clinton High.

The preceding summer, Bill Smith, a 1946 Clinton High graduate, had asked Betty Jo Connolly to marry him. She said yes, and they planned a November wedding. Waller King's mother, Mary, hosted the bridal shower. Bill had attended Mississippi College for three years before dropping out to work at a Jackson clothing store. He and George Sharp had also joined the Marine Corps Reserve unit in Jackson, which paid $21.50 for one weekend drill a month—good money for young men.

Waller joined the same Marine Reserve unit in March 1949, during his junior year of high school. Joe and Homer followed six months later. All three were attracted by the pay and shared the belief that the Marine Corps was the elite among the country's military.[10]

Waller had a great senior year. According to the *Arrow*, "He has captured quite a few honors this year. He was voted 'Most Intelligent,' 'Most Likely to Succeed,' and president of the Key Club." Waller was a member of the Beta Club, Hi-Y and the 'C' Club. As captain of the football team, he "provided that spark that set the Arrows flying. We are looking toward him to go to glory in college."

Waller had signed to play football at the University of Mississippi, planning to study geology. But after visiting the campus and learning that the school had only one geology professor, Waller changed his mind and decided to enroll at Louisiana State University, which had a much larger geology department. When the Ole Miss football coach, Johnny Vaught, refused to release Waller from his commitment and the Southeastern Conference denied his appeal, Waller saw little choice but to stick with his original plan.

The Marine Corps also had plans in the early summer of 1950. Smith and Sharp were sent to Camp Pendleton, California, for training. Joe, Homer, and Waller were slated for two weeks of training at Marine Base Quantico in Virginia. Before his departure, Joe served as a groomsman in his brother's wedding.

The training at Quantico featured drills, time on the rifle range, and intense physical training. During their free weekend, Waller and Homer hitchhiked to New York City, arriving just before dawn on Saturday with each man carrying four dollars in his wallet. They spent the day sightseeing, taking advantage of the courtesy accorded to those in uniform. They were admitted free at the Empire State Building, and a woman and her daughter invited them to a Broadway musical. Just over twenty-four hours after their arrival, Waller and Homer began hitchhiking back to Quantico.[11]

Returning to Clinton, the five Marine reservists expected to pick up where they had left off. Homer would return to Hinds Junior College. Joe was uncertain about a second year at Mississippi College as his romance with Peggy Cain intensified. Waller had reconciled himself to playing football at Ole Miss. Bill Smith would return to his sales job and his pregnant wife. George Sharp would go back to work at Ratliff Motors.

And then North Korea invaded South Korea on June 25, 1950.

Battles on the Potomac

The Marine Corps that Joe, Homer, Waller, Bill Smith, and George Sharp joined as reservists was fighting for its survival after World War II. The Corps had played a glorious role during the war, particularly in the Pacific theater. At the end of the conflict, the Marines numbered more than 474,000 men and women, and two divisions were sent to China to disarm Japanese forces. By the summer of 1946, the number of Marines on active duty had dropped to 155,000, and leadership planned to stabilize the Corps at 108,000 men and women.

Army and Air Force leaders had other ideas. They wanted to scrap the Corps or at least minimize its role in America's military. George Marshall, Dwight Eisenhower, Omar Bradley, and the Air Force's Carl Spaatz—the generals who had won the war in Europe—knew that in the postwar era, the size of the US military had to be reduced, and they were determined to protect their share of military appropriations. They unanimously believed that any reduction in funding should come first at the expense of the Marines.

Bradley and Eisenhower favored reducing the Corps to a ceremonial naval guard force. Bradley believed the atomic bomb had rendered amphibious landings obsolete. Eisenhower's opposition to the Corps was personal. He had resented the Marines ever since they claimed credit for the Allied victory at Belleau Wood in World War I, credit that Ike thought the Army had earned. Eisenhower saw the Marines as a rival second land army and proposed limiting them to the operation of landing craft to bridge "the gap between the sailor on the ship and the soldier on land."[12]

General Spaatz viewed the Marines as intruding into the roles of the Army and Air Force and recommended that the "Marine Corps be limited to small, readily available and lightly armed units no larger than a regiment." Spaatz wanted Marine aircraft. Even President Harry S. Truman, who had served as an Army artillery officer during World War I, had no love for the Marines. He saw the Corps as a duplication—the Navy's "own little Army that talks Navy and is known as the Marine Corps."[13]

Douglas MacArthur was the one general who believed in the worth of the Marines. He had relied on Marine amphibious landings during his World War II island hopping in the Pacific theater and recognized the Marines' unique combat training and performance. MacArthur, however, was in Japan, directing the American occupation and thus avoided the political scramble over military appropriations in Washington, DC.

Army and Air Force opposition to the Corps was formalized in a series of top secret documents written in 1946. The Marine Corps commandant, General Alexander Vandergrift, reviewed the papers and submitted a thirty-four-page response addressing every criticism made by the Army and Air Force. He explained that without the Marines' experience in amphibious warfare, the United States would not have been able to prosecute the Pacific war. Vandergrift reminded the generals that the Army Command and General Staff School committed just 17 hours to amphibious operations, while the Marine Corps devoted 635 hours to the subject.[14]

Marine Corps leaders readily acknowledged that the nuclear age created new problems for amphibious warfare. The landings of World War II required massive concentrations of amphibious and fire-support ships close to the target, making them vulnerable to an atomic attack. To avoid this danger, Marine planners began developing a strategy of dispersion of assault forces. The Marines would use transport helicopters, ferrying troops from distant small-deck carriers. They did not have one helicopter in 1946, but by 1949 the new "vertical assault" concept had become a reality.[15]

In 1946 the US Congress started reorganizing the military services into the new Department of Defense. The Joint Chiefs of Staff (Army, Navy, and Air Force) recommended that the Marine Corps be reduced to one regimental combat team without an air component and with a maximum strength of 60,000 men. Admiral Chester Nimitz, naval chief of staff, opposed the recommendation because it would "eliminate the Marine Corps as an effective combat force." The recommendation became part of Congress's military organization bill. Marine Corps leaders lobbied against the bill, and it was defeated. President Truman expressed his dissatisfaction with the military lobbying against his legislation and told the Marine Corps commandant to "get those lieutenant colonels off the Hill and keep them off."[16]

Truman had a similar bill introduced in 1947 and prohibited Marine Corps officers from testifying against the measure. Corps leaders nevertheless turned to their powerful public relations machinery and defeated the second bill. Truman was furious but compromised by submitting a third reorganization bill that defined the Marine Corps as a separate service within the Navy Department with "the primary responsibility of developing amphibious doctrine and equipment" and the primary mission of "providing fleet marine forces of combined arms, together with supporting arms components, for service with the fleet . . . for the conduct of land operations essential to a naval campaign." This passed as part of the National Security Act of 1947.

The new law represented a victory for Vandergrift, who retired near the end of the year. His successor, General Clifton B. Cates, faced new challenges as Army and Air Force leaders renewed their campaign to render amphibious assaults obsolete, focusing again on the enemy's ability to vaporize attackers in their transports before they could reach the beaches. These officials seemed uninterested in or ignorant about the vertical assault concept and the Marine Corps helicopter program.

Military budget cuts reduced the size of the US Army, which had a little more than one division within the United States and undermanned occupation garrisons in Europe and Japan. In Japan the four divisions were at about 60 percent strength. The small army forced the Joint Chiefs of Staff (JCS) to change their thinking in terms of total war. Their solution was "massive retaliation." Complete reliance on one branch of the military was more economical, and the Army still insisted that the Marines had to go.

Tensions between the services had abated somewhat in 1948 when President Truman issued Executive Order 9981 abolishing racial segregation throughout the military. The Marine Corps had about 1,500 African Americans on active duty, serving in all-Black companies or performing stewards' duties. The Corps complied with the president's order, though the Army delayed any response.[17] In 1950, Black soldiers made up about 12 percent of the Army, and the 24th Infantry Regiment, a part of the 8th Army in Japan, had only African American soldiers.

The battle against the Marine Corps started up again in 1949 when President Truman appointed Louis A. Johnson to replace General Bradley as secretary of defense. An Army veteran of World War I, Johnson shared the president's biases against Marines. At the Pentagon, Johnson focused on "economy," a convenient way to bring the Navy and Marine Corps to heel.

Johnson told Admiral Richard Connally, Navy chief of staff that "the Navy is on its way out. There is no reason for having a Navy and a Marine Corps. General Bradley tells me amphibious operations are a thing of the past. That does away with the Marine Corps. And the Air Force can do anything the Navy can do, so that does away with the Navy." Testifying before the US House Armed Services Committee in October 1949, Bradley declared, "I am wondering whether we shall ever have another large-scale amphibious operation. Frankly, the atomic bomb, properly delivered, almost precludes such a possibility."[18]

Johnson sought to curb the Navy and Marine Corps through administrative and fiscal actions. The 1950 military budget required the Marine Corps to reduce its eleven infantry battalions and twenty-three aircraft squadrons to eight understrength battalions and twelve aircraft squadrons.

For fiscal 1951, the number of battalions would be reduced to six. In an off-the-record speech, Johnson said that he was going to do away with Marine aviation and transfer what remained to the Air Force and Army. Congressman Carl Vinson, chair of the House Armed Services Committee, learned of Johnson's comments and forced him to back off on his aviation threats.[19]

Johnson then resorted to pettiness. He removed Cates from the list of generals who had chauffeurs and limousines and from the list of military leaders accorded special gun salutes on ceremonial occasions. Johnson also attempted to forbid celebration of the Marine Corps birthday on November 10, though he ultimately lacked the authority to do so.[20]

By 1950, the Marine Corps's expeditionary element had dwindled to 27,656 men, a 90 percent reduction from its 300,000 wartime personnel. The 1st Marine Division dropped from 22,000 to 8,000; the 1st Marine Air Wing declined from 12,000 to 3,700; the 2nd Division at Camp Lejeune, North Carolina, had 9,000 men in 1950. The total number of Marines was reduced from 474,680 in 1945 to 93,053 in 1947 to 74,279 in 1950.[21]

General Cates protested each reduction, warning that the Marine Corps could not fulfill its mission if further cuts were made. Committed to maintaining the Corps as a force in readiness for any future wars, Cates's only recourse was to rely on the Marine Corps Reserves, which meant that the Corps could not respond immediately to any conflict.

Cates had strong support from members of Congress and the media. Pro-Marine organizations like the American Legion, the Marine Corps League, and the National Rifle Association opposed Johnson's assaults on the Marines' budget. The Corps had historically cooperated with Hollywood in making war movies, and in 1950, *Flying Leathernecks*, featuring America's favorite Marine, John Wayne, was in production. Marine leaders intended to use the movie as a public relations weapon.[22]

Meanwhile, the vertical assault program moved forward. Fixed-wing advocates in Washington, mainly from the Army and Air Force, opposed funding helicopters, but the Marines prevailed. Planners determined that the Marines would need two types of helicopters: an assault helicopter to deliver infantry, and a larger transport machine to supply those troops with food, ammunition, and heavy weapons. The Experimental Helicopter Squadron was activated at Quantico, Virginia, in January 1948.[23]

While Marine Corps leaders fought their battles in Washington, active Marine Corps units completed the surrender of Japanese forces in China and safeguarded the evacuation of American civilians during the civil war raging there.

Korea, 1945–1950

Korea was truly a hermit kingdom in 1945. Few Americans knew of the country, and those who did had only limited knowledge. Located on a peninsula adjacent to China and close to Japan, Korea had a special relationship with China dating back to ancient times. The Chinese had imposed a Confucian father-son relationship on Korea, bestowing a rich legacy of ethics, arts, and literature that survived for more than a thousand years. Some equated the influence of China on Korea with that of Roman law on Britain.

Americans first thought of Korea as a vassal state of China, but after defeating Russia in 1905, Japan annexed Korea and turned it into a semi-industrialized Japanese colony. The Japanese built reservoirs and power plants and a school system to develop an efficient workforce. Instruction was in Japanese, and Koreans rebelled. The Japanese exiled nationalist leaders and maintained strong control over the country.[24]

Two Korean nationalist leaders, Syngman Rhee and Kim Il-sung, emerged between the two world wars. When the Japanese exiled Rhee in 1904, he migrated to the United States and studied at Princeton University. He subsequently divided his time between the United States and Geneva, Switzerland, petitioning the League of Nations for Korean independence. He was pro-Western, while Kim was a Communist who fought alongside the Chinese Communists against the Japanese during the 1930s and against the Chinese nationalist government of Chiang Kai-shek during the Chinese Civil War.

During the November 1943 Cairo Conference, US president Franklin Roosevelt, British prime minister Winston Churchill, and Chiang agreed that Korea should be free and independent. Roosevelt, Churchill, and Soviet leader Joseph Stalin discussed a trusteeship arrangement for Korea during the February 1945 Yalta Conference. Rhee and other Korean nationalists were encouraged by these public statements.

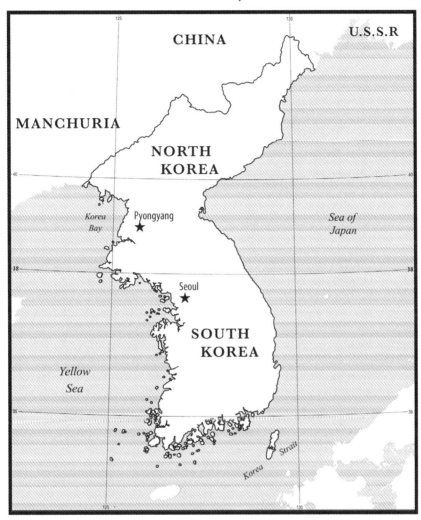

Korea, 1950.

As World War II drew to a close in the summer of 1945, the United States, Great Britain, and the Soviet Union agreed to a joint trusteeship for Korea. American troops would accept the surrender of Japanese forces south of the 38th Parallel, while Soviet forces did so to the north. The United States and the Soviet Union agreed to set up a joint commission to establish a provisional government.

These arrangements ended Korean dreams of immediate independence and eventually made Koreans north and south of an arbitrary line into

implacable enemies at a time when Korea was one of the most homoge-
neous and united countries in the world. Its borders had been fixed for
centuries, and it had no dispossessed minorities. Allied diplomats ignored
those realities when they divided Korea into two artificial zones.[25]

The Soviet Union declared war on Japan on August 8, 1945, and Soviet
troops swept into Manchuria and entered Korea two days later, occupying Wonsan, the largest port along the Korean eastern seaboard, and
then moving to the 38th Parallel. On September 3, 1945, the day after the
Japanese surrendered, US general John R. Hodge accepted the surrender
of all Japanese forces south of the parallel.

The American zone included about 42 percent of Korea's land but
two-thirds of its 30 million people. Primarily a farming area, the South
provided food for the entire peninsula. The Soviet zone had rich mineral
deposits and most of Korea's manufacturing as well as the country's only
petroleum processing and cement plants and Japanese-built hydroelectric
works that were among the best in the world. The North provided nearly
all of the South's electric power.

In the American zone, the US occupying forces reestablished the colonial
national police, collaborators with the Japanese, and brought Rhee back
from exile in the United States. During a December 1945 foreign ministers'
conference, the Soviet Union and the United States agreed to a five-year
bilateral trusteeship for all of Korea, but it quickly became a pawn in the
developing Cold War. The United States laid the Korean issue before the
United Nations in September 1947.[26]

The United Nations adopted a resolution calling for free, all-Korea
elections and the creation of a UN temporary commission to supervise
the elections. The Soviet military refused to allow the UN commission to
enter North Korea. Elections took place in the South in May 1948, a con-
stitution was drafted, and the National Assembly elected Rhee president
of the Republic of Korea. General Douglas MacArthur, commander of
US forces in East Asia, formally proclaimed the new republic on August
15, the United Nations recognized it in December, and nearly all UN
members gave it diplomatic recognition.[27]

P. I. Lipsey's *Clinton Parade* published several stories on these events
and featured the president of South Korea in one issue. Rhee had come to
Lipsey's Geneva apartment looking for a free meal when both men were

in Switzerland, bouncing Lipsey's daughters on his knees while waiting for the meal.[28]

In September 1948, the Soviets recognized the newly formed Democratic People's Republic of Korea, with Kim as prime minister, north of the 38th Parallel. The North claimed sovereignty over all of Korea, and the Soviet Union and its East European satellites immediately recognized it as the legitimate government of the entire peninsula. Weeks later, the Soviet Union announced the withdrawal of its troops from North Korea, leaving behind large numbers of Soviet advisers. The UN General Assembly responded by calling for the withdrawal of US forces from South Korea.

The Soviet Union completed its withdrawal in December 1948, but Rhee asked the United States to maintain occupation forces in South Korea and assist until the South Korean military was capable of defending against threats within and without the country. North Korean guerrilla warfare in the South had already started. The United States agreed to give limited military support but refused to supply aircraft or tanks. The JCS feared that Rhee would launch an attack on the North if equipped with offensive weapons.

The United States found itself supporting a Korean leader who was an uncompromising anti-Communist but who seemed to have lost touch with his country. Rhee was married to an Austrian, and when he returned to Korea in 1945 under American sponsorship, Koreans in the South had little interest in him. Rhee had been away for forty years and had not shared in the pain of the brutal Japanese occupation.

The United States had no clear policy toward South Korea in 1949. MacArthur did not think it feasible for the Republic of Korea to build an army capable of repelling a North Korean attack. His priority was the defense of Japan. MacArthur suggested that the United States complete its withdrawal by May 10, 1949, the anniversary of the general elections.

With some misgivings, Truman agreed to pull US troops from Korea by June 30. Ten days before that date, General Bradley said he wanted a policy stating that any aggression by North Korea against the South would be considered a threat to international peace and that action by the UN Security Council "might be introduced to check the aggression." The other members of the Joint Chiefs of Staff disagreed, and Bradley's concerns were dropped. Withdrawal took place on schedule.

US policy toward Korea was further confused when Secretary of State Dean Acheson, in a speech to the National Press Club in Washington, described America's line of defense in East Asia: a defensive perimeter that ran along the Aleutians to Japan and the Ryukyu Islands and then south to the Philippine Islands. Korea was excluded. Acheson's statement accorded with the views of the JCS and MacArthur. The secretary of state implied that if an attack on South Korea occurred, the United States would take the matter to the United Nations. Some observers later contended that Acheson's speech encouraged the North Korean attack on the South.

Acheson's exclusion of Korea from the line of defense and the Joint Chiefs' position were based on global warfare strategy, ignoring the Cold War military and political implications of a Communist attack on and occupation of South Korea and the danger it would pose.[29]

During the winter of 1949–50, the North Korean government began planning an invasion of the South. In early 1950, the North received large shipments of modern military equipment from the Soviet Union, including 150 T-34 tanks, more than 100 Yak fighter aircraft, heavy military equipment, and artillery. The Korean People's Army numbered 135,000 soldiers organized into seven infantry divisions and one armored brigade. It was trained by Soviet advisers and modeled after the Soviet army. More than 90,000 North Korean soldiers were veterans of the Chinese Civil War.

By the summer of 1950, the Republic of Korea's army reached the level of an upgraded paramilitary force of 95,000 men. The South had mortars and light artillery but no tanks or aircraft. Four undersized divisions were deployed along the 38th Parallel, with four additional divisions scattered across the rest of the county.

General J. Lawton Collins, the US Army chief of staff, traveled to Japan in May 1950 to evaluate the 8th Army's recent training efforts. In his view, improvements had only reached the battalion level, and the inevitable slackness resulting from occupation duty still had to be addressed. But he also believed that given sufficient time, the deficiencies in combat readiness could be corrected.

In early June, Johnson and Bradley traveled to Japan and met with MacArthur and his staff. Reports of a possible North Korean invasion of the South were routine, but Johnson later said that he had seen no hint of an imminent attack. Many observers felt a sense of urgency about Korea, but no one thought an attack would come that summer.

At the time, most of Washington was consumed by Senator Joseph McCarthy's charges of a massive Communist presence in the US State Department. The Wisconsin senator's misleading accusations that Communists were influencing American foreign policy and were responsible for the "loss" of China to the Communists unnerved President Truman at a time when the Cold War was heating up.

In June 1950, the United States presented the United Nations with clear evidence that the Soviet Union had shot down an unarmed patrol bomber over the Baltic Sea, killing ten American airmen. At the same time, Communist China renewed its threats against the Nationalist Chinese government in Taiwan. A Gallup poll reported that a majority of Americans feared the country would soon be at war.

The North Korean government continued preparing to attack the South. On June 19, 1950, it called for the "peaceful unification of Korea through free elections." Three days later, North Korea's military was ordered to proceed with an invasion of the South.

The attack began at 4:00 a.m. on Sunday, June 25 with a massive artillery barrage followed by tank and troop movements across the 38th Parallel toward Seoul and other major cities. The South Korean army was caught by complete surprise, and the four divisions defending the 38th Parallel offered little resistance. Some units had as many as 40 percent of their soldiers on leave.

In Tokyo, Major General Edward Almond, MacArthur's chief of staff, arrived at his office early on Sunday. Twenty minutes after his arrival, he received a report of a border incident on the 38th Parallel. Over the next three hours, he received reports of six other border incidents and ordered an aide to inform MacArthur.[30]

At 9:00 that morning, John J. Muccio, the US ambassador in Seoul, signaled the State Department that an "all-out offensive against the Republic of Korea" had begun. Muccio later ran into United Press correspondent Jack James and told him of the attack. James immediately cabled the United Press office in San Francisco to announce the invasion. The message was relayed to the United Press headquarters in New York at about the same time the State Department received Muccio's cable. In the United States, it was still Saturday evening, June 24.[31]

Truman was at his home in Independence, Missouri, when Acheson called with the news of the North Korean attack. Acheson advised the president to request an emergency meeting of the UN Security Council to consider the threat to peace. Truman agreed, made plans to return to Washington, and instructed Acheson to arrange a Sunday evening dinner conference with principal advisers from the State and Defense Departments.[32]

The UN Security Council met at 2:00 p.m. on June 25 in New York to consider the Korean situation. The Soviet delegate was absent, having abstained from all council meetings since January 1950, when the body refused to unseat Nationalist China. The council unanimously approved a resolution condemning the North Korean attack and demanding a withdrawal of all North Korean forces to north of the 38th Parallel, calling on all members to assist in the execution of this resolution. When the North Koreans did not respond, the Security Council met again on June 27 and called on all UN member nations to support to the Republic of Korea.[33]

The attendees at Truman's Sunday evening dinner conference agreed that the invasion of South Korea was the latest in a series of acts of Communist aggression that had occurred in Iran, Turkey, Greece, and Berlin. General Bradley said a firm line had to be drawn somewhere, and Korea was it. Truman ordered the service chiefs to prepare the necessary orders to meet the threat. The 7th Fleet was to move to East Asia, with additional air units joining it. MacArthur was instructed to send a survey party to Korea to assess the situation and was placed in command of all military action in Korea the next day.

The United States responded to the North Korean invasion of the South because Acheson and Truman saw it as a threat to American prestige and political economy. They later justified intervention because the aggression threatened to upset the balance of power in Asia. The administration saw the heavy hand of the Soviet Union in the invasion of South Korea and linked it to the security of America's allies in Europe.

Chapter 2

AMERICAN INTERVENTION, JUNE–AUGUST 1950

The 24th Infantry Division was the first unit sent to Korea. In their initial
contact with the enemy, the Americans were routed. They retreated from
the enemy, suffering losses. By mid-July, the Americans were in full
retreat. It was among the darkest hours in the history of the U.S. Army.
—**James Warren**, *American Spartans*

Waller King, Joe Albritton, and Homer Ainsworth, fresh from Marine
summer camp, learned of the North Korean attack from the front-page
headline of the June 25, 1950, *Jackson Clarion-Ledger*: "War Declared."
Mississippi was twelve hours and a calendar day behind Korean time.
The paper reported that 60,000 North Koreans had invaded South Korea
along a two-hundred-mile front, adding that South Korean president
Syngman Rhee was prepared to appeal to General Douglas MacArthur
for immediate aid.

Few people in Mississippi were familiar with Korea. Some Clinton
residents remembered the Lipsey articles in the *Clinton Parade* about
Rhee's efforts to gain League of Nations recognition of Korean independence during the 1930s. Rhee gained a half victory when he took control
of South Korea. Now he was threatened.

Clinton had a large number of young men in the Mississippi National
Guard and the US Army, Air Force, Navy, and Marine Corps Reserves.

Most of them had given little thought to being called up to fight in a war, and the conflict in Korea was ominous—they might be called to active duty. Waller, Joe, and Homer did not know that the rush of events in Washington had included no role for the Marine Corps in Korea.

Korea would be a land war, and the Joint Chiefs of Staff (JCS) planned to use Army occupation troops in Japan to meet the Communist aggression. Army commanders knew that these soldiers were not prepared to fight, and their lack of readiness was obvious from the beginning. The JCS conveniently ignored the one service branch always prepared for war: the Marines.

Hours after the UN call for assistance, President Harry S. Truman announced that South Korea would receive military aid. On June 27, the US House of Representatives voted 315–4 to extend the draft for one year and authorized the president to call up reservists from all services. The Senate approved the bill the next day, 70–0. Truman had congressional support for intervening in Korea but did not ask for a declaration of war.[1]

When asked during a June 29 press conference, "Are we at war, or are we not?" Truman replied, "We are not at war." When the reporter followed up with, "Would it be possible to call this a police action under the United Nations?," Truman embraced the description: "Yes, that is exactly what it amounts to, a police action taken to help the UN repel a bunch of bandits." *Police action* became the operative words for US involvement.[2]

After the United Nations endorsed Truman's decision to send forces to Korea on June 27, Australia, Canada, New Zealand, the Netherlands, and Great Britain promised military assistance. Other members joined them over the next few weeks, and in early July the UN Security Council authorized the formation of a UN command and asked Truman to name a commander.[3] The president chose General Douglas MacArthur, already commander of US forces in the Far East.

The president earlier authorized MacArthur to send units of the 8th Army to Korea, and on June 29 MacArthur flew to Suwon airfield, south of Seoul, to evaluate the military situation. He recognized that without immediate US help, South Korea would quickly lose control of its territory. At the time, the 8th Army had four poorly trained divisions spread across Japan under the command of General Walton Walker. MacArthur requested and Truman approved sending two divisions to Korea, a momentous step that meant that Americans would fight Communists on a battlefield for the first time in the Cold War.

From the beginning, some observers questioned MacArthur's appointment as commander of UN forces in Korea. Columnist James Reston of the *New York Times* raised the point that MacArthur

> was being asked to be not only a great soldier but a great statesman, not only to direct the battle, but to satisfy the Pentagon, the State Department, and the United Nations in the process. . . . Diplomacy and a vast concern for the opinions and sensitivities of others are the political qualities essential to this new assignment, and these are precisely the qualities General MacArthur has been accused of lacking in the past.[4]

Reston's questioning had merit but was quickly forgotten.

MacArthur, as general of the Army, with five stars, outranked but still reported to the JCS, who reported to the president. MacArthur also had the UN mandate. And he was no ordinary general, accustomed to following orders. As supreme commander of the Allied forces in Japan, he had been solely responsible for policy during the occupation. MacArthur was the real ruler of some eighty-three million Japanese, directing the country's foreign policy and receiving foreign diplomats when they visited. His absolute rule over a foreign state was unique in US military history.

While the United States and United Nations worked together to rescue South Korea from military collapse, the North Korean invaders continued their advance, taking advantage of the fact that they had five times as many troops as the South Koreans did at critical points on the attack line. North Korea's tank-led offensive on the western sector moved rapidly toward Seoul and Inchon. The soldiers of South Korea, known formally as the Republic of Korea (ROK), were in disarray and offered little resistance. North Korean Yak-3 fighters buzzed Seoul and bombed the train station while a tank regiment came within twenty-five miles of the capital on the first day of the invasion. American personnel were ordered to evacuate Seoul on June 27, and the city fell the next day.[5]

The North Korean army advanced south, meeting weak resistance from ROK forces on the ground. Control of the air was another matter. US 5th Air Force planes from Japan provided air cover at the airfields at Kimpo and Suwon during the evacuation of Seoul. Four American fighter jets shot down seven YAK piston-driven aircraft in the war's first air combat. American aircraft controlled the skies over South Korea from the beginning.

Three branches of the American military—the Army, Navy and Air Force—were engaged in the initial defense of South Korea. Marine Corps leaders wanted a role, and pressured Admiral Forrest Sherman, chief of naval operations, to remind the JCS that the Marines were available and ready to fight. Sherman radioed Admiral C. Turner Joy, commander of naval forces in the Far East, advising him that a Marine regimental combat team could be made available for service in Korea if General MacArthur wanted one. Two days later, Sherman asked Fleet Marine Force Pacific's headquarters in Honolulu how long it would take for the Marines to deploy a reinforced battalion or a reinforced regiment.

Colonel Victor "Brute" Krulak received Sherman's cable two days after reporting as Force Pacific's operations officer. Krulak responded to the cable: "(a) 48 hours. (b) five days for a regiment including a Marine air group." When Colonel Gregon Williams, the Force Pacific chief of staff, later asked how Krulak knew that such a quick deployment was possible, he answered, "I don't, but if we can't, we're dead."[6] The Marines had to be part of this war to justify their existence.

MacArthur had the Marines in mind in his early planning. He invited the Marine commandant, General Clifton B. Cates; Marine General Lemuel Shepherd; and Admiral Arthur Radford to a meeting in Tokyo on July 10. After a briefing on Korea, MacArthur spoke of the need for an early counteroffensive and brought up the Marines who had served under him in Japan during World War II. MacArthur then pointed to Korea's west coast on a map and said, "If I had the 1st Marine division now, I could stabilize my front and make an amphibious envelopment here—at Inchon on the west coast." Shepherd encouraged MacArthur to make the request to the JCS.[7]

MacArthur still had to reckon with the deteriorating military situation. The ROK army was in steady retreat and in danger of being pushed to the sea by the North Korean invaders. Moving two American divisions to Korea probably could not take place quickly enough to stop the enemy advance. As a stopgap, MacArthur had a small contingent of American soldiers led by Lieutenant Colonel Brad Smith flown to Pusan, South Korea, on July 5. Task Force Smith had two rifle companies and a depleted artillery detail—a total of 406 officers and men—to check the leading elements of a North Korean division of 9,000 soldiers.

Task Force Smith lacked effective antitank weapons, and its ammunition came from supplies that had been stored since World War II. Smith used Korean trucks to move his soldiers north to Osan, about twenty miles south of Seoul on the highway to Pusan. The task force took positions on the highway, but a North Korean tank column easily smashed through the American defenses, followed by an infantry division. After slowing the enemy advance somewhat and suffering about 150 casualties, the Americans withdrew south toward Taejon, ending the first American land engagement of the Korean War.[8]

The delaying action allowed the 34th Infantry Regiment of General William Dean's 24th Infantry Division to arrive by air and move north from Pusan by train, hoping to stop or delay the advancing North Korean column south of Osan. The 34th was poorly trained and equipped, and when advancing North Korean infantry began an enveloping maneuver, many soldiers dropped their weapons and fled in what became known as Operation Bug Out. Newspapers back in the United States reported on the fiasco.[9]

Dean replaced the regimental commander and began preparing for the defense of Taejon, the next major city on the Seoul-to-Pusan highway and the temporary capital of South Korea after the fall of Seoul. Taejon (population 130,000) lay in a north-south valley below the Kum River 100 air miles from the capital and 130 air miles from Pusan. When North Korean troops reached the Kum River on July 14, they were twenty miles northwest of Taejon.[10]

While units of the 24th Infantry Division continued their retreat toward Taejon, General MacArthur had one brief triumph. On July 10, a flight of F-80 jets from the 5th Air Force came upon a large convoy of enemy tanks and vehicles stopped bumper-to-bumper on the north side of a destroyed bridge. Flight controllers quickly scrambled every available combat plane—B-26 light bombers, Mustang F-51s, F-82s, and F-80 jets—and they destroyed 38 tanks, 7 half-tracks, and 117 trucks, the greatest destruction of North Korean armor in one day during the entire war.[11]

Air Force power had less success in interdicting enemy troops on the ground in the early weeks of the war. Infantry units lacked forward air controllers to direct attacks on North Korean positions, and attempts to provide air cover for the infantry too often resulted in friendly fire on

American positions, causing casualties among retreating US and ROK soldiers. Air-ground coordination was a major strength of the Marine Corps.

The North Korean forces paused at the Kum River before beginning their advance on Taejon on July 19. Most South Koreans fled the city as the enemy approached, while those who remained hid in their homes and hoped for the best. North Korean infantry and tanks began to encircle Taejon, and the main attack began the next morning.

The city's defenders were the badly mauled and weakened 24th Division. The American soldiers again could not hold their positions and began a disorderly withdrawal. General Dean found himself in the streets directing attacks on enemy tanks, but in the confusion, Dean's jeep was separated from the main convoy. He was injured in a fall and became separated from his staff. After wandering behind enemy lines for more than a month, General Dean was captured and held prisoner for the next three years.[12]

The fall of Taejon was another disaster for the 24th Infantry Division. Of the 4,000 soldiers engaged in the defense of the city, 1,150 were dead, wounded, or missing. In the seventeen days since Task Force Smith first engaged the enemy at Osan, the 24th suffered 30 percent casualties and lost enough equipment to supply an entire division.[13]

After the fall of Taejon, the North Korean command moved to execute a double-envelopment strategy for all of South Korea still held by American and ROK forces. One North Korean division undertook the west-side envelopment along the Yellow Sea and through southwest Korea, while another division moved down the east coast road along the Sea of Japan. ROK defenses in both sectors were undermanned, and the North Korean command directed its divisions to drive all-out for Pusan. The rest of the North Korean army pressed against the central front held by American and ROK troops.[14]

The US Army's 25th Infantry Division arrived in Korea on July 12, and the 1st Cavalry Division completed its landing ten days later, with both units joining the depleted 24th Division in defending the central sector against the main North Korean force. Fortunately for American and South Korean forces, the North Korean command wasted days searching for ROK forces that did not exist on the eastern front while committing troops to occupy small ports on the southwestern corner of the Korean peninsula. ROK forces, aided by US and British naval bombardment and UN air strikes, managed to stop the North Korean advance along the east coast, giving General Walker time to strengthen the defensive lines protecting the port of Pusan.[15]

Walker and Rhee had moved their respective headquarters further south to Taegu before the attacks on Taejon began. MacArthur flew to Pusan and met with Walker for several hours. Despite the perilous situation, MacArthur was confident that his troops could hold the line. His staff in Tokyo estimated that 270 of North Korea's 300 tanks had been destroyed, greatly weakening the enemy's offensive capabilities.

Meeting with Walker, MacArthur insisted that there would be no evacuation, no Korean Dunkirk or Bataan. Walker agreed the time for retreat had passed. When he later met with his division commanders, the general repeated MacArthur's vow. Additional Army forces and the First Marine brigade were about to arrive in Korea, which MacArthur and Walker believed would give them enough personnel to develop a continuous defensive line and complicate the enemy's efforts at further envelopment movements. The generals agreed that the army's attitude of easy retreat in the face of the enemy had to change. American forces had to hold the line.

In early August, the 8th Army's three divisions retreated south of the Naktong River and set up a defensive line starting at Potsung (now Pohang), a port city on the east coast about sixty miles north of Pusan. The line followed the Naktong as it flowed west and then south to its confluence with the Nam River. This defensive line was 140 miles long and covered a rectangular area on the tip of South Korea, 100 miles north-south and about 50 miles east-west—the Pusan Perimeter.

North Korea had failed to reach its goal of conquering the South within thirty days. The North Korean forces had the ROK army and the Americans in retreat but had not driven them into the sea. The North Koreans had the initiative, but the ROK army and the three American divisions now had numerical parity with the invaders. Moreover, the American soldiers had not performed well, and it was not clear that they could hold the perimeter.

The Fire Brigade

When General MacArthur requested a Marine division in Korea, the JCS objected, arguing that reducing Marine forces elsewhere in the world might

encourage the Soviets to take advantage of American weakness and act in
Europe. On July 3, with MacArthur's request on the table, General Cates
crashed the JCS meeting and answered all questions about Marine readiness. The JCS then recommended that the president mobilize the Marine
Corps Reserve and authorize a provisional Marine brigade (one regiment)
for MacArthur. On July 19, the president called up 33,528 members of the
organized Marine Corps Reserve and an additional 50,000 volunteer
reserves on August 7. Two additional regiments were being organized to
complete the division MacArthur requested.[16]

General Edward Craig assumed command of the 1st Provisional Brigade,
still in its formative state, on July 22. By definition, a Marine brigade was
a tactical force of three to six battalions with supporting artillery, tanks,
and aircraft. The 5th Marine Infantry Regiment at Camp Pendleton,
California, became the core of the brigade. Commanded by Lieutenant
Colonel Raymond Murray, the regiment was not at full strength, but with
the Marine Reserve call-up and Marines drawn from different depots on
the West Coast, the 5th quickly reached combat-readiness.

Navy medic Herbert Pearce was assigned to the 5th Marine Regiment
and became the first young man from Clinton, Mississippi, to go to Korea.
Pearce, the son of a college professor, wanted to become a doctor and
enlisted in the Navy after graduating from high school. Since the Navy
provided medics for the Marine Corps, Pearce found himself in a Marine
uniform with the 5th.[17]

Marine Air Wing MAG-33, commanded by Brigadier General Thomas
Cushman, was part of the provisional brigade. The wing had three fighter-
bomber squadrons of late model F-4s and Corsairs and an observation
squadron that included four Sikorsky helicopters. Lieutenant Colonel
Murray's regiment was reinforced with tanks and amphibious companies
and an artillery battalion. Altogether the brigade numbered 6,534 Marines,
not much larger than a standard infantry regiment of World War II.[18]

The 1st Provisional Brigade landed at Pusan on August 2, 1950. It had
been pulled together so fast that Murray left his regiment's trucks and
heavy equipment back at Camp Pendleton and had to borrow from
the Army. The 5th Regiment was short three infantry companies but
did have a reinforced artillery battalion, a tank company, a weapons
company, and motor transport personnel. All units were undermanned
but ready to fight.

North Korea Attacks the Pusan Perimeter, June–August 1950.

According to *Time* magazine, in an issue that featured General Edward Craig of the Marines on its cover, "The Marines, who carried along with their shiny new equipment, a large ration of glory in their packs, arrived at a critical moment in the Korean fighting. . . . As they landed, some of them exchanged the usual banter with the watching doggies (as they call Army men). You can go home now, Junior. Us men have taken over." The magazine quoted Craig as saying that his men "are ready for anything that can be thrown at them."[19]

The Marines of the Provisional Brigade were well trained and disciplined. More than half were veterans of World War II. The others had received the same training Marines endured in the 1930s and 1940s. In contrast, the US Army had lowered its training standards after the war, and the soldiers of the 8th Army were poorly trained and disciplined.

The Marine brigade arrived at Pusan at a critical time. The soldiers of the 8th Army were dispirited and barely holding on. The Marines came prepared to fight, and their readiness was about to be put to the test. The expectation that the course of the war would now change fueled Army-Marine competition at all levels, from the generals in command to the soldiers and Marines on the ground. The media enjoyed playing on the rivalry. The Marine Provisional Brigade and later the 1st Marine Division were under Army command.

General Walker welcomed the Marines and immediately sent the brigade to the southwestern sector of the Pusan Perimeter to defend the strategic city of Masan. Marine aircraft, flying off aircraft carriers, had already attacked an advancing North Korean division with bombs, rockets, and strafing. The brigade teamed with units of the Army's 25th Infantry Division, and for the first time, Americans outnumbered North Koreans on a front. The US force stopped the North Korean advance after six days of heavy fighting and pushed the North Koreans west back to Chinju.

The Marines' "flying artillery" played a critical role in the fight. Forward air observers placed in each Marine battalion directed air strikes against the enemy within minutes of a request. This air-ground coordination gave the Marines an asset the US Army did not have and made the difference between advancing against a pulverized enemy and being stopped by an entrenched enemy.[20] Marine air cover gave General Walker his first victory in the war.

The first encounter between the Marines and the North Koreans was a learning experience for both. Fighting in temperatures of over one hundred degrees, the Marines recognized the enemy as tenacious and skilled at camouflage, infiltration, and night fighting. The North Koreans in turn realized that the Marines were different from soldiers of the 8th Army. Marines wore camouflaged helmets and leggings in place of high-top boots. Marines did not retreat. They did not drop their weapons and run. Marines carried their dead and wounded from the battlefield.

The Marine brigade came out of its initial fight physically tough and psychologically hard. It experienced heavy losses in the attacks that week: 66 killed in action (KIA), 240 wounded, and 9 missing. The Marine observation squadron of helicopters played a vital role in artillery spotting and in scouting enemy positions, evacuating wounded, and transporting supplies. MacArthur read the reports of the Marines' performance and concluded that the Marine attack had secured the southern approaches to Pusan and indicated that the North Koreans would not hold when under attack.[21]

While Marines strengthened the US line on the southwest sector of the perimeter, the Army's 24th Division came under attack from the North Koreans along the Naktong River. The enemy crossed the river, the last natural barrier to the supply line between Taegu and Pusan, on August 6. The 24th fell back twenty-five miles to Miryang, one of the last outposts guarding the supply line. Walker ordered the Marine brigade to Miryang and persuaded Rhee to evacuate his government from Taegu to Pusan on August 15.

The Marine brigade was placed under the command of General John Church, commander of the Army's 24th Infantry Division. The situation at Miryang was critical. If the North Koreans could not be stopped there, Taegu would be lost, and the threat to Pusan would become even more serious. The Marines attacked North Korean forces on August 18, forcing the enemy to pull back. After a North Korean counterattack, the brigade resumed its offensive and forced the North Koreans back across the Naktong River, achieving the US objective. Marine casualties in the second engagement were 66 KIA, 278 wounded, and 1 missing. The enemy left behind more than 1,200 dead.[22]

General Walker detached the brigade from the 24th Infantry and made it a part of the 8th Army Reserve to give the Marines a break. The brigade moved back to an area near Masan known as the Bean Patch. The 11th Marine Regiment, the brigade's artillery unit, was temporarily assigned to the Army's 25th Infantry. While the Marines enjoyed a brief rest, 800 replacements began to arrive to fill the depleted ranks. In addition, helicopters flew in hot food, letters from home were delivered, and new equipment was issued.

While the brigade was at the Bean Patch, Marine leaders flew to Tokyo to meet with MacArthur and discuss plans for an amphibious landing at the South Korean port of Inchon. General Oliver Smith, the designated commander of the 1st Marine Division, met with MacArthur and his chief of staff, General Edward Almond, on August 22. The 1st Marine Division remained fragmented: the 5th Regiment was fighting in the Pusan Perimeter; the 1st Regiment had just left the United States for Korea, and the 7th Regiment was still being assembled from Marines pulled from embassy duty and from Navy ships and was not due to arrive in Asia until the middle of September. Smith had reservations about MacArthur's vision of the amphibious landing. MacArthur described the Inchon landing as a Marine operation that could win the war within a month. He explained to Smith that the enemy forces had been concentrated at Pusan, leaving Inchon virtually undefended. MacArthur visualized Smith's Marines taking Inchon and driving on Seoul within days.

The Marines' Smith and the Army's Almond started a contentious relationship during the Tokyo meeting. Almond, who was only three years older than Smith, repeatedly addressed him as *Son*. Almond also claimed the high ground of greater military experience, though Smith's record as a combat commander overshadowed Almond's. Almond's aggressiveness stood in sharp contrast to Smith's reserved approach.[23]

When the two men met to work out arrangements for the Inchon landing, Smith asked Almond to release the Marine brigade from the Pusan Perimeter by August 23 to prepare for the Inchon operation. In his capacity as MacArthur's chief of staff, Almond responded that the release of the brigade "would be bad for the morale of the Eighth Army and, in any case, would be dependent on the tactical situation." When Smith repeated his request on August 30, fifteen days before the invasion, he was told that General Walker was unwilling to give up the brigade because of the tenuous situation in the Pusan area. Almond advised Smith that the brigade commander (Lieutenant Colonel Murray) should negotiate his release directly with Walker, the 8th Army commander. Smith refused to accept this suggestion and officially requested that MacArthur release the brigade to prepare for the Inchon operation.[24]

MacArthur approved Smith's request. When notified that the brigade would be removed from his command, Walker said, in effect, "If I lose the 5th Marine Regiment, I will not be responsible for the safety of the front."[25] MacArthur assured Walker that additional Army units were on their way to Korea. Walker considered pulling the Pusan Perimeter inward to strengthen the Army's defenses after the Marine brigade's departure.

President Truman sent the Army chief of staff, General J. Lawton Collins, to Japan on August 21 to be briefed on the details of the planned Inchon landing and to evaluate the Army's performance in Korea. The Collins team arrived in Tokyo the day before MacArthur's meeting with Marine leaders. General Collins flew to Korea the next morning and carried out inspections of improvements General Walker had made in his command. In the interim, Army and Marine units had scored victories over the North Koreans. Collins reported that the 8th Army should be able to hold the Pusan Perimeter and expressed concerns about withdrawing the Marine brigade from the perimeter. After a briefing by MacArthur on the Inchon landing, Collins noted the many "handicaps" facing the invading forces. He recommended using the 70,000-plus soldiers and Marines currently assigned to the Inchon landing for the continued defense of the Pusan Perimeter.[26]

Walker's last battlefield use of the Marines came after the North Koreans launched attacks along the perimeter line on September 1. Thirteen undersized North Korean divisions (75,000 men) overran several Army defensive positions, forcing 2nd Army Division units to fall back to Yongsam. The enemy opened a hole six miles wide and eight miles deep in the line, creating another bulge. Walker turned to the Marine brigade to stop the North Korean advance, another humiliation for the Army since the Marines had taken this territory from the enemy earlier.

Meeting with General Craig, who wore one star, Lawrence Keiser, the commander of the 2nd Army Division and a two-star general, said, "General, I'm horribly embarrassed that you have to do this. My men lost the ground you took in a severe fight." Craig responded, "General, it might have happened to me." When Keiser brought up the idea of breaking the Marine brigade into smaller units and distributing them among the Army units, Craig argued strongly against the concept and stood firm. The brigade would fight as a unit.[27]

The Marines attacked the North Korean positions on September 3. Air-ground coordination was decisive in the fighting, pushing the enemy back across the Nakong. The Marines recovered an enormous amount of weapons and equipment that had been abandoned by the Army—tanks, trucks, artillery pieces, heavy mortars, and stockpiles of ammunition. Three days of fierce fighting resulted in heavy Marine casualties: 148 KIA, 750 wounded, and 9 missing (7 of whom were later confirmed dead). Navy corpsmen serving as medics with the brigade suffered 11 casualties.⁴⁰ A new defensive line was established, and during the night of September 5, the Marine brigade moved south to Pusan to join other units of the 1st Marine Division for the Inchon operation.

The Marine brigade accomplished much in one month of fighting along the Pusan perimeter. It traveled 380 miles in three difficult operations, facing an overwhelming and previously successful enemy that enjoyed numerical superiority. In its initial fight in the southwest sector, the brigade repelled a major enemy offensive. Its second battle, at the Naktong River, resulted in the destruction of a North Korean division, with Marine air and artillery contributing significantly to the victory. In their next fight at the Naktong, the Marines coordinated their offensive with the Army and drove two enemy divisions back across the river. The Marines had inflicted more than 9,000 casualties and captured massive amounts of equipment, leading Walker to dub the Marines his Fire Brigade because they put out conflagrations along the Pusan Perimeter. The Fire Brigade later won a Presidential Unit Citation for its service in the Pusan Perimeter operation.

Much to the chagrin of Army officials, the American media played up the Marines' role as the "Minutemen of 1950." The brigade force of 6,000 outshined the Army's 90,000 troops in defending Pusan.

While the Marines prepared to withdraw from 8th Army, US Army reinforcements continued to arrive at Pusan, and in September the first allied ground forces arrived. The United States had been fighting with British and Dutch ships and Australian air support since the early days of the war. Now 8th Army had the British 27th Brigade, a unit of 1,600 men who began arriving piecemeal in July. The British were placed in the battle line near Taegu in late August. The North Koreans now faced an army fighting under the United Nations banner.

The Marine brigade reached the docks of Pusan on the morning of September 7, rested for five days, and was then dissolved. The 5th Marine Regiment and its supporting units now became part of the 1st Marine Division and were joined by 1,135 officers and enlisted men who had arrived as replacements. A Korean Marine Corps regiment of 3,000 well-trained men was attached to the Marine division.

General MacArthur reorganized his military structure, bringing the 1st Marine Division and the 7th Army Infantry Division together into X Corps under the command of his chief of staff, Almond, an arrangement that gave MacArthur direct control of the newly formed unit. When units of the Army's 7th Infantry were ordered to Pusan, many of the men cheered, thinking they were going back to Japan. Their enthusiasm quickly faded when they learned they were to be part of Operation Chromite, the amphibious landing at Inchon.

The 8th Army carried out the American fighting in Korea in July. The 1st Marine Brigade arrived in August and bore the brunt of the fight during that time. Marine historians view August 1950 as the Marines' fight, in which they received assistance from various Army regiments. Army historians have described the 8th Army's courageous defense of the Pusan Perimeter, making brief mention of the Marines in different battles.

But neither Marines nor soldiers knew that the war was being censored back home. CBS news anchor Edward R. Murrow traveled to Korea that summer and witnessed the disorderly Army retreat to Taegu and the desperate fighting to maintain the Pusan Perimeter. He was shocked by the poor performance of American soldiers, which was nothing like what Murrow had witnessed when covering World War II in Europe. He recorded a newscast highly critical of the Army's leadership and blamed General MacArthur for bad decisions that caused unnecessary casualties. In Murrow's opinion, MacArthur had decided that he needed a victory and recklessly ordered attacks against an entrenched enemy.[29]

Prior to the show's airing, the head of CBS News reviewed a transcript and immediately called a high-level conference that included the president of the network and chair of its board. They decided to kill the story. Murrow angrily objected to the censorship but did not resign or go public. Members of the Overseas Press Club learned of Murrow's muzzling and cabled protests to General MacArthur, whom they believed was responsible for the censorship. *Newsweek* eventually leaked the story.[30]

Also during the summer of 1950, President Truman recklessly picked a quarrel with the Marine Corps in the continuing Battle of the Potomac. The president had already come under heavy fire for American forces' obvious lack of preparedness in Korea and Japan. After the Marine Brigade won the first battle at the Naktong, Congressman Gordon L. McDonough of California wrote to President Truman praising the

Marines' battlefield performance over the years and their valiant response to the Korean crisis. McDonough raised the possibility of having the Marine Corps commandant serve on the JCS with the Army, Air Force, and Navy chiefs.

Truman, sensitive to the widespread attacks on his administration over Korea, sent a frustrated reply that was not screened by his advisers, telling McDonough, "For your information, the Marine Corps is the Navy's police force and as long as I am President that is what it will remain. They have a propaganda machine that is equal to Stalin's." McDonough placed the president's letter in the *Congressional Digest*, and members of Congress and senators, Democrats and Republicans alike, attacked Truman. Wisconsin senator Joseph McCarthy called Truman's letter "a fantastically unpatriotic thing to say about the boys who are dying in Korea." The press chimed in with damning editorials and feature articles on the president's views of the Marines.[31]

The uproar coincided with the national convention of the Marine Corps League, an organization of Marine veterans and supporters, which was taking place in Washington, DC, and at which the president had been invited to speak. The Marine Corps League demanded that the president apologize to the American people for insulting the Marine Corps. Truman's staff advised him to go to the convention and apologize personally, and he reluctantly agreed. When he entered, however, the bugler refused to play "Hail to the Chief," claiming that his dentures had fallen out. Speaking before an otherwise respectful crowd, Truman declared, "I sincerely regret the unfortunate choice of language which I used in my letter to Congressman McDonough." After the president's departure, attendees voted to accept his apology and adopted a resolution calling for the Marine Corps commandant to join the JCS.[32]

In September, Senator Paul Douglas and Representative Mike Mansfield sponsored a bill giving the commandant that status. Admiral Forrest Sherman opposed the idea, asserting that as chief of naval operations, he represented the Corps in the same manner as the submarine arm and the air arm. Senators Leverett Saltonstall and Ralph Flanders then asked whether the commandant would be present at a JCS meeting if the military were to consider another major amphibious operation like the Inchon landing. Sherman answered that he would not. The status question remained unresolved.

Truman also had political problems at home and with General MacArthur during the first months of the Korean conflict, mainly over a role for Nationalist China. Chinese Nationalist leader Chaing Kai-shek had offered to send troops to assist South Korea after the invasion, and Truman had entertained the offer until Secretary of State Dean Acheson warned that Nationalist Chinese involvement might draw Communist Chinese intervention. Truman ordered the US 7th Fleet to the Straits of Taiwan to defend the island against any mainland threat—and to prevent Chaing from taking action against the mainland.

On August 1, MacArthur visited Taiwan without the knowledge or permission of Washington. He subsequently made a brief statement to the press about the trip that caused little stir. However, Chaing announced that they had engaged in talks regarding not only the defense of Taiwan but also "Sino-American military cooperation," hinting at future actions against mainland China and declaring that victory over the Chinese mainland armies was now assured.[33]

Such a public announcement shocked the Truman administration, and on August 6, the president sent national security adviser Averell Harriman and General Matthew Ridgway of the JCS to Tokyo to meet with MacArthur. Harriman was instructed to advise the general that Truman sought to avoid war with China and to find out what MacArthur needed to win in Korea. Ridgway was sent to appraise the military situation.[34]

MacArthur expressed surprise at the controversy his meeting with Chaing had caused and claimed that they had discussed only routine matters, offering assurances that "I will obey any order I receive from the president." Despite the cordiality of the talks, Harriman reported to Truman that MacArthur would never "fully embrace" the administration's policies regarding Taiwan.[35]

Ridgway found the military situation in Korea deplorable. Divisional and regimental commanders were too old and gave poor leadership to the soldiers, who were demoralized and "suffered from a lack of infantry fundamentals." He privately advised Harriman that General Walker should be relieved of his command of 8th Army.[36]

Truman subsequently ordered MacArthur to refrain from any discussions of foreign policy and to withdraw a statement urging the defense of Taiwan. Though the president's communication was intended to be confidential, it was leaked and later made public in the *Congressional Record*.

The Veterans of Foreign Wars (VFW) reacted by endorsing MacArthur's integrity and military ability, a slap at the president. Truman, in contrast, saw his letter as a "friendly pat on the back" to MacArthur as well as a reassertion of the White House's control of foreign policy. According to the media's interpretation, the president wanted to clarify MacArthur's understanding of White House policy while allowing him to save face. Truman later said at a press conference that he and MacArthur saw "eye-to-eye" on Taiwan. The VFW invited MacArthur to its annual encampment in Chicago at the end of August. Unable to attend, the general sent a message to be read to the gathering in which he declared, "Nothing could be more fallacious than the threadbare argument by those who advocate appeasement and defeatism in the Pacific that if we defend Formosa, we alienate continental Asia. Those who speak thus do not understand the Orient. They do not grant that it is the pattern of Oriental psychology to respect and follow aggressive, resolute and dynamic leadership . . . and they underestimate the Oriental mentality."[37]

MacArthur had not cleared this message with the JCS, the president, Acheson, Secretary of Defense Louis Johnson, or any other top foreign policy official. An angry Truman met with these advisers to decide how to proceed. Acheson thought MacArthur was insubordinate, but given MacArthur's role in the upcoming Inchon landing, the group decided that Johnson, as MacArthur's boss, would order the general to withdraw his message to the VFW because "various features with respect to Formosa are in conflict with the policy of the United States and its position in the United Nations."[38]

MacArthur replied to the reprimand by protesting that his message supported the president's June 27 order regarding Taiwan. The general added that Taiwan was being discussed around the world and that his message expressed his personal views. Though the incident did not result in MacArthur's dismissal for insubordination, it did make Truman aware that Johnson was conspiring to have Acheson ousted as secretary of state and forced the defense secretary's resignation on September 12.[39]

The Clinton Homefront

After Waller King, Joe Albritton, and Homer Ainsworth returned home from Marine camp, the rest of the summer of 1950 passed quickly. Jackson's Marine Reserve unit, C Battery of the 105mm howitzer Battalion, 7th Regiment, received official notification of the call-up of reservists on July 24, ending any speculation about the immediate future for Waller, Joe, and Homer as well as Bill Smith and George Sharp.

Waller would not be reporting to Oxford for the start of fall football practice at Ole Miss. Joe would not be returning to Mississippi College. Homer would not be returning to Hinds Junior College. Bill would not be there when Betty Jo Smith gave birth to their first child. And George would no longer have to endure the tedium of his job at Ratliff Motors. All five would probably be fighting in Korea.

Waller King sold his 1938 black Chevrolet for one hundred dollars and reported to the reserve unit on August 11, only to be sent home to await the official call-up on August 28. Homer devoted a lot of time to his family. His mother celebrated her birthday in early August, and the family attended a revival his father preached near the end of the month before heading to the Gulf Coast for a weekend of fishing.

Joe tried to persuade Elwood Ratliff to join the Marine Reserve unit, but his father insisted that he return for his second year at Mississippi State, where he was in the ROTC program. Joe also continued his secret courtship of Peggy Cain.

On August 10, the *Jackson Clarion-Ledger* ran a front-page story on the activation of C Battery effective August 28, with the unit's departure for the West Coast Training Center at Camp Pendleton around September 1. The accompanying photo showed the unit's commander, Captain Gordon Worthington of Brandon, reading the order calling the unit into active service.[40]

Marine Battery C was the first military reserve unit in the Jackson area called to active duty. The city of Jackson and the Jackson Jaycees staged a celebratory parade led by the Forest Hill band during which the reservists marched from the Marine Reserve facility behind the Old Capitol building to City Hall, where Captain Worthington presented a flag to Mayor Allen C. Thompson, who proclaimed Battery C Day in the city. The members of the battery then boarded a train at the Illinois Central depot on West Capitol Street.[41]

After a six-day train trip from Jackson to San Diego, the five young men from Clinton got off a bus at midnight at Camp Pendleton. Despite their fatigue, they were told to stand on yellow-painted footprints on the concrete walk. A Marine sergeant made sarcastic remarks about the group of more than fifty young men looking like a bunch of girls. He began calling off their names and assigning them to training companies. George Sharp went directly to twelve weeks of combat training, while Bill Smith was assigned to the 4th Battalion, 11th Artillery Regiment, which would leave for Korea in October. Waller, Joe, and Homer were sent to boot camp, Homer and Joe to one company, Waller to another.[42]

The five were about to begin the great adventure of their lives.

Fallen Comrade, sketch by Dr. Samuel M. Gore, 2009. Courtesy of the family of Dr. Samuel M. Gore; original sketch in Gore Gallery Collection, Mississippi College.

Joe Albritton with his new Leica camera, 1950. Photo by Waller King; courtesy of Clay King.

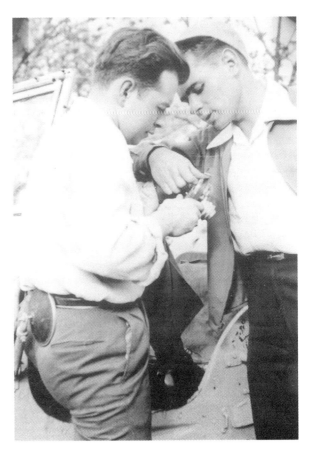

Joe Albritton (*left*) and Homer Ainsworth, 1950. Photo by Waller King; courtesy of Clay King.

Joe Albritton (*left*) and Waller King just before they were called to active duty, 1950. Courtesy of Clay King.

(*left to right*) George Sharp, Waller King, and Joe Albritton in front of the Bank of Clinton, May 1950. Photo by George M. Black; courtesy of Margaret Anne Black.

Waller King, 1950. Photo by George M. Black; courtesy of Margaret Anne Black.

Joe Albritton and Homer Ainsworth onboard a Navy ship on their way to Korea, March–April 1951. Courtesy of the family of Peggy Albritton Sharp.

Homer Ainsworth onboard a Navy ship on his way to Korea, March–April 1951. Photo by Joe Albritton; courtesy of the family of Peggy Albritton Sharp.

Homer Ainsworth during basic training at Camp Pendleton, California, 1950–51. Photo by Joe Albritton; courtesy of the family of Peggy Albritton Sharp.

(*left to right*) Homer Ainsworth, George Hardy, and Joe Albritton during basic training near Bishop, California, winter 1950–51. Courtesy of the family of Peggy Albritton Sharp.

(*left to right*) John Wayne and Joe Albritton during the filming of *Fighting Leathernecks*, spring 1951. Courtesy of the family of Peggy Albritton Sharp.

(*left to right*) Joe Albritton, George Hardy, and Homer Ainsworth during basic training, Camp Pendleton, California, 1950–51. Courtesy of the family of Peggy Albritton Sharp.

Joe Albritton, Korea, 1951. Courtesy of the family of Peggy Albritton Sharp.

Joe Albritton on patrol, May 15, 1951. Courtesy of the family of Peggy Albritton Sharp.

Waller King on an outpost, Korea, 1951. Courtesy of Clay King.

1st Marine command post on the road to Hongchon, just south of the No Name Line, May 1951.
US Marine Corps; National Archives, ID 127-GR-155-A8728.

Chosin Reservoir observation post, 1950. Oliver P. Smith Collection, COLL/213, Archives Branch, Marine Corps History Division, Quantico, VA.

Marines on the road between Yudam-ni and Toktong Pass, November 1950. Oliver P. Smith Collection, COLL/213, Archives Branch, Marine Corps History Division, Quantico, VA.

Tractors towing 155mm howitzers to Hagaru-ri, November–December 1950. RG 127, General Photograph File of the US Marine Corps, National Archives, College Park, Maryland; Local ID 127-N-A5670.

5th and 7th Marines withdrawing from the Chosin Reservoir, December 1950. RG 127, General Photograph File of the US Marine Corps, National Archives, College Park, Maryland; Local ID 127-N-A4852).

Chapter 3

INCHON AND SEOUL, SEPTEMBER–OCTOBER 1950

Amphibious landings are among the most complicated maneuvers in a war,
requiring intense planning, choreography and timing–a Marine's specialty.
—**Victor Krulak,** *First to Fight: An Insider View of the US Marine Corps*

While the Fire Brigade wrapped up its operations in the Pusan Perimeter
in early September, Waller King, Joe Albritton, and Homer Ainsworth
began boot camp at Camp Pendleton in San Diego, California. Joe and
Homer started training immediately, while Waller was assigned to a platoon tasked with building twelve-man squad tents for other new arrivals.
Two weeks behind Joe and Homer in the training cycle, Waller did not
see either of them until they were home on Christmas leave.

Boot camp was a physical and mental challenge for the Clinton boys.
Joe and Waller had played football in high school and knew about physical
conditioning, but now they trained sixteen hours a day. When they ran,
they ran in combat boots—a total of 90 miles during the twelve weeks
of boot camp. They also marched more than 250 miles, ran the obstacle
course ten times, did at least seventy hours of calisthenics, swam for a
minimum of sixteen hours, and spent ninety hours in field training.[1]

Their drill sergeants instilled discipline by separating trainees from
their civilian habits and mindsets. Waller, Joe, and Homer were now in a
hostile environment designed to prepare them to function during intense

harassment and confusion, much like conditions they would face in combat. They gained the instinct of quick and total obedience, something with which they—and especially Joe—were not familiar. Joe's record of mischievous behavior did not bode well for him in boot camp, but from all accounts he adapted and proved to be a good Marine.

Waller felt he was reduced to a dog during the first weeks of boot camp, stripped of his pride and self-esteem as the drill sergeant sought to change Waller into a mean, dirty, fighter. Because Waller was six feet, three inches tall, he was selected as the leader of his twelve-man squad even though he was only seventeen years old. The squad also included Eddie Gomez, whom Waller described as a "no-good . . . kid from Omaha, Nebraska" who caused his leader untold grief: "He could do nothing right, and I was the one punished for every infraction."[2]

Waller, Joe, and Homer still knew little about what was taking place in Korea. Their drill sergeants never mentioned the conflict, and the only outside news came from the weekly arrival by mail of the *Clinton News*. They knew that Herbert Pearce, a 1948 Clinton High graduate, was serving as a medic with the 5th Marine Regiment and that Eugene S. Harris, son of Hendon M. and Florence Harris, a missionary couple living in Clinton, had been reported missing in action in August 1950. Harris was killed on September 26, 1950.[3]

The three knew nothing of the amphibious landing that was about to commence as they started boot camp. The landing at Inchon was General Douglas MacArthur's grand plan to bring the war to a close as quickly as possible, but those opposed to the idea included his own staff, the Navy and Marines, and the Joint Chiefs of Staff (JCS) in Washington, DC.

The barriers to an Inchon landing seemed insurmountable. An invasion force would have to move through a narrow, mined channel and twist its way through mudflats; a high seawall; Wolmido (Moontip) Island, which blocked the harbor entrance; and the most extreme tidal range in the world—thirty-two feet. Wolmido Island would have to be neutralized before the landing. Since both operations could not be carried out during the same favorable tide, eleven hours would lapse between the attack on the island and the landing.[4]

MacArthur had an answer for every argument against his plan. North Korean forces were concentrated at Pusan, leaving Inchon vulnerable to an attack, and he predicted that the landing would save 100,000 lives. Given that the only alternative was a frontal attack from the Pusan Perimeter, which would be costly in terms of casualties, the JCS reluctantly agreed to MacArthur's operation.

MacArthur believed that the Navy and the Marines could carry out the landing—he had more confidence in them than in his own soldiers, though he would never publicly say so. He gave General Edward Almond, his chief of staff, command of the Inchon landing but overruled his suggestion that elements of the 7th Army Division carry out the amphibious landing. Navy and Marine leaders balked, and MacArthur agreed that the Marines would make the landing with the Army following.

MacArthur made a mistake in judgment when he gave command of the landing operation to Almond rather than to General Lemuel Shepherd of the Pacific Marine Force. However, another Marine general, Oliver Smith, had the presence of mind and strong will to compensate for Almond's many errors during the Inchon operation. Smith's Marines were part of the 8th Army's X Corps, commanded by Almond.

Smith had already compiled a distinguished military record. He had commanded the 5th Marine Regiment in the Pacific theater during World War II and was part of the 10th Army team that planned the invasion of Okinawa. Smith was serving as assistant commandant of the Marine Corps when the Korean War broke out and received his second star when he took command of the 1st Marine Division in July 1950.[5]

Almond, a Virginia native and graduate of the Citadel, had commanded an all-Black division in Europe during World War II. Considered one of MacArthur's "fair-haired boys" and fiercely loyal to him, Almond was clearly out of his element at the helm of the Inchon landing.

Almond decided to war-game the Inchon operation eight days before the scheduled landing—timing that made the exercise senseless. The Marine operations officer, Colonel A. L. Bowser, recognized the absurdity of the idea and told Almond's subordinate to take the directive back to his commander.[6]

Almond's next gaffe was his request for 100 Marines to team with Army rangers and British commandos to paddle ashore at night, move ten miles over land, and capture the Kimpo airfield. Smith initially tried to explain to Almond that the boats could not move forward against six knots of tidal current and then finally rejected his scheme outright, telling Almond that the Marines were not available. Almond dropped the idea.[7]

Operation Chromite's 260-ship invasion force left Japan on September 8, 1950. Those deployed included the 1st Marine Regiment, which had just arrived from the States. Vessels carrying the 5th Marine Regiment joined the invasion fleet as it passed the bottom of Korea and moved up the west coast. The fleet encountered severe weather when it entered the Yellow Sea but kept on schedule. The 7th Marine Regiment was still en route to Korea and would not be available for the initial landing on September 15, which was the only day of that month when Inchon's tides would permit a landing.

MacArthur's planners carried out a series of deceptive moves to confuse the North Koreans about the landing's exact location. The battleship *Missouri* shelled the east coast port of Samchok, while carrier aircraft struck the small port of Kunsan, one hundred miles south of Inchon. Other attacks took place on the western coast of North Korea at possible landing sites near the capital of Pyongyang. On September 7, a British frigate carried out an amphibious feint at Kunsan.[8]

Navy and Marine aircraft began bombing and strafing runs in the Inchon sector on September 10 as the fleet continued toward Flying Fish Channel, the narrow twelve-mile passage to Inchon that had to be navigated with precision. MacArthur, aboard the *Mount McKinley* as it reached the entry channel, received word that the president had fired Louis Johnson, the secretary of defense. MacArthur also received a last-minute communique from the JCS asking him to reevaluate his plans, a request that he believed had originated with President Harry S. Truman. MacArthur replied with an assurance that the landing would succeed.

General Almond continued to show his ignorance of amphibious operations. While standing on the deck of the *Mount McKinley* at dawn on September 15 and watching the unloading of amphibious landing craft for the attack on Wolmido Island, Almond made a comment that indicated his unawareness that the vehicles could float. Colonel Victor "Brute" Krulak was appalled.[9]

Repeated air attacks by Marine and Navy aircraft destroyed all visible fortifications and burned off vegetation on Wolmido Island by September 14, and the Marine assault began around 6:30 a.m. on September 15, after a heavy naval bombardment and air strikes on the island. The estimated 300 North Korean troops who had survived the earlier attacks could give only token resistance as the 3rd Battalion of the 5th Marines (3/5) went ashore.

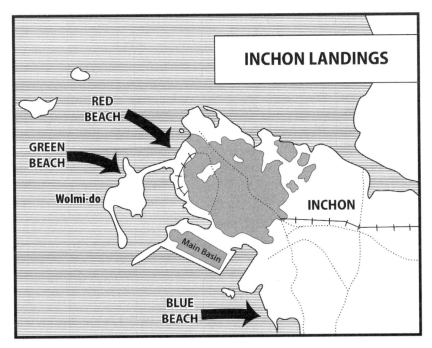

Inchon Landings, September 1950.

The island was secured in two hours. The battalion and nine tanks of the 1st Marine Tank Battalion then moved over the causeway connecting the island with Inchon and set up a front at Red Beach, while the invasion fleet waited in plain sight for the tide to return.[10]

The bombardment of Inchon harbor began later that morning, and the waterfront was soon burning. With the afternoon tide, the landing began. Despite the predictable chaos—several landing craft became mired in the mudflats, and some friendly-fire casualties occurred—the initial landing was accomplished by the end of the day. Seeing the American flag flying on the highest hill on Wolmido Island, MacArthur sent a message to Admiral Arthur Dewey Struble: "The Navy and the Marines have never shown more brightly than this morning."[11]

Colonel Lewis "Chesty" Puller's 1st Marine Regiment landed at Blue Beach, an industrial area three miles southeast of Red Beach, where the 5th Marines under Lieutenant Colonel Ray Murray made their landing, using scaling ladders to climb the high seawall blocking the shore. By nightfall, 13,000 Marines had come ashore, suffering 20 KIA and 179 wounded.

The forces began moving into Inchon the next morning and secured the city within three hours. As the Marines moved from the beachhead into towns around Inchon, enemy resistance stiffened.

The 5th Marines moved on Kimpo airfield, sixteen miles away, while the 1st Marines went up the highway to Yongdungpo, an industrial suburb across the Han River from Seoul. Soldiers of the Army's 7th Division came ashore on September 18, followed days later by the just-arrived 7th Marine regiment.[12]

General Smith set up his command post onshore and quickly restored civil government in Inchon. Officers from the Republic of Korea (ROK) Marine regiment screened local residents for loyalty. Smith installed a provisional municipal government that began to bury the civilian dead, care for orphans, distribute food and clothing, and establish a hospital and a police force.[13]

General MacArthur came ashore on September 16 along with his staff, war correspondents, and photographers. Smith cautioned MacArthur that enemy fire remained intense and expressed concerns regarding his safety and that of his entourage, which included Truman's special envoy Frank Lowe and Marguerite Higgins, a reporter for the *New York Herald Tribune* who went on to win the 1951 Pulitzer Prize for her coverage of the war. Within a day, photographs of the landing appeared in newspapers across the United States. *Time, Life, Newsweek,* and other publications followed with feature stories on the Inchon landing and the ensuing events.[14]

A North Korean division in Seoul had been about to depart for the Pusan Perimeter when the Inchon landing began but was ordered to remain to defend the capital. The division consisted of 12,000 soldiers (most of them recruits with little training), few tanks, and no air cover. In the early hours of September 17, a North Korean column led by six tanks made its way along the Inchon-Seoul highway to attempt a counterattack on the Marines but soon came under fire from Marine tanks and artillery. The North Korean tanks were destroyed, and the soldiers scattered. Within hours, General MacArthur and his entourage visited the battle site; after they left, Marines captured seven armed soldiers hiding nearby.[15]

The 5th Marine Regiment and the ROK Marines continued to move toward Kimpo airfield, a strategic target that US/UN forces wanted to use for air-ground support, transportation of supplies, and evacuation of wounded. The airfield and three Soviet-built fighter aircraft were captured on September 18, and several enemy counterattacks failed to dislodge the Marines. The airfield was in surprisingly good condition, requiring only minor repairs. The 5th Marines set up their command post at Kimpo: when a Marine helicopter landed later that morning, it became the first US aircraft to touch down there since the June evacuation.[16]

General Smith had all three regiments of his division together for the assault on Seoul. The 5th Marines under Lieutenant Colonel Murray were to cross the Han River north of Kimpo and then swing east along the north side of the river and attack Seoul from its flank. The 1st Marines under Colonel Puller would first secure Yongdungpo, then cross the Han north of the suburb and join the 5th Marines in the flanking attack. The 7th Marines, under the command of Colonel Homer Litzenberg, were to go to a line north of the 5th Marines.

Murray's 5th Regiment started the Seoul offensive on the night of September 19, when a swim team crossed the Han River to reconnoiter its northern bank. They found no enemies in the area and signaled for landing vehicles to start the crossing. When the engines started, however, the well-concealed enemy forces responded with heavy artillery fire, preventing any landing. The swim team pulled back south of the river. The Marines brought in their own heavy artillery and close air support, clearing the hillsides north of the river and carrying out the crossing on September 20.[17]

The 1st Marines captured Yongdungpo on September 22 after a three-day fight. Second Lieutenant Henry Commiskey of the 1st Marines, a native of Hattiesburg, Mississippi, led his platoon in a head-on assault against North Korean defenders on Hill 85. Commiskey outran the platoon and found himself alone and armed only with his service .45 automatic weapon. After reaching the top of the hill, Commiskey leaped into a North Korean machine-gun emplacement, shooting four soldiers and killing a fifth with his bare hands. He then picked up several enemy rifles and advanced on another machine-gun nest, killing two Koreans. The remaining North Korean soldiers abandoned the hill. Commiskey later received the Congressional Medal of Honor for his actions in what became known as the Madman of Hill 85 incident.[18]

After capturing Yongdungpo, the 1st Marines crossed the Han and began to move along the highway to Seoul. The 5th Marines regrouped after crossing the Han and prepared for their march to the capital. At the

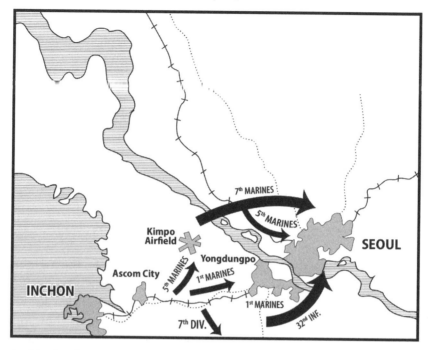

Retaking Seoul, September 1950.

same time, General MacArthur and his party made another appearance in the combat zone. The general was pleased. He had just received a message reiterating the JCS's doubts about the landing and warning that if the operation failed, the US/UN effort in Korea might be plunged into serious difficulties. But MacArthur remained nonplussed: "I and all of my commanders and staff officers, without exception, are enthusiastic and confident of the success of the enveloping operation."[19]

Litzenberg's 7th Regiment reached Inchon on September 21 and saw its first action the next day. Units of the 7th gave backup support to both the 1st and 5th Regiments after they crossed the Han River. General Smith decided to hold the 7th back briefly, giving the regiment time to adjust to the new surroundings before committing it to the attack on Seoul.[20]

In Pusan, General Walton Walker's 8th Army launched a major assault on North Korean forces along the perimeter line on September 16. The enemy soldiers strongly resisted the US/UN attack, unaware of the Inchon landing and expecting the arrival of support troops from Seoul. But the reinforcements had been held back to defend the capital.[21]

After a week of US/UN counterattacks, the North Koreans began to panic as they recognized the danger of being enveloped as the Marines advanced on Seoul. The North Koreans' discipline broke down, and the retreat northward turned into a near rout.[22]

The 1st and 5th Marine Regiments continued their assault on Seoul. Impatient with the Marines' progress, General Almond told General Smith that the Marines had twenty-four hours "to make headway" before the Army's 32nd Infantry Regiment and the ROK Marine Ranger Regiment would cross the Han River southeast of the capital and advance from that direction. Almond wanted to capture Seoul by September 25, the three-month anniversary of the invasion. Smith replied that his troops would do their best, but "I can't guarantee you anything. I leave that up to the enemy."[23]

Relations between Almond and Smith continued to deteriorate. When Almond broke the chain of command by giving orders directly to Marine regimental commanders, Smith politely mentioned that he preferred to command his own regiments. When Almond continued to interfere, Smith angrily denounced the Army general's actions during a meeting in the presence of other officers and correspondents. Almond, now on the defensive, took Smith aside and assured him that a misunderstanding must have occurred because he had never given orders to his regimental commanders.[24]

Colonel J. D. Coleman, who served in the Army under Almond, said that his style was "to bully, to meddle, and to constantly interfere with the normal chain of command. He had an enormous ego and he spared no one—officers or soldiers—in his efforts to demonstrate his superiority."[25]

The battle for Seoul represented urban warfare at its most intense. When the 1st Marines captured Hill 66, the heart of the North Korean defenses, on September 26, the enemy lines collapsed, and the North Koreans began a pullout. Half of Seoul was now secured. Marine attacks against western defenses, coupled with attacks by the Army's 34th Infantry Regiment and the ROK Marine Regiment from the southeast, forced the main North Korean army to evacuate Seoul on September 26, but the fight for the capital was not yet over.

General Almond had been almost pathological in his quest to capture Seoul by September 25. That evening, he prematurely issued a press release announcing the liberation of Seoul, though fighting in the city continued for another four days.[26]

The remaining North Korean forces in Seoul set up barricades of sandbags at intersections and used machine guns and antitank guns to sweep the streets, making any Marine movement dangerous. Fighting block by block and neutralizing every barricade they encountered, the Marines engaged in a series of nasty street fights that took a heavy toll on both sides. The Marines improvised a method for destroying the barricades, calling on Marine and Navy aircraft to strafe the positions and hit them with rockets. While the North Koreans were pinned down, Marine tanks advanced and destroyed the barricade. Sometimes it took an hour to break a barricade, leaving the area burning and littered with dead bodies. Colonel Chesty Puller's 1st Marine Regiment did most of the heavy fighting in capturing Seoul.[27]

By the morning of September 27, Seoul was a dying city. North Korean snipers still commanded the rooftops, and street-to-street fighting continued as the Marines and units of the Army's 7th Infantry slowly took possession of the city.[28]

MacArthur wanted a ceremony replete with honor guards when the Rhee government returned to Seoul. The JCS learned of his plans and sent a message admonishing the general for acting without higher authority. But MacArthur—the highest US/UN authority in Korea—retorted, "Your message is not understood. I have no plan whatsoever except scrupulously to implement the directive I have received." He pointed out that the UN Security Council had called on all its members to assist the Republic of Korea in repelling the armed attack and restoring the country's security.[29] The United Nations had recognized the Korean government's legality, and he was returning Seoul to that government. MacArthur was a step ahead of the JCS.

On September 29, Marine guards lined the route from Kimpo airfield to the capitol in Seoul. At 10:00 a.m. General MacArthur and his wife, Jean, landed at Kimpo and were escorted to the first of five waiting staff cars, followed by five jeeps for the press corps. The procession drove toward the government building on roads lined with Korean civilians. Rhee and his party arrived later that morning, flying in from Taegu.[30]

UN officials, diplomats, South Korean officials and military leaders, and US military officers filled the National Assembly room in the capitol for the ceremonies. The US contingent included three full rows of army generals but only four Marine officers—Generals Oliver Smith and Edward Craig and Colonels Lewis Puller and Ray Murray. Despite suffering more than

700 casualties in the fight for Seoul, the Marines were scarcely represented; in fact, Colonels Litzenberg and Brower were still fighting.[31]

MacArthur opened the ceremonies by praising the men fighting under the UN banner. Enemy artillery thundered in the background as the general asked the audience to stand and join him in the Lord's Prayer. Then MacArthur turned to Rhee and said, "Mr. President, my officers and I will now resume our military duties and leave you and your government to the discharge of civil responsibilities." The two men embraced, and Rhee told the crowd, "We admire you. We love you as the savior of our race! How can I ever explain to you my own undying gratitude and that of the Korean people?"[32]

MacArthur left Korea after the ceremony and began to question Washington's thinking on Korea:

The golden moment to transmit our victory at Inchon into a political peace had arrived. Yet, it appeared that diplomatic inertia had set in, and we were failing to grasp the possibilities of ending the war and moving towards a decisive peace in the Pacific. The rule of the day was timidity and appeasement, which would not end the war, but increase the military efforts against us. I discussed my fears with General Walker, who agreed completely.[33]

The Inchon-Seoul campaign began on September 15, 1950, and ended on October 7. A total of 19,494 Marine and Navy personnel were engaged in the operation. The Marines suffered 366 KIA, 49 dead of wounds, 6 missing in action, and 2,029 wounded. Estimated enemy casualties were 13,666 killed and wounded and 6,492 captured.[34]

Inchon was MacArthur's last stroke of genius. According to David Rees, author of *Korea: The Limited War*,

Inchon, then, could not have happened under any other commander but MacArthur. It sprang from his overpowering personality and self-confidence, and his plan was supported by no one else for it looked back to an age of warfare unencumbered by specialist objectives and peripatetic Joint Chiefs. . . . [I]t was a triumph not of military logic and science, but of imagination and intuition. It was justified on no other grounds but the overwhelming, most simple; it succeeded and remains a Twentieth Century Cannae ever to be studied.[35]

Military and civilian leaders only reluctantly endorsed MacArthur's plan. General Omar Bradley, chair of the JCS, called Inchon "the luckiest military operation in history." But luck had nothing to do with it. Planning and execution brought success. Bradley later admitted, "In hindsight the JCS seemed like a bunch of nervous Nellies to have doubted."[36]

According to Admiral James Doyle, the Navy commander responsible for the amphibious landing, "The assault itself was successful only through the perfect teamwork that existed between the participating Naval and Marine elements." Success demanded that an incredible number of individual and coordinated tasks be performed precisely as planned. Only the Marine Corps, with its specialized training in amphibious warfare, and the Navy had the required know-how to formulate and execute plans flawlessly without additional training or rehearsal. For the 1st Marine Division, the Inchon landing and the liberation of Seoul constituted another chapter in the glorious story of the Marine Corps at war. General Smith's team worked with speed and precision, an acceleration of men and events made possible by the experiences of a Navy–Marine Corps team that had long worked together in the Pacific.

At the time of the Inchon-Seoul operation, the Marines were still the only military service with helicopters, and they carried out 643 helicopter and light aircraft surveillance flights over 515 hours. In addition, helicopters evacuated 139 seriously wounded men, who owed their lives to the speed and ease with which they were transported to the hospital.[37]

What General MacArthur and the 1st Marine Division accomplished was heresy to that group of military thinkers who believed that nuclear and aeronautical sciences had diminished armies, navies, and humans as insignificant in waging war. These advocates of the push-button theory of warfare were thoroughly disillusioned by what took place at Inchon on September 15, 1950.

Inchon and Seoul were psychological and political victories for the American public as well. MacArthur restored confidence in the US military, and the country believed that the North Korean invaders would quickly be pushed back across the 38th Parallel and the status quo ante bellum restored. That, however, was not the Truman administration's objective. Containment had been achieved. The new goal was liberating North Korea.

In deciding to intervene in Korea, the Truman administration knew that the North Koreans would certainly be defeated. Weeks before the

Inchon landing, senior officials debated whether the 8th Army should invade North Korea after liberating the south. They considered possible Soviet or Chinese intervention if US/UN forces crossed the parallel but agreed that the Soviet Union would not risk global war over Korea and that China was too weak militarily to fight the United States.[38]

The approaching midterm elections in the United States also influenced the decision to cross the parallel. The administration knew a decisive victory in Korea would be politically profitable for Democrats. Eliminating Soviet influence on the peninsula would have a positive impact on other Asian countries flirting with Communism, and the rescue of some 2,700 American prisoners of war would give Washington the moral high ground.

On September 1, 1950, the National Security Council recommended that the president authorize MacArthur to cross the 38th Parallel, destroy the North Korean army, and provide for the unification of Korea via free elections. Truman approved the document ten days later. General MacArthur received a summary of the plan on September 15, the day of the Inchon landing. He was cautioned not to implement any action without the specific "approval of the President."[39]

When the US recommendation was introduced in the United Nations, the British initially objected because of concerns about a possible Chinese attack against Hong Kong, a British colony. Other resolutions called on UN forces to stop at the 38th Parallel, but when the General Assembly took up the question on September 29, forty-seven nations voted to approve going north of the parallel, the five Soviet-bloc countries voted no, and eight countries abstained.[40]

The JCS provided MacArthur with specific instructions for crossing the 38th Parallel: "Your military objective is the destruction of the North Korean armed forces." MacArthur was not to make any statements about unifying Korea and under no circumstances was he to use air or naval forces to attack Manchuria or Soviet territory. MacArthur had to clear all movements northward with the JCS and have ROK units cross the parallel first, with Americans following. The general was on a leash.

North Korean forces retreating north from Pusan hoped to reach the 38th Parallel before being cut off by American forces moving east from Seoul. Their commanders did not know that the US/UN army intended to pursue them across the parallel.

General Walker had not been in contact with MacArthur during the breakout from Pusan and had no orders regarding what to do after reaching the 38th Parallel. Walker developed a plan predicated on the X Corps being placed under his direct command. Once his army reached the Parallel, X Corps would lead the drive to capture Pyongyang, the North Korean capital, and then would head east to the port of Wonsan. The 8th Army and X Corps would then carry out an offensive north to the Yalu River, which formed the border between Manchuria and North Korea.

MacArthur had other ideas. X Corps would remain an independent force under General Almond and responsible to MacArthur. MacArthur wanted the 1st Marine Division to ship out from Inchon and make an amphibious landing on the east coast at Wonsan. The Army's 7th Division, meanwhile, would travel south from Seoul to Pusan, where they would board ships for Wonsan. X Corps would be positioned to move west to join with the 8th Army and march to the Yalu River.

MacArthur considered different factors in his planning. The animosity between Walker and Almond prevented either man from serving under the other. Keeping X Corps separate and under Almond's direction allowed MacArthur to reward his chief of staff for his loyalty while keeping the direct control that MacArthur relished. The Inchon landing had won MacArthur accolades around the world, and another amphibious landing would not only repeat that strategy but also give him a third port for supplying US/UN forces in Korea.

MacArthur's plan also had many weaknesses. An ROK Army Corps moving up the east coast of Korea would already be in position to capture Wonsan long before a Marine landing could take place. Loading the Marines onto ships at Inchon would tie up the port for up to fifteen days, preventing it from receiving vital supplies for the 8th Army. Sending the 7th Division down the already crowded Seoul-to-Pusan highway would create major traffic problems and delays. And the idea of sending X Corps west from Wonsan across treacherous mountain terrain to join up with the 8th Army more than fifty miles away was not logical.

Army, Navy, and Marine Corps officers voiced opposition to MacArthur's plan. General Dave Barr, commander of the 7th Division, favored General Walker's plan. X Corps was positioned to carry out hot pursuit of enemy forces, exploit their weaknesses, and prevent them from regrouping.

MacArthur's plan would throw away that opportunity. Admiral C. Turner Joy warned that Wonsan Harbor was probably mined, delaying any landing for days. General Smith, who chafed at having to continue serving under Almond, questioned MacArthur's strategy that would send a Marine division along miles and miles of poor roads with units unable to assist each other when attacked.

MacArthur refused to listen. Still basking in the glow of his success at Inchon, he allowed no debate on the merits of the landing at Wonsan. He refused to meet with Joy in Tokyo headquarters and let Almond deal with Generals Barr and Smith in Korea. Almond flippantly dismissed their concerns and even moved the Wonsan landing up from October 20 to October 15.

After the US/UN forces retook Seoul, the Chinese government warned that they should not cross the 38th Parallel and invade North Korea. In late September, Beijing announced that "battled-trained Koreans from Manchuria" had been released from the Chinese Army "to defend their motherland." On September 25, the Chinese charged that a US plane had dropped twelve bombs on Antung, just across the Yalu frontier. On the same day, Chinese premier Chou En-lai told the Indian ambassador to China that the country would intervene if UN/US forces crossed the 38th Parallel.[41]

American officials heard the Chinese warnings but did not heed them. Secretary of state Dean Acheson did not take them seriously because he did not trust the Indian ambassador, who had a reputation for overreacting. Others in the administration doubted that the Chinese would give advance warning if they intended to intervene. Some saw China's statement as an attempt at "diplomatic blackmail" and a "war of words" intended to deter an invasion of North Korea.[42]

Moreover, the 38th Parallel was not sacrosanct. American aircraft had crossed the line repeatedly when ordered to do so soon after the North Korean invasion, and American ships had sailed north of the parallel. US leaders argued that the parallel had no legal or logical basis, an argument that the UN General Assembly accepted on October 7 when it approved a resolution that stated, "The artificial barrier which has divided North and South Korea has no basis for existence in law or in reason. . . . The North Koreans, by armed attack upon the Republic of Korea, have denied the reality of any such line."[43]

ROK forces crossed the parallel on October 1 on the east coast at the same time that MacArthur announced the UN command's surrender terms to the head of the North Korean Army. MacArthur did not receive a direct response, but North Korean president Kim Il-sung made a fiery radio speech in which he declared that he would not surrender.

The Truman administration had no reliable way to verify China's intentions. The United States had no high-level spies in Beijing. Moreover, Chinese radio communications were in the Mandarin dialect, and the US Army intelligence staff in Tokyo had no Mandarin linguists; the Pentagon rejected requests to have Nationalist Chinese linguists assist in translating.

Relying solely on aerial surveillance, MacArthur's intelligence service believed it could provide an accurate picture of Chinese movements toward the Yalu River. US/UN aircraft controlled the North Korean skies and could detect any aggressive movement by the Chinese. But American intelligence did not consider Chinese forces' ability to camouflage their movements. Photographs taken in early October 1950 indicated that about 210,000 Chinese soldiers were deployed north of the Yalu River.

When US/UN troops crossed the 38th Parallel, the United States passed the point of no return in Korea, symbolically laying down the gauntlet to China and the Soviet Union. The United Nations endorsed the invasion, and MacArthur believed he had the means to win the war. The general had seven US divisions (about 125,000 men), six ROK divisions (about 60,000 men), and about 3,000 British Commonwealth soldiers under his command. His ground forces had the support of six aircraft carriers, the battleship *Missouri*, six cruisers, and hundreds of destroyers, landing craft, and other vessels as well as the US 5th Air Force and Navy and Marine aircraft. MacArthur faced the remnants of thirteen divisions of the North Korean army. With two reserve divisions, the North Koreans were defending their country with about 100,000 demoralized and ill-equipped troops. North Korea had no naval craft or airplanes.

ROK divisions moved slowly north of the 38th Parallel on September 30, meeting little resistance. They had the cover of the US 5th Air Force, which conducted unfettered bombing and strafing of North Korean targets. The offensive continued smoothly until October 8, when two US fighter aircraft pursuing enemy planes attacked a Soviet airfield sixty-two miles north of the Yalu River, near Vladivostok. Such an attack was not part of Washington's plan. Provoking the Soviets was not in America's interests. Fortunately for the United States, there were no major diplomatic repercussions.

On October 9, the JCS directed MacArthur to engage with Chinese troops in Korea as long as China had not publicly announced it was intervening. MacArthur was empowered to act as long as he felt confident that he could defeat the Chinese forces without calling for reinforcements. He was not to attack Chinese territory under any circumstances unless he received specific instructions from Washington to do so.

The question of Chinese intervention, coupled with the unauthorized American attack on the Soviet airfield, led Truman to decide on a face-to-face meeting with MacArthur. According to John Spanier, Truman wanted "to establish a more cordial and harmonious relationship with his field commander." The president wanted to convey his foreign policy goals to the general in an attempt to prevent him from ignoring them. Truman's advisers cautioned him to meet with MacArthur somewhere in the Pacific, far from Washington, DC, so that he could not stir up Republican opposition so close to the midterm congressional elections.[44]

MacArthur's staff thought that the meeting was unnecessary and believed that the president was seeking to bask in the glow of the Inchon triumph. With congressional elections approaching, Democrats wanted all the positive press they could get.[45]

The president was scheduled to make a speech in California, so the meeting was set for October 15 on Wake Island, a dot in the middle of the Pacific Ocean. Though wartime meetings between presidents and their military commanders had a history that dated back to the US Civil War, this one was different. Many observers at Wake Island thought that the commander in chief and his subordinate seemed to be meeting as equals.

MacArthur arrived first and welcomed Truman when his plane landed. The general did not give the traditional salute to the president, a slight that Truman remembered. They conferenced privately for an hour in a Quonset hut near the beach, where, according to Truman, they discussed the situation in Korea and Japan. Truman received assurances that the Korean conflict had been won and that Chinese intervention was unlikely. The president also said they reached complete agreement on the general's support of Truman's foreign policy.[46]

Truman and MacArthur then moved to another building for a meeting that included the president's military and diplomatic advisers. Though no official transcript of the meeting was made, a secretary to Philip C. Jessup, Truman's ambassador-at-large, took notes from an adjacent room. MacArthur did not know that notes had been taken until several months later, when Truman used them to refute statements MacArthur made after being relieved of his command.[47]

According to the notes, the discussions centered on Korean rehabilitation, economic, and unification problems. MacArthur addressed a number of strictly military matters, including his plan to use X Corps to drive from Wonsan on the east coast to Pyongyang to the west. He believed that North Korean resistance would end by Thanksgiving and hoped to withdraw the 8th Army to Japan by Christmas, leaving two divisions and detachments from other countries as an occupation force. When Truman asked about the chances of Chinese intervention, MacArthur responded, "Very little. Had they interfered in the first or second months it would have been decisive. We are no longer fearful of their intervention. We no longer stand hat in hand. The Chinese have 300,000 men in Manchuria, not more than 100,000 to 125,000 are distributed along the Yalu River. They have no air force."[48]

The meeting ended with Truman's statement that the talks had been satisfactory and that "there is complete unity in the aims and conduct of our foreign policy." The president's words implied that MacArthur was an equal in policymaking, though the president missed the subtlety.

MacArthur later wrote in his memoir, *Reminiscences*, that his assurances of China's nonintervention were based on a purely military evaluation, whereas the question of intervention was primarily a political one. He claimed to have told the president that this evaluation could not be a guarantee. MacArthur's military intelligence on Korea was faulty, He pointed out that neither the State and Defense Departments nor the Central Intelligence Agency had at any time furnished him with any "political intelligence" indicating that the Chinese Communists would pursue a course contrary to the one he had predicted and that General Bradley had already raised the question of transferring troops from East Asia to Europe. MacArthur suspected that the Wake Island meeting had been called for political purposes and feared that the president was "being swayed by constant whispers of timidity and cynicism."[49]

Truman's hopes for the meeting did not pan out. The president may have given too much credence to MacArthur's opinions on the question of Chinese intervention. The general's military intelligence on Korea was faulty, though the Central Intelligence Agency's readings were no better. MacArthur had proven himself right about the Inchon landing, and Truman hoped that the same would hold true for China.

MacArthur returned to Japan and the war, while Truman flew back to Washington optimistic that the conflict would soon be over. He did not know that on the night of his departure from Wake Island, major elements of the Chinese 4th Army crossed the Yalu River into North Korea. Other Chinese units followed under the cover of darkness during the next two weeks, and by the end of October, 180,000 Chinese soldiers were on Korean soil, with another 120,000 still in Manchuria and ready for war against US/UN forces.[50]

The Chinese had determined early in the war that if North Korea faltered, they were obligated to come to its aid. Koreans had fought in the Chinese Revolution, the anti-Japanese resistance, and the Chinese Civil War. China's commitment to North Korea would be honored. The Chinese government informed the Soviet government of its intentions.

After returning to Tokyo from Wake Island, MacArthur learned the North Koreans had mined Wonsan Harbor, meaning that the Marine landing would be delayed. He consequently changed his plans: instead of moving laterally from Wonsan and joining with 8th Army for the advance northward, X Corps would now move north from Wonsan to Hungnam and proceed toward the Chosin Reservoir and from there to the Yalu River. The Army's 7th Division would be diverted to Iwon, a port about 100 miles by sea north of Wonsan in an area already controlled by ROK units. MacArthur also ordered the Army's 3rd Infantry Division, his command's only reserve force, to Wonsan to protect the coastal area after the Marines moved north. The 3rd was understrength and had 8,500 Korean draftees added to bring it up to combat strength. It became part of X Corps.

The JCS in Washington still questioned MacArthur's planning, especially the immense logistics problems caused by moving X Corps from the Seoul area to Wonsan. Another puzzling question was MacArthur's decision to move the 7th Division to Iwon, where the unit would not be in position to support the 1st Marine Division in any move to the north.

Chapter 4

CHINESE INTERVENTION, OCTOBER–NOVEMBER 1950

No, I hold no grudge against anyone about going to Korea to chase the North Koreans back across the 38th Parallel. It was supposed to take two or three months. Then, we were to go home. But after we had done that, why did we start heading north for the North Korean–Chinese border, especially with the oncoming Korean winter? Doesn't anyone read history? Both Napoleon and Hitler broke their picks on brutal Russian winters. Why was an invasion of North Korea going to be any different?
—**Lieutenant Colonel Harold Roise,** Commander, 2nd Battalion, 5th Marine Regiment, 1st Marine Division

Marine Corps boot camp at Camp Pendleton gave Homer Ainsworth, Joe Albritton, and Waller King their most challenging physical and mental training ever in the fall of 1950. Their awareness of what was going on in Korea was limited to the one column on the front page of the *Clinton News* that covered the war. Their parents' letters kept them informed about Herbert Pearce, who was part of the Inchon landing with the 5th Marines, and Bill Smith, who shipped out to Korea in October and joined the 1st Marine Division at Wonsan. They knew that George Sharp was near the end of his twelve weeks of combat training at Camp Pendleton.

In Korea, the 1st Cavalry Division, the 24th Infantry Division, and the 1st Republic of Korea (ROK) Division of I Corps all moved across the 38th Parallel on October 9, 1950, bringing an immediate response from the Chinese foreign office: "The American war of invasion in Korea had been a serious menace to the security of Korea from its very start . . . the Chinese people cannot stand idly by." American intelligence discounted the warning.[1]

North Korean forces stubbornly resisted the US/UN advance until it reached the Seoul-to-Pyongyang corridor, when their efforts weakened and they abandoned the capital. As they retreated, the North Koreans took with them hundreds of American and ROK prisoners held there. ROK troops occupied Pyongyang on October 19.[2]

General Douglas MacArthur and the Joint Chiefs of Staff (JCS) had agreed that the advance would stop when it reached a line stretching from Pyongyang in the west to Wonsan on the east coast. After the North Korean capital fell, MacArthur arbitrarily moved the stop line sixty miles north and advised Generals Walton Walker and Edward Almond on October 24 that all restrictions on moving northward were lifted because of the enemy's refusal to surrender. The 8th Army and X Corps were now authorized to use any and all ground forces necessary to secure all of North Korea.

The JCS learned of MacArthur's unauthorized actions through Army back channels and reminded him that he was acting outside their previous instructions. MacArthur replied that there were military reasons for his move and that he was acting in accord with his instructions from George Marshall, who had succeeded Louis Johnson as secretary of defense, and from the Wake Island meeting. Secretary of state Dean Acheson was furious at MacArthur's violation of President Harry S. Truman's direct order. Nevertheless, the JCS backed off, and MacArthur's move toward the Yalu continued.

The 8th Army's 24th Division reached the city of Chonju, on the western coastal road about forty miles from the Yalu, on October 29. From there, a battalion of the 21st Regiment spearheaded the drive to the Chinese border, getting to within eighteen miles of the river before a tank-led North Korean force counterattacked at Taechon. The advance stopped while Air Force planes destroyed enemy tanks. The eighty-nine prisoners taken at Taechon included two Chinese men, who were sent back to the division's command post for further interrogation, even though no one believed they were Chinese. The 24th Division's commander received orders to halt when he reached Kusong on October 31.

Three ROK divisions on the right flank of the 8th Army moved northeast toward the Yalu on October 25. Their advance was uncoordinated, and the divisions had little contact with each other. The 1st Division stopped at the town of Usan when it came under enemy attack. ROK commanders thought they were fighting North Koreans, but prisoners captured during the fighting said they were part of a Chinese division of 10,000 men. The prisoners were sent back to the 8th Army's command center and interrogated further, but General Walker's staff still discounted the information that there were Chinese in North Korea.

The ROK's 6th Division, positioned to the right of the 1st Division, sent patrols north to the Yalu and reached the river on October 26. Some soldiers filled bottles with Yalu water to present to President Syngman Rhee; others urinated in the river to show their defiance of the Chinese. The 6th Division then came under heavy attack from the Chinese, and the South Korean soldiers broke ranks and fled. The Chinese forced all three ROK divisions to retreat, inflicting heavy losses. The command structure of the 6th Division, which bore the brunt of the Chinese attack, collapsed.

By the end of October, US/UN forces were deep into North Korea and confident that the war was coming to an end. Several units had reached the vicinity of the Yalu River, but the 8th Army's supply lines were overextended; in addition, despite military officials skepticism, the continuing reports of a Chinese presence in North Korea created tension among US/UN forces.

The retreating North Koreans foiled MacArthur's plans for a second Marine amphibious landing at Wonsan. The 1st Marine Division reached Wonsan on October 19 and found the harbor heavily mined. Troop transports moved up and down the coast for six days while the harbor was cleared. When the Marines finally came ashore, GIs assigned to the ROK forces occupying Wonsan taunted them about having missed the action. Bob Hope put on a USO show at Wonsan while the Marines remained shipbound during which he cracked, "This is the first time I've been ashore waiting on the Marines." General Oliver Smith of the Marines was frustrated that the Army had planned his landing. The Marines came ashore on October 26, the same day ROK soldiers reached the Yalu.

The two ROK divisions that had captured Wonsan moved north after the Marine landing and captured the port city of Iwon on October 28. The Army's 7th Infantry Division, sailing from Pusan, landed there the next

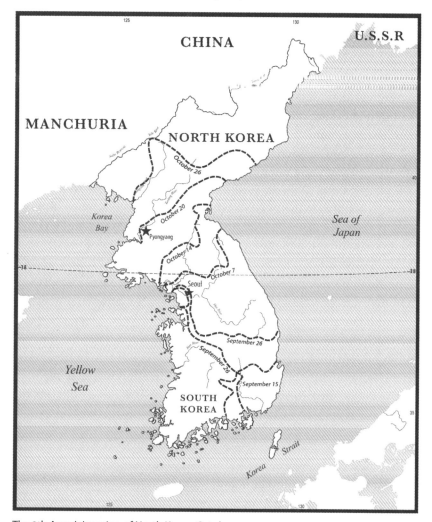

The 8th Army's Invasion of North Korea, October 1950.

day. X Corps now had two American divisions, two ROK divisions, plus supporting elements for a total of about 83,000 men on the east coast of North Korea. MacArthur ordered the Army's 3rd Infantry Division to join X Corps, adding another 19,000 soldiers, including about 8,000 Korean draftees. Almond's X Corps had more than half the personnel of General Walker's other three corps in the 8th Army combined.

Both the 8th Army and X Corps remained in denial about the Chinese presence in North Korea. A regiment of the ROK's 3rd Division unexpectedly encountered Chinese forces while moving north from Hamhung on the narrow road to the Chosin Reservoir on October 29. The regiment retreated and took defensive positions south of the reservoir. Almond flew by Marine helicopter to the ROK command post and learned from ROK interrogators that sixteen captured Chinese soldiers had claimed to be part of a two-division force. Almond relayed the information to General MacArthur's headquarters in Tokyo, where intelligence officers continued to insist that a few Chinese prisoners did not necessarily mean that China had intervened in the war.

But China had intervened. Soldiers of the Chinese 4th Field Army began crossing the Yalu River on the night of October 15. The Chinese force was divided into six army groups, each consisting of four 30,000-man armies. Each army, in turn, had three divisions of 8,000 to 10,000 men. The Chinese had 180,000 soldiers in Korea by the end of October.

The Chinese soldiers were peasants with limited artillery, tanks, and aircraft support. They moved on foot instead of wheels and lived in a world where the enemy always controlled the skies. They were masters at camouflage, trained not to move when an airplane passed overhead. Each Chinese soldier carried eight to ten pounds of gear and supplies— a week's worth of rice, small bits of fish and meat, and eighty rounds of ammunition. They had won a brilliant victory over Chiang Kai-shek's better-equipped Nationalist Army in 1949. Military historians viewed the Chinese army in 1950 as one of the great infantry forces of the modern era.

General Charles A. Willoughby, MacArthur's head of military intelligence, placed no value on South Korean intelligence and thus declared reports that the Chinese were in Korea "unconfirmed and thereby unaccepted." He flew to X Corps headquarters to interview the Chinese prisoners. Confident that American aircraft would have detected the Chinese crossing the Yalu, Willoughby said that the prisoners were "stragglers" or "volunteers" of no real significance. This unwillingness to acknowledge the obvious came at a time when the 8th Army was in a vulnerable position, with the 24th Infantry and 1st Cavalry Divisions spread across the northwest sector below the Yalu River with gaps in their lines. Their supply lines were dangerously overextended, they had no winter clothing, and ammunition supplies were low.

Brigadier General John Chiles, an operations officer under General Almond, criticized Willoughby's intelligence assessments, later writing,

"MacArthur did not want the Chinese to enter the war in Korea. Anything MacArthur wanted, Willoughby produced intelligence for. . . . In this case, Willoughby falsified the intelligence. . . . He should have gone to jail."[3]

American commanders from the regimental down to the company levels were convinced that the Chinese were in Korea, however. Confirmation came on the night of November 1 when two battalions came under attack from thousands of Chinese near the village of Unsan. American soldiers had their first experience with an enemy attack signaled by bugles, horns, and whistles. Confused and terrified, the Americans fought in darkness against an enemy that seemed to be everywhere. Survivors fled to the surrounding hills, leaving behind artillery pieces and equipment. Some eight hundred Americans were killed or missing at Unsan, a devastating defeat in the first direct fight between Chinese and American soldiers.

The Unsan disaster left no doubt about China's presence in Korea. The JCS and some in the Truman administration wanted to blame General MacArthur for faulty judgment, but guilt lay with American intelligence, civilian and military. The Chinese army was a phantom, difficult to detect when it chose to cloak its movements in darkness and camouflage its positions during daylight. Until MacArthur had a major clash with the Chinese, his intelligence sources would not recognize that uniqueness of the Chinese army.

After Unsan, the JCS requested more information. MacArthur now conceded that Chinese intervention was a "distinct possibility" to give cover to the North Koreans. He then ordered the 5th Air Force to bomb the twelve bridges across the Yalu on the Korean side, a violation of an earlier JCS directive to stay clear of the Manchurian border. Before the bombing raid was to start, General George Stratemeyer of the US Air Force passed word of the impending operation to Air Force chief of staff Hoyt Vandenberg in Washington.[4]

The JCS and the State Department were appalled at MacArthur's violation of the JCS directive and responded immediately, ordering the general to postpone the bombing, the first time they countermanded one of his orders. MacArthur fired back that the restrictions would lead to "a calamity of major proportion for which I cannot accept the responsibility without [President Harry S. Truman's] personal and direct understanding of the situation."[5]

MacArthur later wrote, "For the first time in military history, a commander had been denied the use of his military power to safeguard the lives of his soldiers and safety of his army." He considered asking to be relieved of his command but was persuaded not to take that step by General Doyle Hickey. MacArthur conveyed the impression that Washington was dictating policies and refused to accept responsibility for the outcomes.[6]

The question of Chinese intervention now answered, the Truman administration remained puzzled by Chinese leaders' intentions. Did they seek to push US/UN forces back below the 38th Parallel or to drive them out of the country and unify all of Korea under a communist regime? In the absence of information from military sources or the Central Intelligence Agency, the president's advisers concluded that Chinese intervention meant that the Soviet Union and China accepted the risk of global war and that Europe, not Korea, would be the battleground. These advisers' continuing focus on Europe hamstrung their analysis.

Truman ultimately authorized the bombing of the bridges on the south side of the Yalu but warned MacArthur that it was "in the national interest of the U.S. to localize the fighting in Korea, [and] it was important that extreme care be taken to avoid violating Manchurian territory and airspace and to report promptly hostile action from Manchuria."[7] These recommendations were forwarded to MacArthur on November 6, the day before the congressional elections. Although the Democrats lost seats, they retained control of both the Senate and the House.

Still refusing to accept that large numbers of Chinese had intervened, MacArthur responded to the JCS on November 7. He saw bombing the Yalu bridges as a defensive measure, essential to preventing a Chinese buildup, and assured the JCS that he would not violate the Manchurian or Soviet borders or destroy hydroelectric installations. He added that he intended to resume the offensive within ten days. Later in the day, MacArthur reported that enemy aircraft operating out of Manchuria had attacked US airplanes before fleeing back to the "sanctuary" north of the Yalu. He warned that unless corrective measures were taken, the air problem could become serious. The Chinese should not have a safe haven behind the Yalu.

The JCS agreed with MacArthur's "sanctuary" assessment, but the president would not allow American aircraft to pursue the enemy north of the Yalu and thereby widen the war. State Department and Pentagon advisers pushed the idea of the 8th Army and X Corps setting up a line of resistance at the neck of the Korean peninsula from Pyongyang to Wonsan while negotiators and diplomats attempted to settle the Korean conflict. Events on the battlefield were dictating changes in US objectives in Korea.[8]

On November 8, the JCS cabled MacArthur to get his latest plans before a National Security Council meeting, implying that MacArthur's mission might have to be reexamined in light of the Chinese intervention. MacArthur angrily replied that "it would be fatal to weaken the fundamental and basic policy of the United Nations to destroy all resisting armed forces in Korea and bring that country into a unified and free nation." He mentioned the British desire "to appease the Chinese Communists" and referenced the "historic precedent in the action taken at Munich," again invoking the idea of appeasement and World War II.[9]

When the National Security Council met the following day, it considered two options: (1) continuing the fight to unify Korea or (2) solving the problem by "political means." The JCS recommended that "pending further clarification as to the military objectives of the Chinese Communists and the extent of their political commitments," MacArthur's mission "should be kept under review, but should not be changed." MacArthur was free to continue operations, including the 8th Army offensive, as he saw fit.[10]

The JCS still had concerns about the fifty-mile gap between the 8th Army and X Corps. In early November, patrols had taken five days to span the gap and make contact between the two forces. At the time, X Corps had orders to go north of the Chosin Reservoir to the Yalu River. The Joint Chiefs' concerns were relayed to MacArthur's staff, and on November 15 MacArthur directed General Almond to develop an alternative plan for redirecting his attack to the west.[11]

In early November, the Chinese disappeared into the North Korean mountains, where neither American patrols nor aerial surveillance could locate the forces. The Chinese later said that their First Phase Offensive had come to an end, but in reality, they abandoned the fight because their supply lines were overextended. Transportation and logistics limitations meant that they could sustain an attack only for about ten days before they needed to draw back, resupply, and regroup. This pattern continued through most of the war.

General MacArthur mistakenly attributed the withdrawal to heavy battle losses and believed that his air offensive had prevented the Chinese from reinforcing their armies already in Korea. MacArthur planned to begin the Yalu River offensive on November 15 and expected it to be completed in ten days. The 8th Army's logistics problems caused a delay, however. On November 17, MacArthur told John Muccio, the US ambassador to Korea, that the offensive would begin within a week and estimated that China had about 30,000 troops in Korea—10 percent of the actual number.

X Corps Operations

In the X Corps sector to the east of the 8th Army, General Almond outlined the Marine mission for the next phase of General MacArthur's war plan to General Smith on October 25. The Marine division was to move north to the port of Hungnam and then follow a road north toward the Chosin Reservoir. From there, the Marines would move to the west side of the reservoir and begin an advance to the Yalu River, occupying the northeastern corner of North Korea. The 7th Army Division would give support from the east side of the reservoir and lead the drive to the Yalu. Almond ignored the challenges of the terrain in that part of North Korea, which included few inland roads and the Taeback Mountains, which rose to eight thousand feet. The mountains were already experiencing subfreezing temperatures.[12]

Almond wanted to beat the 8th Army to the Yalu River and did not question MacArthur's plan, but Smith recognized the danger of stretching his division along a narrow road that turned into a sixty-four-mile dirt path from Hungnam to the southern tip of the reservoir. Marine units would not be able to assist each other if attacked. Smith feared that the Chinese were setting a trap, but Almond minimized the threat, urging Smith to proceed at full speed. It proved to be the most dangerous operation the Marines would undertake in Korea.

Smith and Almond had already clashed during the Inchon landing and the battle for Seoul. Smith was cautious, always concerned about the safety of his Marines, whereas Almond was headstrong, arrogant, and reckless. After the landing at Wonsan, Almond detached the Korean Marine Corps regiment from Smith's division and assigned it to the Army's 7th Division, further alienating Smith. The US Marines had trained the Koreans and won their confidence, only to lose them to the Army. The

Marines, from General Smith to the lowest private in the ranks, regarded Almond as militarily unintelligent. Martin Russ, a Marine veteran of Chosin, later wrote that Almond was at the top of every Marine's "shit-list." They disliked his living quarters, which featured a refrigerator, hot-water shower, and flush toilet. They despised his eating with fine china and linen, silverware, and napkins and were furious that Far East Command transport planes delivered fresh fruit, vegetables, and meat daily for his headquarters' mess. Marine Colonel Lewis "Chesty" Puller remarked that Almond's headquarters required the support of 3,000 men—almost a regiment of soldiers. Almond's love of luxury caused resentment among Army ranks as well.[13]

General Smith assigned Puller's 1st Regiment to remain in the Wonsan area to secure the supply line. The rest of the division moved by local train up to Hamhung, some eighty miles north of Wonsan. At night, the temperatures dropped below freezing, so Smith ordered cold-weather gear issued. The 7th Regiment was partially outfitted because it would lead the advance, while other units received the gear over the next few weeks.

Each Marine was issued a mountain sleeping bag, a parka lined with alpaca wool, windproof trousers, several pairs of heavy woolen socks, and shoe-pacs, which were like duck hunter's boots—rubber on the bottom with leather uppers. Marching in shoe-pacs caused the feet to sweat, so Marines needed to change their socks frequently to avoid becoming vulnerable to frostbite. Despite the approaching cold weather, Army units throughout Korea still wore their summer uniforms.[14]

Chinese soldiers wore two-piece reversible uniforms of quilted cotton—white on one side, mustard-yellow on the other—and cotton caps with fur-lined earflaps. They wore canvas shoes with crepe soles. Later arrivals wore half-leather shoes.[15]

The 7th Regiment started the advance north from Hamhung on November 1. Colonel Homer Litzenberg received information that the ROK regiment at the town of Sudong, twenty-nine miles to the north, had come under attack from the Chinese. He gathered his officers and stressed the importance of winning their first battle with the Chinese. "We want the outcome to have an adverse effect on Moscow as well as Peking."[16]

The road from Hamhung to the Chosin Reservoir became the main supply route (MSR) for the Marines. A mountain stream bed ran along the road, with hills on each side averaging between one thousand and fifteen hundred feet above the valley floor. Litzenberg had his Marines cover the hill sight lines on both sides while tanks, artillery, and supply trucks moved along the road. Marine Corsairs flew sorties during daylight hours, covering the regiment's advance. The Marines initially had no contact with the enemy and felt that the advance was like a military parade. They were unaware of the Chinese division just beyond the ridges that was about to surround them.[17]

Lieutenant Colonel Ray Murray's 5th Regiment followed the 7th Regiment's advance on an alternate road to the east. Murray's objective was to move through the Sinhung Valley, five miles north and fifteen miles east of the 7th Marines, to relieve an ROK regiment and then continue north, seeking a route to the Chosin Reservoir or the Fusen Reservoir to the east. The 7th Regiment reached Sudong on November 2 and dug into a defensive line at a bridge.

Colonel Litzenberg assigned one battalion to the high ground, another to the slopes to the left, and the third to guard the regiment's rear. Around 11:00 p.m., the Chinese started probing the Marine defenses, and at midnight, flares and bugle calls announced an attack from both sides of the road. The Chinese broke through Marine defenses at several points, but by morning the enemy had withdrawn. In a "fog of war" situation, a North Korean T-34 tank operated by Chinese soldiers appeared, and the Marine guards on the road mistook it for a bulldozer and waved it through. The tank did considerable damage before the Marines forced it to withdraw with heavy antitank fire.[18]

The Marines learned in that initial fight that if they could withstand Chinese night attacks and maintain their positions, Marine air support would force the Chinese to withdraw by daybreak. After five days of attacks and counterattacks, the battle at Sudong ended with the Marines driving the enemy back into the mountains. Five North Korean tanks were lost in the battle, abandoned because they could not navigate the Funchilin Pass nine miles north of Sudong. The 7th Regiment won its first encounter with the enemy at a cost of 50 KIA and 200 wounded out of a force of 3,000. The Marines counted about 1,500 enemy dead from a division of some 9,000.[19]

The Chinese forces in the Chosin Reservoir area pulled back, just as they had done in the 8th Army sector. Other than minor skirmishes with patrols on both sides, the Chinese did not launch a major attack again until November 27, when the 5th and 7th Marine Regiments started their offensive from Yudam-ni.[20]

On the east side of the Chosin Reservoir, the Army's 7th Division, commanded by Major General Dave Barr, occupied a thirty-mile front anchored on its west at the Fusen Reservoir, east of Chosin, and linked to ROK I Corps at Hysenjin on the east. Many on MacArthur's staff in Tokyo thought X Corps was too fragmented and recommended that General Almond forgo the drive to the Yalu and move due west from the Chosin Reservoir and support the 8th Army in its offensive to the north.

MacArthur initially approved his staff's recommendations, but Almond objected, arguing that lateral roads were not available and that such a move would position his X Corps to the rear of 8th Army, thereby neutralizing any coordination he could give it. Almond ultimately was ordered to draw up alternate plans for reorienting his attack to the west and was to advance only "minimum forces" to the Yalu.

Almond's "minimum forces" were two Army regiments, the 32nd and 17th, which spearheaded the drive to the Yalu through mountainous terrain with temperatures below zero at night. Enemy forces resisted the 17th's advance, but one company-size unit reached the Yalu on November 21. Reporters joined Generals Almond and Barr for the ceremonial urinating in the Yalu, captured by *Life* magazine and Army photographers. MacArthur cabled his "heartiest congratulations" to Almond for his triumph.[21]

Almond's recklessness in sending two regiments forward to the Yalu River was compounded by problems the 17th and 32nd Regiments faced when they attempted to withdraw from the area. Heavy snowstorms made the trails nearly impassable, and the division's transportation unit could move only one battalion at a time while the war in Korea had just taken a disastrous turn for the 8th Army.

The 1st Marine Division continued its slow move up the MSR to the Chosin Reservoir. When the 7th Regiment moved north from Suwon, they found the bridge over the Funchilin Pass intact. Because the Chinese should have destroyed the bridge to delay the Marine advance, Smith recognized a trap. Marines on foot continued forward, but tanks and heavy equipment had to wait while the road north of the pass was improved.

The column reached the Koto-ri plateau on November 10. The Marines opened a small airstrip capable of handling light aircraft and started organizing a supply dump. Bitter weather struck and the temperature fell below zero. Patrols sent into the surrounding hills found only a scattered enemy presence. Despite the conditions, the Marines of the 1st Division celebrated the birthday of the Corps with cake.[22]

General Almond attached the Army's 65th Infantry Regiment, the ROK's 27th Regiment, and two battalions of the Korean Marine Corps to the 1st Marine Division on November 10. When General Smith learned of the transfers to his command, he contacted the leaders of his new units to set up command lines, only to learn that Almond had given the commanders detailed instructions on their new assignments. While the 7th Regiment continued its advance toward Hagaru-ri at the base of the Chosin Reservoir, the 5th advanced through the Sinhung Valley, where they captured a stray Chinese soldier found sleeping in a house about ten miles east of Koto-ri. According to the prisoner, six Chinese armies—a total of twenty-four divisions—had been committed to the Korean War, information that was relayed to Smith and Almond.

By November 8 Murray's 5th Regiment was stalled, unable to find a usable road from the valley to either the Chosin or Fusen Reservoir. Smith ordered the regiment to move west and relieve the 7th Regiment, which was about to depart Koto-ri for Hagaru-ri. The 5th moved cross-country along a one-lane road following the ridgeline, encountering North Korean and Chinese company-size forces that retreated into the hills. Bitter cold further complicated the troop movements.[23]

General Almond issued new orders on November 11 for the Marine division to lead the X Corps drive to the Yalu from the west side of the Chosin Reservoir. The Army's 7th Division would advance from the center, and the ROK's I Corps would come from the east. General Smith directed the 7th Regiment to take Hagaru-ri and prepare to advance to Yudam-ni on the west side of the reservoir. The 5th Regiment would protect the MSR at Koto-ri and be prepared to pass through Hagaru-ri and move east of the reservoir. The 1st Regiment would protect the MSR from the south at Chinhung-ni and Koto-ri.

Colonel Litzenberg's 7th Regiment reached Hagaru-ri on November 15, finding only a few huts still standing after Marine air attacks. The Marines found a sawmill nearby and started building temporary wooden shelters and setting up tents. Marines could see Chinese soldiers in the distance; the blue ice covering the reservoir was thick enough to hold a jeep.

Hagaru-ri straddled the MSR, which forked to the left and right of the Chosin Reservoir. Smith decided to make his command post at the village and ordered division engineers to move forward from Koto-ri, improving the road for tanks and bulldozers needed to build an airstrip to resupply his division and evacuate its wounded. C-47 transport aircraft required four thousand feet of runway, but engineers believed that three thousand feet would suffice.

Frustrated with Almond, Smith wrote to General Clifton Cates, commandant of the Marine Corps, on November 15,

> I have little confidence in the tactical judgment of X Corps or in the realism of their planning. . . . Time and time again I have tried to tell the Corps Commander [Almond] that in a Marine Division he has a powerful instrument, and that it cannot help but lose its effectiveness when dispersed. . . . I believe a winter campaign in the mountains of North Korea is too much to ask of the American soldier or marine, and I doubt the feasibility of supplying troops in this area during the winter or providing for the evacuation of the sick and wounded.[24]

Later that day, Rear Admiral Albert Morehouse, chief of staff of US naval forces, Far East, helicoptered to Hagaru-ri to meet with Smith, who again shared his concerns about Almond's unrealistic planning and tendency to ignore enemy capabilities.[25]

On November 17, Almond flew by Marine helicopter to Hagaru-ri to give Smith new orders. The 5th Regiment would take the fork to the east side of the reservoir, while the 7th would go west and advance to Yudam-ni. When Smith objected, Almond pretended not to hear. After Almond left the meeting, Smith told his staff, "We're not going anywhere until I get this division together and the airfield built."[26]

Ignoring Almond's order, Smith kept one battalion of the 5th Regiment at Hagaru-ri to guard the road to the right of the reservoir while the other two battalions moved behind the 7th Regiment on the road to Yudam-ni. The 7th Marines moved slowly—about a mile a day—in their advance to Yudam-ni, taking time to set up supply dumps along the way. After being relieved by an Army task force, the battalion defending the east fork at Hagaru-ri rejoined the 5th Regiment.

General Almond became impatient with the slow Marine advance and flew to Hagaru-ri for an inspection. He questioned why an airfield was being built and was told that it was needed to evacuate casualties. Almond did not believe that there would be any casualties and refused to provide Army engineers to assist in the airstrip construction.[27]

The road from Hagaru-ri climbed through the Toktong Pass four miles to the northwest before descending into a narrow valley that led to Yudam-ni. Smith gave Colonel Litzenberg orders to leave a company at the pass to defend the road. On November 23, General Almond ordered the Marine division to advance west from the Chosin Reservoir at Yudam-ni on November 27 and then move to Mupyong-ni and north to the Yalu.

Almond's latest order placed the Army's 7th Division on the right flank of the Marines on the east side of the reservoir. The 7th was ill prepared to launch an attack. Most of the 17th and 32nd Regiments remained eighty air miles from the reservoir and probably twice as far by road. It would take several days to redeploy the three Army regiments, artillery, and armor over miserable clogged roads and prepare for a major offensive in another direction.

Almond directed a battalion of the 32nd Regiment to the east side of the reservoir to relieve the Marine battalion guarding the road. Two other battalions from the 31st Regiment would follow, supported by two artillery batteries and a tank company, making up Task Force MacLean, named for Colonel Allan MacLean, commander of the 31st Infantry Regiment. The redeployment occurred as roads were unstable and jammed with vehicles in bitterly cold weather. The first Army battalion reached Hagaru-ri on November 24 and moved east of the reservoir, with the other two battalions following.

Thanksgiving fell on November 23—Bill and Betty Jo Smith's first wedding anniversary. Bill had arrived in Korea in October as part of the Wonsan landing and spent the day in the Kajon-Dong area, where he and the other Marines were treated to a turkey dinner with all the trimmings—shrimp cocktail, mashed potatoes, dressing, cranberry sauce, and mince pie. Though the temperature was freezing, as much of the food as possible was served hot.[28]

The Marines' 7th Regiment reached Yudam-ni on November 25, with the 5th Regiment right behind. The 1st Regiment had one battalion on the

Hamhung-Hagaru road at Chinhung, one battalion at Koto-ri, and one at Hagaru-ri. As General Smith had feared, his division was strung out along the MSR from Hamhung to the Chosin Reservoir. Army units on the east side of the reservoir also occupied a dangerous position. Smith was convinced the Chinese had large numbers near the reservoir, though Almond and his X Corps staff believed the opposite. Almond "doubted" that the Chinese had even one or two divisions with a maximum of 20,000 soldiers in the area. In reality, there were twelve Chinese divisions with about 120,000 men.[29]

The Home by Christmas Offensive

General MacArthur's offensive was scheduled to start on November 24. The Truman administration supported the move, believing that the United States needed to occupy a position of strength to bring the Chinese to a conference table. Acheson and others supported a British proposal calling for a demilitarized buffer zone at the neck of North Korea on a line from Pyongyang to Wonsan.

The 8th Army had 118,000 men—eight infantry divisions and two brigades organized into three corps on a seventy-mile front. They faced an enemy with at least 180,000 soldiers and another 40,000 guerrillas operating behind US/UN lines. Because he lacked sufficient numbers to carry out a frontal attack, MacArthur split his army into two segments with a fifty-mile gap between them. This was a gamble, but MacArthur still believed he faced a weakened North Korean army supported by Chinese volunteers.

MacArthur knew he had to complete the operation before the worst of the Korean winter set in. To prevent further Chinese advances into North Korea, the 8th Army and X Corps had to be dug in along the Yalu before the river froze over. MacArthur admitted to the US ambassador to Japan that if the offensive failed and the Chinese continued moving into North Korea, the United States would have to bomb key targets in Manchuria, which could bring the Soviet Union into the war. The stakes were high, but the general remained confident.

The JCS in Washington recognized the fifty-mile gap between the 8th Army and X Corps as a major weakness to MacArthur's plan but okayed the offensive on November 21. MacArthur placed ROK divisions on the right flank of the 8th Army, thinking that their experience in fighting in Korea's mountains would somehow neutralize the gap and ignoring the South Koreans' previous performance when facing the Chinese.

MacArthur's successes at Inchon and Seoul and his position as commander on the ground caused the JCS to defer to him. Several thousand miles away, the Joint Chiefs were reluctant to reverse the American tradition that military considerations take priority over political factors.

MacArthur flew to Korea on the morning of November 24 and met with General Walker and staff. The offensive began later that day with a massive artillery barrage along the front, followed by the three corps moving forward. According to later accounts, MacArthur quipped to a reporter that he would have American troops home by Christmas, but MacArthur denied having said that. After the offensive started, MacArthur left on a plane that did a flyover of North Korea and then followed the Yalu River before dropping south to survey the Chosin Reservoir and then finally heading on to Japan. MacArthur saw no enemy activity during the flight and remained optimistic about ending the war.

The 8th Army offensive initially went well, but on the night of November 25, the Chinese counterattacked the ROK 8th Division in a flanking movement, near the gap between the 8th Army and X Corps lines. Within two days, the Chinese had routed the South Koreans and penetrated to the rear of IX Corps, threatening the entire 8th Army line. Chinese troops attacked the Army's 25th and 2nd Divisions at the same time. The collapse of the Korean divisions on the right endangered the 2nd Division, which faced wave after wave of attacking Chinese infantry while other enemy units moved around the ROK division and threatened to envelop the 2nd Division. If the Chinese could drive to the Yellow Sea, most of the 8th Army would be surrounded.[30]

The 8th Army's withdrawal was complete chaos. Language difficulties led to the premature pullout of a Turkish brigade that had been ordered to hold the town of Wawon to cover the 2nd Division's withdrawal, making the division's situation even more critical. The Chinese encircled the 2nd and fought off attempts by other forces to break through and rescue the division. Its destruction seemed imminent, but the soldiers finally broke out, running a gauntlet of seven miles under concentrated enemy fire and suffering heavy casualties that included the loss of 5,000 men and most of its artillery, vehicles, and equipment.[31]

Chapter 4

On November 28, as the 8th Army fought to survive, Generals Walker and Almond were summoned to Tokyo for a council of war. MacArthur told his two field commanders that he believed the Chinese could push back the 8th Army and X Corps and be in a position to launch a massive spring offensive and drive both forces out of Korea. MacArthur authorized Walker to go on the defensive. Walker said he could hold Pyongyang and establish a defensive line north and east of the city.

Almond, in contrast, said that the 1st Marine Division and the Army's 7th division could continue their offensives from both sides of the Chosin Reservoir and drive to the Yalu. MacArthur disagreed with his assessment and ordered the withdrawal of X Corps to the Hungnam area on the Sea of Japan. The meeting ended at 1:30 a.m. on November 29.

MacArthur then sent an ominous message to the Pentagon:

The developments resulting from our assault movements have now assumed a clear definition. All hope of localization of the Korean conflict . . . to North Korean troops with alien token elements can now be completely abandoned. The Chinese military forces are committed to North Korea in greater and ever-increasing strength. No pretext of minor support under the guise of volunteerism or other subterfuge now has the slightest validity. We face an entirely new war.[32]

American newspapers were already calling MacArthur's offensive a disaster when General Omar Bradley received this message early on the morning of November 28. He relayed MacArthur's message to the president, admitting that the situation was serious but denying that it was the catastrophe the press reported. When Truman later met with his staff, he referred to MacArthur's cable and called Korea "the worst situation we have had yet."

With the 8th Army in general retreat, General Walker planned to create an enclave around Pyongyang and establish a defensive line across the western sector of the peninsula. The withdrawal was complicated by poor roads and refugees moving on foot as well as by Chinese soldiers pressed so close to the retreating Americans that artillery could not be used against the enemy forces.

While the withdrawal continued, Walker drew four fallback lines on his map. The first line, Able, was north of Pyongyang and was overrun before it could be staffed. Walker knew that his army could not make a defensive line at Pyongyang if the Chinese attacked in force, so he made the controversial decision to abandon Pyongyang on December 5, destroying more than 10,000 tons of supplies before withdrawing. Discipline deteriorated, and soldiers began raping and looting during the retreat. Turkish and British troops felt let down by their American allies.

Walker's next line, Baker, ran below the 38th Parallel along the Imjin River north of Seoul. The geography here was favorable to a defense, but if the line could not hold, Walker would withdraw farther south, to the Han River, the Kum River, and all the way back to the Naktong River and the Pusan Perimeter if necessary.

The Washington Front

In retrospect, the National Security Council's November 8 decision to allow MacArthur to continue the 8th Army offensive was one of the Truman administration's major mistakes of the war. The president's advisers could not agree on what to do in Korea: continue the objective of uniting the country or take stronger control over the direction of the war and deal with MacArthur as a subordinate. China had intervened.[33]

As Acheson later wrote, "The JCS should have taken firmest control of the Korean War and dealt with MacArthur bluntly. . . . At the very least the chiefs should have canceled MacArthur's planned offensive. Instead we let ourselves be misled by MacArthur's wildly erroneous estimates of the situation and his eloquent rhetoric, as well as by too much wishful thinking of our own."[34]

After news of the Chinese counteroffensive and the collapse of 8th Army in Korea reached Washington, the president convened an emergency meeting of the National Security Council on November 28. State Department officials, the JCS, and presidential advisers feared defeat. Secretary of Defense George Marshall advised getting out of Korea "with honor." At the end of the meeting, Truman announced that he would submit a supplementary appropriations bill to Congress requesting an additional $16.8 billion, bringing the total military appropriations for fiscal 1951 to $43 billion.

On November 30, the president intensified the crisis when he told reporters that the United States would use all its resources to win the war in Korea. Asked whether the atomic bomb was a possibility, Truman answered, "There has always been active consideration of its use. I don't want to see it used. It is a terrible weapon and should not be used on innocent men, women, and children, who have nothing whatever to do with this military aggression—that happens when it's used."[35]

The White House press corps offered Truman a chance to back off, but the president failed to take advantage, stating that the Pentagon would make any decision about using the bomb and that the United States would never do so unless the United Nations approved. The press then reported to the world that the United States was actively considering use of the atomic bomb in Korea.

British officials were shocked that General MacArthur might have authority to use the bomb: they wanted Truman to have final say. Clement Attlee, the British prime minister, hurried to Washington to meet with Truman in early December. A supporter of Communist China, Attlee had long backed the country's bid to be seated at the United Nations in place of Taiwan as well as the island's return to mainland Chinese control. Truman assured Attlee that the United States would not use the atomic bomb in Korea but rejected the idea of abandoning the Chinese Nationalist government.

The furor over the possible use of the atomic bomb was soon eclipsed by MacArthur's statements published in *U.S. News and World Report* in early December. According to the general, the prohibition on operations beyond the Yalu gave the enemy privileged sanctuary and were "an enormous handicap, without precedent in military history." He argued that the United States was mistakenly focusing military and economic resources on Western Europe, where there was no war, at the expense of East Asia, where there was a war. MacArthur believed that he should have been allowed to bomb and blockade North Korea after its invasion and expected to receive permission to bomb and blockade China after it intervened in the war. Historians later termed MacArthur's statements "posterity papers," designed to blame others for the reversals in Korea.[36]

Truman recognized MacArthur's words as self-serving, an attempt to sidestep the failure of his offensive. The president later wrote that he should have sacked MacArthur at that time. Firing, however, would have caused a public uproar. Republicans and the China lobby, which lionized

MacArthur, would have faulted Truman and Acheson and demanded a congressional investigation. Dismissing the general would certainly undermine public support for the war and might cost the Democrats the 1952 presidential election.

General Matthew Ridgway was appalled at MacArthur's behavior and at the Joint Chiefs' failure to take charge of the situation. Instead, they continued to make timid suggestions to MacArthur, who treated their recommendations with contempt. Ridgway told the JCS that "they had all spent too much damn time on debate, and it was time to take action. They owed it to the men in the field."[37]

But Truman's only option was to issue a new set of directives ordering all government officials to reduce the number of public speeches related to foreign and military policy and to obtain prior approval from the State Department and the White House. State and Defense Department officials overseas were to exercise "extreme caution" in public statements and to avoid communicating directly with the media. These December 5 directives specifically sought to silence General MacArthur.

Administration officials, fearful that war with the Soviet Union was imminent, examined different scenarios centering on a negotiated cease-fire with China. One plan called for building an impregnable defensive line across the peninsula before inviting the Chinese to negotiations. If the Chinese refused to talk, planners considered establishing two enclaves, one around Seoul-Inchon and the other on the east coast around Hamhung-Hungnam. The worst case was a fallback to the Pusan Perimeter.

The Truman administration sent General J. Lawton Collins, the Army chief of staff, to Tokyo on December 3 to evaluate the situation and acquaint MacArthur with the new restrictions on public statements. MacArthur had begun making defeatist remarks, and officials feared that he had lost the will to fight. Acheson wanted Collins to stay in Tokyo indefinitely, and Dean Rusk, the assistant secretary of state for Far East affairs, proposed that the president appoint Collins "field commander" in Korea and restrict MacArthur to "full time" duty in Tokyo, where he would work on the Japanese peace treaty and other routine matters.

After meeting with MacArthur in Tokyo, Collins flew to Korea and met with General Walker and his staff. Walker proposed withdrawing to the Pusan Perimeter and asked that X Corps be placed under his command, assuring Collins that Pusan could be held indefinitely.

Collins next flew to Hungnam to meet with General Almond. The 1st Marine Division's survival was still in question, but Almond remained optimistic about establishing an enclave at Hamhung-Hungnam for the winter and launching another offensive in the spring. He was not pleased to learn of Walker's request that X Corps be placed under his command.

After meeting with Almond, Collins returned to Tokyo for a final meeting with MacArthur. The two men discussed the issue of X Corps, with MacArthur initially opposing the idea of placing it under Walker's command. "After thinking it over," however, MacArthur gave his approval, which was then conveyed to both Walker and Almond. Collins and MacArthur also considered different options for containing the Chinese, with the general requesting at least 75,000 additional troops and saying that if they were not sent quickly, the 8th Army should pull out of Korea.

Back in Washington, Collins reported to the president and the JCS that while the military situation in Korea remained serious, it was no longer critical. He shared MacArthur's views that the United States had three possible courses of action in Korea: (1) continue the war within limits; (2) enlarge the conflict by bombing the Chinese mainland, blockading the Chinese coast, and allowing Nationalist Chinese soldiers to fight in Korea and in South China; (3) negotiate with the Chinese to stop at the 38th Parallel. According to Collins, MacArthur saw the first option as "surrender," favored the second, but would accept the third if it could be arranged.

Truman was disturbed that MacArthur's thinking diverged so sharply from the administration's position that the war should continue with restrictions, but the president was willing to allow MacArthur to share his views privately. Problems arose when the general continued making his views known to the public.[38]

Chapter 5

THE SAGA OF THE CHOSIN RESERVOIR, NOVEMBER–DECEMBER, 1950

> The Korean name for the reservoir was Changjin. The Marines used Japanese maps for the area that named the reservoir Chosin. It rhymed with "frozen" so Chosin remains uncorrected in the history books.
> —**Martin Russ,** *Breakout: The Chosin Reservoir Campaign, Korea 1950*

Army General Edward Almond received the distressing news that the 8th Army's offensive had been shattered and its retreat turned into a rout on November 26 but did not share the information with Marine General Oliver Smith.[1] X Corps's offensive was scheduled to start the following day. Smith learned from a captured Chinese prisoner that the Chinese would attack when the Marines reached Yudam-ni, seize the main supply route (MSR) north and south of Koto-ri, and effectively isolate the three Marine outposts. As was the case with other intelligence gleaned from Chinese prisoners, X Corps headquarters ignored this information.

Despite reversals in the western sector, Almond held to the second part of MacArthur's offensive, sending the 7th and 5th Marine Regiments to the west from Yudam-ni and moving Army Task Force MacLean north on the east side of the reservoir. Almond helicoptered to the Marine position at Yudam-ni on November 26 and once again violated the chain of command by telling the regimental commanders, Colonel Homer Litzenberg and Lieutenant Colonel Ray Murray, "Don't let a bunch of Chinese laundrymen stop you." Almond's words had no effect on the more realistic Litzenberg and Murray, who had firsthand experience with Chinese capabilities.[2]

General Smith arrived at Yudam-ni later that morning, still unaware of the full extent of the 8th Army's reversals. He was skeptical of Almond's orders to go on the offensive and directed Litzenberg to hold his position while Murray's 5th Regiment passed through to spearhead the offensive.

The X Corps offensive called for the Marine division to drive west from Yudam-ni to Mupyong-ni, forty to fifty miles away, on roads that might or might not exist. Mupyong-ni was a village on the Chongchon River, in the 8th Army's sector. According to General MacArthur's plan, the Marines would link up with the 8th Army forces and encircle any Chinese troops in the area and cut off their escape. The harshness of the terrain and the below-zero temperatures rendered the plan absurd.[3]

On November 27, the 1st Marine Division had 14,708 Marines on the ground: 8,200 with the 7th and 5th Regiments around Yudam-ni; another 190 guarding the road rising to the top of Toktong Pass; and the 218 Marines of Fox Company who were dug in at the pass. Three thousand Marines and 600 GIs protected Hagaru-ri, while another 1,500 Marines and 1,000 soldiers defended Koto-ri. Smith had 1,600 Marines and 4,500 GIs farther south on the MSR at Chinhung-ni. The Chinese had twelve divisions—estimated between 60,000 and 120,000 soldiers—in the ridges and mountains on the roadsides from Chinhung-ni in the south to Hagaru-ri and on to Yudam-ni, a distance of roughly thirty-five miles.[4]

Almond placed Task Force MacLean under General Smith's command but continued to give orders to the group. Lieutenant Colonel Don Faith had his battalion of the 31st Infantry Regiment at Hudong-ni on the east side of the reservoir when the task force commander, Colonel Allan MacLean, arrived late on the night of November 27 and positioned his two battalions below Faith's. Task Force MacLean comprised approximately 3,500 soldiers.

The Marine division was broken into a group of isolated garrisons, and General Smith was not comfortable with the situation. He knew the Chinese had overwhelming numbers of soldiers against his division, and he wanted it withdrawn from Korea's far north as quickly as possible. General Almond seemed oblivious to the Chinese threat. His decisions

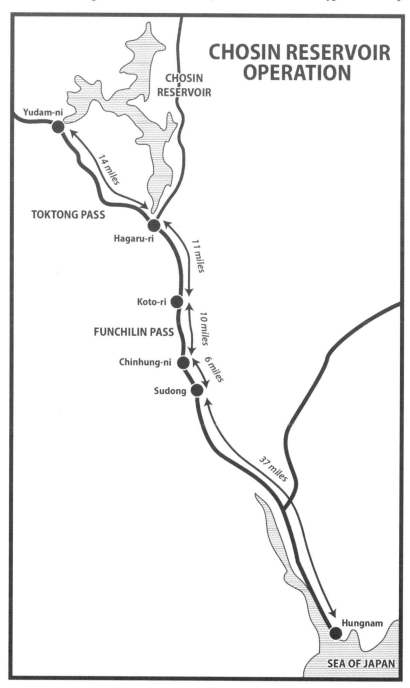

Chosin Reservoir Operation, December 1950.

gave the Chinese the opportunity to inflict what could be the worst defeat in American military history—the destruction of a Marine division.

Monday–November 27

Yudam-ni. The temperature was zero degrees Fahrenheit when the offensive began, led by elements of the 5th Marine Regiment, which were followed by the 7th under Marine air cover. The advance stopped after less than a mile because of a Chinese roadblock. Colonel Litzenberg aborted the offensive and pulled back to the defensive perimeter of the previous night and prepared for a night attack. It came around 11:00 p.m. with the temperature twenty degrees below zero and heavy snow falling. The Chinese first probed the Marine perimeter, then called in mortar fire and attacked, overrunning several hilltop positions and making temporary breakthroughs along the perimeter. Hand-to-hand fighting resulted in heavy casualties on both sides.[5]

Toktong Pass. Three Chinese divisions positioned themselves around Yudam-ni and the Toktong Pass with the intent of destroying the 7th and 5th Regiments. By taking control of the pass, the Chinese could cut off any Marine line of retreat. They prepared for an assault on a hill overlooking the pass, Fox Hill, named for the Marine company occupying it. Captain William Barber, Fox Company's commander, expected a Chinese night attack and had his men dig foxholes deep into the frozen ground, while the artillery battery at Hagaru-ri zeroed in on the ridges opposite Fox Hill to provide support when needed. The company was on a 25 percent watch (one of every four Marines would be awake at any time).

Hagaru-ri. General Smith's command post sat in a natural amphitheater that had a circumference of four miles and was surrounded by mountains. The battered village was vulnerable from East Hill, a high ridge overlooking the outpost. Marine engineers worked around the clock to build an airstrip there. Smith placed Army Lieutenant Colonel Thomas Ridge in command of the defending Army/Marine task force, which included 3,000 Marines, 500 soldiers, and about 800 support personnel—engineers, medical staff, military police, communications staff, and transport staff.

Koto-ri. Colonel Lewis "Chesty" Puller had one battalion of his 1st Regiment at Koto-ri with support personnel and 1,000 soldiers of the 7th

Division to defend the supply dump and small airstrip. He set up a defensive perimeter and faced enemy fire. The Chinese set up nine roadblocks between Hagaru-ri and the Funchilin Pass, isolating the 1st Regiment.

Task Force MacLean. All units of Task Force MacLean came together, and the Chinese attacked in force late at night, drawing fire from the soldiers but then retreating after determining the defenders' positions. Enemy troops attacked again hours later, overrunning the task force's positions and inflicting heavy casualties before withdrawing at dawn. Task Force MacLean remained surrounded by Chinese forces.[6]

Tuesday–November 28

Yudam-ri. Daybreak revealed hundreds of dead Chinese scattered across the ground, causing Litzenberg and Murray to realize that they were surrounded by a large Chinese force and to suspend any further advance. General Smith sent a message affirming their decision and requested that a column be sent to clear the road to the Toktong Pass; however, heavy enemy fire forced the relief column to turn back. The defensive perimeter was compressed, and the Marines prepared for another attack, which came that night. The Chinese attacked with bugles blaring and in greater numbers than on the first night. Because they were shooting flares to light up their targets, the Marines were able to call in air support as well as artillery.[7]

Toktong Pass. Marine guards fired on a Chinese column coming down the road around 4:00 a.m., beginning the battle for the pass. Chinese soldiers swarmed up the hill in columns, throwing grenades and firing snub-nosed burp guns. The enemy broke through the perimeter at several points but withdrew by daylight. Chinese bodies littered the hill. Heavy clouds prevented Marine air support during the morning, but during the afternoon, Marine Corsairs fended off further Chinese attacks. Fox Company suffered 20 KIA, 54 wounded, and 3 missing during the morning's action. The Marines were low on ammunition and had to retrieve cartridge belts and bandoliers from the dead and weapons and ammunition from Chinese bodies. The Marines also stacked frozen corpses in front of their positions for added protection. A Marine transport airplane dropped medical supplies and ammunition in the afternoon.[8]

When Captain Barber learned that the relief column from Yudam-ni had been turned back, he knew that his company would have to defend the pass for a second night. The Chinese attacked at dusk, moving up the reverse slope of the hill with bugles blowing. They broke through Marine defenses and took part of the hill.[9]

Hagaru-ri. When General Almond arrived by Marine helicopter and learned from Smith that he had canceled the advance by the 5th and 7th Regiments, Almond reluctantly agreed and then helicoptered to the east of the reservoir to meet with Colonel MacLean. Lieutenant Colonel Ridge spread the defenders along a perimeter, supported by tanks at unmanned gaps. At night, the temperature fell to fifteen degrees below zero with light snow falling. Ridge set up tents with heaters along the perimeter to allow defenders to thaw out. Engineers continued their work on the airstrip with weapons close by. The unit was on a 100 percent watch. The Chinese attacked at 10:00 p.m. with their usual sound effects, startling the Marine and Army defenders. Flares lit the sky, and mortar rounds pounded the perimeter. The enemy moved forward in large columns, penetrating Marine defenses, and fired on the engineers. Clerks, cooks, band members—anyone with a rifle fought the Chinese that night. By 3:00 a.m., all breaches in the lines had been sealed, and the Chinese withdrew.[10]

Koto-ri. The Chinese had the 1st Marine Regiment command post surrounded when Smith ordered Puller to send a company-size force up the MSR to meet a tank patrol coming down from Hagaru-ri, but the company had to turn back at a Chinese roadblock a mile north of the Koto-ri perimeter. The 41st Commando Battalion (240 men) of the British Royal Marines, commanded by Lieutenant Colonel Douglas Drysdale, later reached Koto-ri with thirty Army tanks and an Army company set to join Task Force MacLean on the east side of the reservoir.

Task Force MacLean. Colonel MacLean assessed the damage the Chinese had inflicted the previous night and knew that his soldiers were in a desperate situation, lacking winter clothing and vastly outnumbered. The situation became even more dire when General Almond arrived by Marine helicopter during the afternoon. MacLean reported that two Chinese divisions were located on the east side of the reservoir, but Almond replied that China did not have two divisions in all of North Korea. He ordered MacLean to take his soldiers forward—"We're still attacking, and we're going all the way to the Yalu. Don't let a bunch of goddamn Chinese laundrymen stop you!"[11]

Although Task Force MacLean was under General Smith's command and although Almond had agreed to Smith's decision to suspend the offensive on the west side of the reservoir, Almond ordered MacLean to continue the offensive on the east side. The colonel was aware of what had happened to the 8th Army and knew that Almond was minimizing the Chinese threat. Almond had three Silver Stars to award and handed one to Lieutenant Colonel Faith, who said one should be given to a wounded lieutenant sitting nearby. Almond then called over a mess sergeant and gave him the third medal. When Almond departed, a disgusted Faith threw his silver star in the snow.[12]

The Chinese encircled Task Force MacLean after dark and attacked around 10:00 p.m. Strung out on the road, the three battalions could not help one another. The soldiers were hard-hit and dangerously exposed when some 300 South Korean soldiers threw down their weapons and ran. The fighting raged through the night.

Wednesday–November 29

Yudam-ni. The Chinese still occupied two hills at dawn, but Marine counterattacks drove the enemy away. Air cover and artillery fire kept the Chinese at bay during the day. On the west side of the reservoir, the 7th and 5th Marine Regiments had suffered heavy casualties and initially did not have enough tents at medical aid stations to shelter the seriously wounded. An airdrop that day brought in more tents, supplies, and ammunition. Clinton's Herbert Pearce was with the 5th Regiment at Yudam-ni, where he and other Navy corpsmen and Marine surgeons found their work impeded by the severe cold. Wearing gloves caused him difficulty in changing dressings, and clothing could not be cut off of wounded Marines because they would freeze to death. The extreme cold did prove an asset in one way, however: it froze blood in wounds, thereby stopping surface bleeding.[13]

The most common cold-weather injury Pearce dealt with was frostbite, which affected all the combatants during the Chosin Reservoir operation. Frostbite could set in when a wounded fighter was pinned down by enemy fire and could not move or was wounded and lay for too long on frozen ground. The extremities—hands and feet—were the most difficult parts of the body to keep warm and thus were most vulnerable to frostbite.[14]

The Chinese probably suffered more from the cold than did the Marines and soldiers. Although the Chinese soldiers had quilted uniforms that offered some protection from the severe cold, most Chinese had only canvas boots with rubber soles, and many lacked protective gloves. Nearly all Chinese fighters suffered some degree of frostbite during the Chosin operation.[15]

Aware of the mounting casualties at Yudam-ni, General Smith ordered another attempt to clear the road between Yudam-ni and the Toktong Pass, but Chinese roadblocks again turned back the relief column a mere three hundred yards into their march. With Chinese forces entrenched on both sides of the road, Smith ordered Litzenberg and Murray to prepare for a withdrawal to Hagaru-ri. The two colonels looked to the Chosin Reservoir as a path out of Yudam-ni. If the ice were thick enough to support a convoy of trucks, the two regiments could be moved over the ice under air cover without having to blast their way through Chinese roadblocks. But engineers determined that the ice was just three inches thick, not enough to support heavily laden trucks.[16]

Toktong Pass. When dawn came, the Marines again drove off the Chinese. Captain Barber was among the Marines wounded during the fight. Another 200 dead Chinese remained on the hill. Radio reports informed Captain Barber that the 5th and 7th Regiments at Yudam-ni had taken heavy casualties, and he knew that Fox Company could not expect relief. Its only chance for survival was to continue holding Toktong Pass. Enemy mortar and sniper fire during the day kept Fox Company on alert, but the Chinese did not attack during the night.

Hagaru-ri. Daylight revealed hundreds more Chinese bodies, many covered by snow. More than a thousand Chinese soldiers had been killed the previous night. Unaware of the decisions made in Tokyo, General Smith preempted MacArthur's orders, directing the 5th and 7th Marine Regiments to prepare to withdraw from Yudam-ni. After arranging a parachute drop of needed supplies and ammunition at Yudam-ni, Smith ordered Puller to open the road from Koto-ri up to Hagaru-ri and began planning his troops' escape. The two regiments and Task Force MacLean would pull back to Hagaru-ri, then move south in a massive column to

Koto-ri, held by Colonel Puller's Marines and various Army units. From there, they would move to Chinhung-ni, held by another battalion of Puller's 1st Regiment, and then onto Hamhung and the ports of Hungnam and Wonsan.

When Almond returned from his meeting in Tokyo, his headquarters staff at Hamhung briefed him on the status of X Corps. He directed Smith to deploy one Marine regiment from Yudam-ni to Hagaru-ri to assist in the withdrawal of Task Force MacLean and to open the road between Hagaru-ri and Koto-ri. Almond's order was impossible to carry out and revealed his ignorance of the task force's desperate situation. General Dave Barr, assistant commander of the Army's 7th Division, was at Hagaru-ri and agreed with Smith that no Marines at Hagaru-ri could be spared. The base camp was surrounded by a division-sized enemy force.

Almond flew to Hagaru-ri later in the day and conferred with Smith and Barr and General Henry Hodes. Almond ordered Smith to draw up a schedule for the extraction of the task force and then left the meeting. Smith pointed out to Barr and Hodes the absurdity of trying to write a timeline and expressed his disgust at Almond's suggestion that they destroy their heavy equipment and burn the rest of their gear. Smith told the two Army generals that Almond had lost all effectiveness as a corps commander and that the Marines were on their own, adding that anything X Corps said would be taken with a grain of salt: "We are going to have to fight our way out without relying on X Corps." Barr and Hodes agreed with Smith's assessment.[17]

Smith gave Lieutenant Colonel Ridge a free hand in the defense of Hagaru-ri. Ridge faced a serious problem in the 4,000 Chinese on East Hill, who could fire at will on the Marines in the village with machine guns, mortars, and small arms. Ridge consequently sent a 250-man detail of Army, Marine, and Korean soldiers to attack East Hill during the night. After fierce fighting, the detail reached the crest of the hill and found only 80 men still firing weapons. The Chinese had to retreat.

Koto-ri. The Marines had to hold Hagaru-ri at all costs or face certain doom. General Smith ordered Colonel Puller to destroy the Chinese roadblocks and open the road between Koto-ri and Hagaru-ri. The relief column would then become part of Hagaru-ri's defense force. Puller designated Drysdale to lead the breakthrough force (Task Force Drysdale) comprised of 245 British commandos, an Army infantry company, a

Marine company, and 70 men of the Marine division headquarters and signal battalion—the numerical equivalent of a battalion. Task Force Drysdale left Koto-ri at 9:45 a.m. with seventeen tanks in the lead and ten in the rear. British commandos took the first objective, a hill north of Koto-ri, against light opposition. A Marine company moved up and took the next hill. Drysdale planned to leapfrog all the way to Hagaru-ri, with tanks leading the column. The task force met heavy enemy fire about four miles north of Koto-ri. The tanks in the lead had no problems with Chinese mortar fire, but Marine trucks were vulnerable. One truck near the middle of the column was hit, caught fire, and blocked the road. Tanks and trucks in the rear guard were cut off from the middle of the column and returned to Koto-ri. The lead elements continued forward until they ran into heavy Chinese fire within sight of Hagaru-ri, suffering heavy losses: 321 of the 922 men were wounded or killed. Seventy-five vehicles were lost, but the trucks and tanks that had reached Hagaru-ri would be critical during the breakout.[18]

The middle elements of the column, cut off at what later became known as Hell Fire Valley, consisted of 380 soldiers, Marines, and British commandos spread out across about two-thirds of a mile on the narrow road. They were poorly organized and faced concentrated enemy fire. Marine air attacks provided some protection until dark. The Chinese made one assault and then withdrew from the road. The group tried to organize itself into a defensive perimeter as members heard bugles signaling the beginning of the night attack on Hagaru-ri in the distance. The Chinese slowly encircled the US and British forces, preparing to attack. Three Marines and an Associated Press photographer tried to escape but were stopped by a Chinese roadblock. One Marine was allowed to return with orders for the group to surrender, and the Chinese ultimately took prisoner roughly 160 Marines, soldiers, and British commandos.[19]

Major Henry Seeley opposed surrendering and escaped with 20 other Marines. They crossed a frozen stream and fled into a rice paddy out of sight of the road. Seeley's group eluded Chinese pursuers and returned to Koto-ri the next morning, finding the defenders counting the Chinese dead from the previous night's fighting.

Task Force MacLean. When dawn came, Air Force and Marine air support drove the enemy away. Colonel MacLean ordered the two lead battalions to pull back and link up with the third battalion for a withdrawal to

Hagaru-ri. The convoy of sixty trucks moved out at 6:00 a.m. with Marine Corsairs providing cover. The Chinese attacked, and the wounded MacLean was captured. Lieutenant Colonel Don Carlos Faith took command. The task force was blocked by the Chinese to the north and south. The soldiers were in a dangerous position on the edge of the reservoir and running low on ammunition and supplies. The Army detachment at Hagaru-ri sent out a relief column of eleven tanks and a platoon of infantry but was forced back. Hodes asked Smith for Marine assistance, but the Marine general had no forces to spare and could provide only air support. Those Marine Corsairs kept the Chinese at a distance during the day.[20]

When Almond returned to his command post at Hungnam, he was summoned to Tokyo; he returned to Korea the next morning with new orders to withdraw his forces from the reservoir area to the Hamhung-Hungnam area of the coast. During his brief absence, the situation for X Corps had worsened.

Thursday–November 30

Yudam-ni. The Chinese harassed the Marine perimeter with long-range small-arms fire and small probing attacks during the day, while Litzenberg and Murray rearranged their defenses in preparation for the breakout. The 5th and 7th Regiments had to be turned around for the withdrawal, a difficult operation. Colonel Litzenberg came up with the idea of sending a battalion cross-country to relieve Fox Company and keep Toktong Pass open. The battalion would have to move more than four miles, though the distance would be double that because of the steep slopes, while maintaining complete silence. Artillery at Yudam-ni would guide the battalion by periodically firing star shells. The Chinese expected the Marines to remain on the road, so moving cross-country would constitute a surprise.[21]

Toktong Pass. Marine air cover gave protection to Fox Company during the day, and other than sporadic sniper and mortar fire, the Chinese made no attempt to take Fox Hill during the night. The company had a large number of casualties who needed to be evacuated but no means of getting them out of the Chinese encirclement.[22]

Hagaru-ri. Marine Corsairs burned the hill with napalm in the morning, forcing the Chinese to remain hidden in the surrounding mountains during the daylight hours, but after dark, with the temperature at twenty-five degrees below zero, the Chinese made an all-out assault that lasted until first light. At one point, the Marine artillery battery turned its howitzers and mortars to bear directly on the slopes where the enemy was concentrated. The Marines repulsed an attack on East Hill, and the Chinese again withdrew when the rising sun enabled Marine aircraft to bomb the enemy's exposed positions. The enemy dead count was placed at 930. General Smith knew that if the Chinese took control of Hagaru-ri, the 5th and 7th Regiments and the Marine division could not survive. Matters worsened when the Chinese destroyed the bridge at the penstock station at Funchilin Pass. The Marines were now trapped. That bridge had not been guarded during the early days of the Chosin Reservoir operation, and Marine and Army traffic crossed daily. But General Almond had ordered Lieutenant Colonel Richard Reidy, commander of the 2nd Battalion of the 31st Infantry Regiment, which was stalled around the pass, to move the unit. Reidy pointed out the importance of occupying the terrain that controlled Funchilin Pass, but Almond's personal representative ignored Reidy's reasoning. The Chinese then destroyed the bridge.[23]

Task Force Faith (formerly Task Force MacLean). Lieutenant Colonel Faith formed his depleted battalions into a tight defensive perimeter and inflicted heavy casualties when the Chinese attacked during the night.

Friday–December 1

Yudam-ni. The 5th and 7th Regiments completed their turnaround and prepared to start the fourteen-mile withdrawal to Hagaru-ri. The 85 Marines killed in the fighting at Yudam-ni were buried there. Marines policed the area and burned clothing, food containers, and anything else the Chinese could use. The lead elements of the column would complete the march while the last units were still at Yudam-ni. The spearhead of the 7th Regiment, led by the Marines' sole tank, began its advance at 9:00 a.m. and ran into repeated heavy Chinese mortar and small-arms fire. Attacking Corsairs broke up roadblocks, forcing the Chinese into the hills and ridges along the route. When gaps appeared in the column, the Chinese attacked the rear of the forward group. The move toward Hagaru-ri was not a motor march, it was a tactical battle. At the same time, Lieutenant

Colonel R. G. Davis's 1st Battalion moved through rough mountain terrain and deep snowdrifts, traveling for three hours before their first enemy contact. After several firefights, the battalion reached the pass the next morning and was amazed to see an estimated thousand-plus Chinese bodies along the road and at the foot of the hill that Fox Company had defended for five nights.[24]

Toktong Pass. The enemy began probing defenses around Fox Hill at 2:15 a.m. and then launched an assault that broke through the lower Marine positions. Fox Company executed a counterattack and forced the numerically superior enemy forces to withdraw. At first light, the Marines drove the Chinese stragglers off the slope. Captain Barber was wounded a second time during this encounter.

Hagaru-ri. Hagaru-ri would have fallen if Task Force Drysdale had not arrived and become part of its defenses against the three attacking Chinese divisions. That, combined with completion of the airstrip by Army engineers on December 1, was a turning point for General Smith, who could not deal with the overwhelming number of casualties at Hagaru-ri. Helicopters and light aircraft flying from a smaller strip at Koto-ri had evacuated 152 casualties, but Smith had 600 wounded at Hagaru-ri, at least 500 coming from Yudam-ni, and several hundred more Army casualties from east of the reservoir. With the airstrip at Hagaru-ri only about 40 percent complete, Smith ordered a test flight to determine whether the 2,900-foot runway could accommodate a C-47. The test was successful, and three planeloads of casualties were flown out. Flights significantly increased the next day, as planes brought in more than one hundred tons of supplies and ammunition and took out casualties. Marine replacements were also brought in.[25]

General Smith also allowed some Marine dead to be taken out, a decision criticized by Major General Clark Ruffner, Almond's X Corps chief of staff. Smith ignored the protest and later explained, "The Marines have a particular reverence for comrades killed in action. They will make every effort, even risking casualties, to bring in the bodies for a proper burial. We felt it was an obligation, so that these men would not be buried in some desolate North Korean village."[26]

Task Force Faith (formerly Task Force MacLean). Lieutenant Colonel Faith knew that the task force could not survive another night attack. His soldiers were exhausted, almost out of ammunition, and suffering from frostbite. Marine and Navy air cover arrived at daylight, and the Chinese melted away.

An Army tank company attempted once more to move the eight miles north from Hagaru-ri to assist the task force, but Chinese roadblocks again forced the tanks to turn around. Chinese soldiers watched as the demoralized GIs took weapons, clothing, and ammunition from the dead. Faith called his officers together and told them to prepare to pull back around noon. Task Force Faith had a total of nearly 3,000 soldiers, including 600 wounded GIs loaded on thirty operational trucks. As the vehicle column began to form on the road, the Chinese came down from the surrounding slopes and took positions along the breakout route. A flight of four Marine aircraft appeared as the column began its march, opening fire on enemy positions and dropping napalm canisters. One fell at the front of the convoy, killing and wounding several soldiers, a crushing blow to morale. Those leading the column began to fall back. Disorder broke out in the ranks, and many troops tried to climb into trucks already loaded with the wounded. The column rolled south under heavy enemy fire, which targeted truck drivers to immobilize the convoy. Faith was wounded and placed in a truck cab, where he was later fatally wounded. A destroyed bridge about four miles from Hagaru-ri forced the convoy to stop, and the Chinese then methodically destroyed the convoy, truck by truck. Task Force Faith was on the brink of destruction.[27]

Some soldiers survived by escaping across the ice at the southern end of the reservoir, dragging along the wounded.[28] The task force had been given an assignment beyond its capabilities. The unit should have been ordered back to Hagaru-ri after the first Chinese attack. Instead, Almond ridiculed the Chinese and ordered Colonel MacLean to push forward. About 1,000 of the task force's 3,500 Americans were killed, left to die of wounds, or taken prisoner.[29]

Amid the larger disaster unfolding in Korea, the public took virtually no notice of the grim story of Task Force MacLean/Faith. Within Army circles, however, the story became well known. Two commanders were lost, and Faith posthumously received the Congressional Medal of Honor, the only Korean War battalion commander so honored.[30]

Saturday–December 2

On the morning of December 2, accompanied by air cover, a column of Marine jeeps, trucks, and sleds crossed the ice and rescued 319 soldiers, most of them in a state of shock. The Chinese did little to interfere except for an occasional long-range rifle shot.[31]

China's state-controlled international broadcaster, Radio Peking, announced to the world that the destruction of the 1st Marine Division was imminent, causing fear and anxiety in Washington and among the American public. The Chinese relished the propaganda value of destroying one of the most esteemed US military units in Korea. American newspapers, already ridiculing MacArthur's Home by Christmas offensive, warned of the dangers the Marines faced against an enemy that outnumbered them ten to one. Radio reporter Walter Winchell told listeners to pray for those serving in the Marine division in Korea.

General Smith still believed he could save his division. If he could pull his Marines and Task Force MacLean/Faith survivors to Hagaru-ri, they could then fight their way south on the MSR to Koto-ri and on to Hungnam and Wonsan. The last elements of the 5th Marines began withdrawing from Yudam-ni after the artillery battalion fired off most of its ammunition.

Clinton's PFC Bill Smith was in the 4th Battalion of the 11th Marine Artillery Regiment at Yudam-ni. Already suffering from the first stages of frostbite, he marched with the rear elements of the column. The gunners of his battalion were organized into nine rifle platoons that were the last to leave Yudam-ni.[32]

Lieutenant Colonel Davis's battalion, making its way through deep snowdrifts, reached the Toktong Pass early in the morning. Company B relieved Fox Company and took control of Fox Hill, guarding the pass. The Ridgerunners of Toktong Pass, as Davis's Marines later became known, suffered 26 killed, 89 wounded, and 3 missing during their cross-country trek. Fox Company's heroic defense of Toktong Pass was one of the many extraordinary stories of the saga of the Chosin. During four nights of heavy fighting against 6,000 Chinese soldiers, 240 Marines held the pass. Six of the company's seven officers were wounded, among them Captain Barber. The men of Fox Company had done their job.[33]

Sunday–December 3

The lead elements of the Marine 5th and 7th regimental column took two days to cover the seven miles to the Toktong Pass under continuous attack.

Marine Corsairs broke up Chinese roadblocks, scattering the enemy into the surrounding hills during the march. The 1st Marine Air Wing flew 145 sorties covering the Marine column in its final miles to Hagaru-ri. The 1st Battalion of the 7th Regiment, with Fox Company survivors in the front, formed into two columns and marched into Hagaru-ri singing the "Marines' Hymn."[34]

The British commandos welcomed the arrivals as they were escorted to the field mess for hot pancakes and coffee. The rear elements of the column reached the Toktong Pass and were joined by the Ridgerunners for the final leg to Hagaru-ri. The 5th and 7th Regiments had about 1,500 casualties, a third of them from frostbite. The wounded received immediate medical attention at the already crowded Marine hospital in the old schoolhouse. The most seriously wounded Marines were airlifted out, and in some cases, able-bodied men tried to get on the C-47s, leading General Smith to order the field hospital to provide documentation for all of the wounded.[35]

Smith also ordered Lieutenant Colonel Berry Anderson of the Army to organize the physically fit survivors of Task Force Faith into a provisional battalion. Since they had abandoned their weapons and equipment, the Marines had to supply the soldiers.

General Almond flew into Hagaru-ri and proposed that the Marines destroy all equipment and evacuate by air. Smith summarily rejected the idea, pointing out that as the perimeter shrunk during the evacuations, the Chinese could fire mortars and destroy the airstrip and any planes on it, stranding the thousands of Marines still defending the village. Almond dropped his plan.[36]

Monday—December 4

The Chinese made no serious attacks on the last leg of the column leaving Yudam-ni until the movers hauling eight 155mm howitzers at the end of the column ran out of diesel fuel and stopped. In the face of a major Chinese assault, the rear column returned fire, reopened the road, and moved on, leaving the howitzers behind. They reached Hagaru-ri around 2:00 p.m., finally completing the move from Yudam-ni. General Smith knew he had to begin the breakout south as soon as possible and wanted to evacuate as many wounded as he could before giving up the airstrip. Air Force and Marine transports had flown out more than 1,600 casualties on December 2–3, bringing the total to 4,312—3,150 Marines, 1,137 soldiers, and 25 Royal Marines over five days.[37]

Over this period, 537 Marine replacements—most of them recovering wounded who rejoined their original units—had flown into Hagaru-ri. The incoming planes also brought reporters and other visitors, among them Marguerite Higgins of the *New York Herald Tribune*. General Smith promptly ordered her out of the perimeter by nightfall, though he allowed other correspondents as well as camera crews to remain. When a British reporter made the error of referring to the withdrawal as a "retreat," Smith pointed out that a surrounded force cannot retreat; it can only attack in a new direction. The published version of his remarks in the United States became, "Retreat, hell, we're just attacking in a new direction."[38]

Tuesday–December 5

Smith spent the day organizing the breakout. He had more than 10,000 men at Hagaru-ri, including about 1,000 Army personnel, survivors of Task Force Faith, engineers, and others. Lieutenant Colonel Anderson structured Army personnel into a provisional 31st Regiment made up of two battalions with two companies each and assigned to the 7th Marine Regiment. The concentration of aircraft covering the advance to the south from Hagaru-ri was the greatest of the Korean War. Marine aircraft conducted approximately 130 daily sorties, four Navy carriers contributed 100 or more attack sorties daily, and the Air Force added more power with medium and heavy bomber interdictions. This air cover was essential to the success of the breakout.[39]

Wednesday–December 6

The attack to the south began at dawn as units of the 5th Marines cleaned up East Hill. Several squadrons of Marine and Navy aircraft plus one Australian squadron gave air cover. Six Chinese divisions surrounded Hagaru-ri and took positions along the MSR. Colonel Litzenberg's

7th Marines, labeled Division Train No. 1, interspersed with survivors of Task Force Faith, led the advance south. Tanks, trucks, and other vehicles moved on the road while Marines patrolled the ridgelines on both sides. One Marine tank bore a sign reading, "Only fourteen more shooting days until Christmas!"[40]

The Chinese countered with heavy mortar, machine-gun, and small-arms fire, but the column pushed on. As it reached Hell Fire Valley at midmorning, the Marines picked up twenty-two Royal Marine survivors who had concealed themselves in a Korean hut after being separated from Task Force Drysdale on November 29. The 7th Regiment had covered three miles when it lost air cover at nightfall. Chinese attacks continued as the column marched through the night. Led by an artillery battalion of the 11th Marine Regiment, the next segment of Train No. 1 started south at 4:00 p.m. The Chinese struck when the US/UN troops were one mile south of Hagaru-ri, and the gunners fought like infantrymen, using their howitzers to fire at point-blank range, destroying the attackers.[41]

Thursday–December 7

Train No. 2, the last part of the division, started its move from Hagaru-ri after midnight, and the last elements did not leave until the next morning. Engineers and ordinance men destroyed equipment that had to be left behind and burned all supplies, but the train moved slowly because the road was clogged with discarded equipment. Corsair air cover resumed at dawn for the breakout, and both the first and second elements of Train No. 1 reached Koto-ri in the morning, with other units of the Marine division arriving throughout the day until the last elements of Train No. 2 arrived around midnight. The Chinese had thrown all their firepower at the Marines during the preceding thirty-eight hours, and the Marines suffered 103 KIA, 506 wounded, and 7 missing. Thousands of Chinese were killed along the road.[42]

The Marines had problems with some GIs during the breakout. Colonel Litzenberg had assigned the Army battalion to protect one flank of the column, but on numerous occasions when the Chinese attacked, the GIs moved through the vehicles to the other side of the convoy, meaning that Marines had to cover both flanks of the convoy while the GIs walked among the vehicles. Litzenberg realized he could not rely on the GIs to protect the convoy.[43]

Recognizing the gravity of the military situation, Almond flew to Koto-ri and assured Smith that the Army's 3rd Infantry Division would provide maximum protection on the last leg of the breakout from Chinhung-ni to Hamhung. Almond also gave Smith control over Army artillery in that area. With the exception of the 1st Battalion of the 1st Regiment, Smith's three regiments were now together for the first time since the October landing at Wonson. The general's immediate problem was the bridge at the Funchilin Pass, which had a twenty-four-foot gap courtesy of Chinese explosives. The Army had a treadway prefabricated bridge company at Koto-ri: if the Air Force could airdrop eight 2,500-pound bridge sections, Army trucks could then carry the sections to the pass and span the gap.[44] Operation Tootsie Roll, as it was named, would require precise timing by the Marines, Army, and Air Force. The Marine 1/1 at Chinhung-ni would move north to clear the area of Chinese while the division column moved south. Battalion-sized units of the Army's 7th Infantry Division, reinforced by tanks and artillery, would move up from the south, pass through Sudong, and follow the Marines. The Marine and Army battalions sought to capture Hill 1081, which overlooked the Funchilin Pass and thus needed to be under US/UN control before the bridge sections could be brought in.[45]

Friday–December 8

Smith's division resumed the march south from Koto-ri at first light on a day that featured falling snow and a temperature of twenty degrees below zero. Three Marine battalions and one Army battalion led the march: one at the front of the column, two covering the flanks, and the fourth protecting the rear. Company-size units leapfrogged along the high ground on each side of the road. The heavily laden vehicles faced heavy enemy fire during the advance, which stopped after two miles because of darkness.

North Korean civilian refugees followed the columns as they left Hagaru-ri, hoping to follow them all the way to the coast. The Chinese had ousted most of the refugees from their homes to use them for shelter. The Koreans carried what they could on their backs. Navy corpsmen and Army medics gave medical attention to the refugees and delivered two babies on December 8, but the refugee group had been infiltrated by Chinese soldiers, so it was never allowed to enter the Marine perimeter.[46]

The 1/1 Marine Battalion began the six-mile hike from Chinhung-ni to Hill 1081 at 2:00 a.m. With thick clouds blanketing the hill and heavy snow falling, the Marines climbed to the crest of the hill and drove the Chinese off, then held off a Chinese counterattack.[47]

Saturday–December 9

Saturday was bright, clear, and cold. The Marine battalion from Chinhung-ni reached the area south of the pass, where they faced heavy Chinese fire from the surrounding hills. Air cover gave the battalion control of the south side of the pass while allowing other Marines to maintain control of Hill 1081. A battalion of Colonel Puller's 1st Marine Regiment approached the bridge from the road and found Chinese soldiers, nearly frozen, guarding the penstocks and gatehouse below. They surrendered without a fight. The Army's Brockway trucks carrying the bridge sections left Koto-ri at first light and moved to the bridge area, while Army and Marine engineers rebuilt bridge abutments. The engineers spent three hours installing the bridge sections, and the gap was closed. The road on both sides of the bridge was narrow, chiseled out of the cliff. Marine Train No. 1 began its descent to the pass at 3:00 p.m. and crossed the bridge three hours later.

General Smith spent most of the day directing the burying of the dead at Koto-ri. General Lemuel Shepherd, Pacific Marine Fleet commander, flew into Koto-ri and told Smith he wanted to make the last segment of the breakout with the division. Smith argued that he could not adequately lead the Marines while worrying about losing a three-star general, so Shepherd agreed to fly out. Marguerite Higgins also got to Koto-ri and had been asked by the 5th Marines to walk out with them, but once again, Smith refused to allow her to cover the action. Higgins was livid as Colonel Puller led her by the hand to Shepherd and said, "General Smith says take this woman out of his hair and see that she goes out on your plane."

But Higgins was not to be denied. After the plane landed at Hamhung, she hopped a ride on a weapons carrier that took her to the bottom of the mountains near the Funchilin Pass and "hiked up the mountain for about five miles, past the streams of vehicles heading for the sea." She then "climbed far enough to get a sweeping view of the steep road and the valley below it" and then returned to the valley.[48]

Sunday–December 10

Vehicles passed over the rebuilt bridge throughout the night, and at 2:45 a.m. the head of the column reached Chinhung-ni. Colonel Puller pulled out the remainder of his regiment during the afternoon, leaving Koto-ri for the last time with Korean refugees following. The Chinese continued to fire on the column with machine guns and small arms, but Marine air cover drove them away. After all vehicles had cleared the Funchilin Pass, Marine engineers blew up the bridge. One Korean man had been knocked unconscious by Chinese mortar fire and left for dead, but he regained consciousness, and the engineers coached him through the gatehouse above the penstocks. Refugees watched and crossed in the same way.

The last units of the 1st Marine Division passed through Chinhung-ni by 1:00 p.m. and reached the Hamhung-Hungnam assembly areas eight hours later. Higgins wrote that the Marines had come to Hamhung "in good order . . . just as Colonel Murray said they would"; despite setbacks, "their reputation as fighting men remained fully 'secured.'" News reporters described the breakout as a "miracle of deliverance," a "saga," and "epic" and expressed surprise that the Marines and Army troops had never doubted their ability to "slug their way out to the seacoast." *Time* magazine saw the breakout as "a battle unparalleled in U. S. military history," with "some aspects of Bataan, some of Anzio, some of Dunkirk, some of Valley Forge."[49]

General Smith expected his division to be assigned a defensive position in the Hungnam sector but learned that General MacArthur, following General Almond's advice, had ordered the Marines' immediate evacuation. Almond believed the Marine division to be only marginally combat effective and thought the Army's 7th Division was in much better shape. When the Marines reached Hungnam, they marched straight to the docks.

The Evacuation

US military leaders had assembled ships from every corner of East Asia to
evacuate troops and civilians from the Hungnam area. Between December
11 and December 14, twenty-eight transport ships sailed from northeast
Korea to Pusan. Chinese and North Korean soldiers outside the Hungnam
defensive perimeter attacked repeatedly during the evacuation but were
repelled by American artillery and aircraft. The battleship *Missouri* added
its sixteen-inch guns to the firepower of two cruisers, seven destroyers,
and three rocket craft, covering the withdrawal. The last embarkation
beaches were cleared by December 24. Army engineers then blew up
munitions that had to be left behind, including five hundred thousand-
pound bombs and four hundred tons of dynamite that had frozen and
could not be moved.

The breakout from the Chosin Reservoir was a dramatic victory for
the Marine 1st Division. Suffering from the bitter cold, half-dead from
exhaustion, and at the limits of their will, the Marines outlasted the enemy.
They took up their weapons and marched through the enemy's gauntlet
to safety. The survivors of the operation later dubbed themselves the
Chosin Few, and the Navy named a warship the *Chosin*. Marine aviators
had provided critical air cover during the breakout, as General Smith
recognized: "During the long reaches of the night and in the snowstorms,
many a Marine prayed for the coming of day or clearing weather when he
knew he would again hear the welcome roar of [the] planes. . . . [N]ever
in its history has Marine aviation given more convincing proof of its
indispensable value to ground Marines."[50]

For its actions at the Chosin Reservoir, the 1st Marine Division received
the Presidential Unit Citation for outstanding performance under fire, an
honor usually reserved for smaller units.

The Home Front

Navy medic Herbert Pearce was wounded while the 5th Marine Regiment was in Hagaru-ri but made the march to the Hamhung-Hungnam
assembly area and was evacuated to Pusan. He hoped to be rotated back

to the States. PFC Bill Smith also made the march; suffering from frost-bite, he was then sent to a military hospital in Japan. Their families knew that the Marine division had escaped the Chinese encirclement but knew nothing about the men's fates.[51]

Betty Jo Smith had not heard from her husband since his letter written on Thanksgiving Day, though she was in daily contact with his parents. On Christmas Eve, a ham radio operator in Oregon called her to relay the message that Bill was alive and in a Japanese hospital, good news that she immediately shared with his parents.[52] The Pearce family remained confident that Herbert was alive because military representatives had not contacted them to report his death, and they received confirmation in the form of a letter from Herbert, who was again at the Bean Patch near Masan.

While the Marines evacuated from Hungnam, Homer Ainsworth, Joe Albritton, and Waller King completed boot camp and returned to Clinton on leave for Christmas. George Sharp completed combat training, received Christmas leave, and in January shipped out to Korea, where he joined the 5th Marine Regiment at the Bean Patch.

During their two weeks of leave, Homer, Joe, and Waller spent time with family and friends. In addition, Joe secretly married Peggy Cain on December 26. The *Clinton News* did not report the nuptials, but Bea Quisenberry knew about them. Her January 5 "Bea's Buzzzz" column mentioned that Peggy and two other Clinton women had attended a square dance, an event that would not have been newsworthy except that as a married woman, Peggy should not have been going out dancing.[53]

Homer and Waller did not know about Joe's marriage, but they did read a *Jackson Clarion-Ledger* story about a Navy pilot from Hattiesburg who had died in the fighting north of the Chosin Reservoir. Twenty-four-year-old Ensign Jesse L. Brown, the first African American naval aviator, had been "trying to help those poor guys on the ground" when he was shot down on December 2 while giving air cover to the last Marine column leaving Yudam-ni. Brown survived the crash but was injured and pinned in the wreckage. Lieutenant Thomas Hudner, Brown's wingman, crash-landed his Corsair in a nearby rice paddy, but he and the pilot of a Marine rescue helicopter could not pry Brown from the wreckage, and he died. The next morning, at Hudner's request, four Navy pilots from the carrier *Leyte* flew to the crash site and cremated Brown's body in a blaze of napalm.

Hudner later received the Congressional Medal of Honor for his attempt to rescue Brown. Brown was posthumously awarded the Distinguished Flying Cross, and in 1973, the US Navy named a vessel in his honor. The story of Brown and Hudner is told in Adam Makos's 2015 book, *Devotion: An Epic Story of Heroism, Friendship, and Sacrifice*, which was made into a 2022 movie, *Devotion*, starring Jonathan Majors as Brown.[54]

Chapter 6

AN ENTIRELY NEW WAR, DECEMBER 1950–APRIL 1951

No one is blaming General MacArthur and certainly I never did,
for the failure of the November offensive.... But I do blame him
for the manner in which he tried to excuse his failure.
—**Harry S. Truman,** *Memoirs: Years of Trial and Hope*

After General Douglas MacArthur told the Pentagon, "We face an entirely new war" on November 29, the Truman administration faced a questioning American public over the new crisis in Korea. The Chinese counterattack and 8th Army's retreat shocked Americans. *Time* magazine called the disaster "the worst defeat the United States ever suffered." *Newsweek* called it America's worst military licking since Pearl Harbor. Many observers feared that the 8th Army, which represented two-thirds of the entire US Army, would have to be evacuated in a Dunkirk-type rescue.[1]

A wide range of opinions emerged on what the administration should do. No one wanted a major ground war with China or the Soviet Union. The consensus among the president's advisers was that the United States should hold on in Korea. State Department and Pentagon officials agreed that the atomic bomb would not be used. Everything else hinged on China's behavior. If China used air power from Manchuria on US/UN forces, they would have to counterattack across the Yalu and consider a naval blockade of China.

The administration also had to deal with General MacArthur, who in communications with the Joint Chiefs of Staff (JCS) and in statements to reporters blamed the military reversals on the restrictions placed on his command. The president hoped that his December 5 order requiring the State Department or the Pentagon to clear all public announcements touching on national policy would muffle the general, but MacArthur refused to comply.

Even though China was the enemy on the ground, the administration continued to fear war with the Soviet Union. The specter of Soviet intervention—and use of nuclear weapons—in Korea led the administration to allocate twenty atomic bombs for use against Soviet military targets if retaliation was necessary. The warheads were placed on American bases on Guam, Saipan, and Tinian. Military procedure called for these options to be shared with the theater commander to give him time to plan, but the White House did not share this information with MacArthur.

The thirteen Arab and Asian members of the United Nations proposed a cease-fire agreement for Korea that reached the Security Council on December 13 and the full General Assembly the next day. The Chinese Communist government, confident of victory in Korea, rejected the proposal on the grounds that all UN actions without China's participation were illegal.[2]

The perceived Soviet threat led President Truman to declare a state of national emergency on December 15, 1950. He told Americans that the Soviet Union was behind China's intervention in Korea, that the United States would increase the size of its military to 3.5 million, and that American industrial production would be placed on a war footing. The declaration resulted in the activation of national guard units across the country, including the Mississippi National Guard. Thirty-six Clinton men were called up and sent to Fort Jackson, South Carolina, for basic training.[3]

The Soviet Union reacted to the US emergency declaration with a series of mid-December radio broadcasts directly threatening Japan, increasing fears of a global war. According to *Life* magazine, "Our leaders are frightened, befuddled and caught in a great and inexcusable failure to marshal the strength of America as quickly and as strongly as they ought to have done in recent months."[4]

General Walton Walker evacuated Pyongyang and by December 13 had pulled the 8th Army below the 38th Parallel to defensive Line B on the Imjin River. The Chinese stopped their counteroffensive north of the parallel because of logistical problems, but they were within a day's march of Line B: when the next attack came, Walker would be forced back to Seoul and the Han River.

General Oliver Smith's 1st Marine Division rested at Masan, twenty-seven miles from Pusan. For a couple of weeks, they had free time to play tag football and enjoy the autumnal weather, a major change from the freezing conditions during the Chosin operation. The Marines received fresh food every day and enjoyed a good Christmas as they recovered physically and mentally from the rigors of early December. Draftees from the United States filled the division's depleted ranks.

Smith had rifle ranges built and continued training exercises to keep his troops battle-ready. New equipment and uniforms were handed out. Among the visitors to Masan was Hollywood director John Ford. An activated Navy reservist, Ford began filming a documentary on the Navy and Marines and told the general that Hollywood was going to make a movie, *Retreat Hell!*, based on Smith's remarks during the Chosin withdrawal. In addition, Colonel S. L. A. Marshall, an Army historian, carried out several interviews with Marine survivors for a classified report on the Chosin Reservoir operation.

The Marines instituted a rotation system after arriving at the Bean Patch in December. Based on combat time, 5 officers and 600 men were scheduled to return to the States. One of the first to be rotated was General Edward Craig, commander of the Fire Brigade in the early months of the war and assistant divisional commander. He received a promotion to major general, followed by a farewell dinner and celebration. Promoted to brigadier general, Lewis "Chesty" Puller replaced Craig as assistant commander of the 1st Marine Division, while Colonel Francis McAlister took command. On that same day, the 1st Korean Marine Corps Combat Regiment rejoined the 1st Marine Division.[5]

As 1950 ended, the American people still supported the war in Korea. *Time* magazine named the "American Fighting Man" its Man of the Year, but some people began to question the wisdom of "limited war" and worried about the ever-increasing loss of American lives.[6]

To date, American and South Korean soldiers had turned in disappointingly poor performances, and everyone looked for someone else to blame. Moreover, although President Truman had desegregated the armed forces in 1948, some units, among them the 24th Infantry Regiment of the Army's 25th Infantry Division, remained predominantly Black, and African Americans continued to face discrimination. The commander of the 24th Regiment claimed that his soldiers had "bugged out" during the retreat, but Black officers in the 25th Division contended that the regiment's problems resulted from the incompetence of the unit's white commander.

On December 23, 1950, General Walker was killed in a vehicle accident while inspecting UN positions along Line B. MacArthur and General J. Lawton Collins, the Army chief of staff, had previously agreed that if anything befell Walker, General Matthew Ridgway would take over command of the 8th Army. Ridgway was the Army's deputy chief of staff for operations in Washington and knew General MacArthur well.

Ridgway arrived in Tokyo on Christmas Day and had a long meeting with MacArthur about Korea. Ridgway agreed with MacArthur's repeated requests to carry the war to China and use Chinese Nationalist troops. When Ridgway asked whether MacArthur would object to the launching of an attack, MacArthur replied, "The Eighth Army is yours, Matt, do what you think best." After having overruled many of Walker's decisions, MacArthur seemed willing to turn over command to Ridgway.[7]

Ridgway arrived in Korea just as the US 5th Air Force regained control of the skies. The North Koreans had introduced the Soviet-made MiG-15 jet fighter, and it dominated the American F-80 Thunderbolt. The December introduction of the F-86 Sabre tipped the scales back toward the United States, which remained dominant for the duration of the war.[8]

Ridgway immediately began preparing for the coming Chinese offensive. He met with each corps and division commander to discuss the military situation and composed a message to be read to every soldier in the 8th Army, asking two questions: "Why are we here?" and "What are we fighting for?" The answers: to contain the spread of Communism, which threatened world peace and the security of the United States.[9]

Ridgway also conducted an aerial survey of the Korean terrain. What he saw was not comforting to a general commanding a mechanized army: "The granite peaks rose to 6,000 feet, the ridges were knife-edged, the slopes steep, and the narrow valleys twisted and turned like snakes. The roads were trails, and the lower hills were covered with scrub oaks and stunted pines, fine cover for a single soldier who knew how to conceal himself. It was guerrilla country . . . a miserable place for road-bound troops who moved on wheels."[10]

Ridgway believed that his soldiers had lost confidence, were too soft, and were too dependent on vehicles to fight an enemy that had no wheels. Soldiers perceived the Chinese as invincible. Ridgway recognized the need to increase the soldiers' toughness of soul and body. They could not abandon vehicles and equipment at the first sight of the enemy. They had to travel on foot and shave and clean up. Ridgway relieved a general who offered contingency plans for retreat and then chewed out the corps and division commanders and ordered them to lead from the combat zone, not from their rear command posts.[11]

Ridgway was appalled that field commanders had so little intelligence regarding the enemy's strength. The first intelligence report he received indicated that 176,000 Chinese soldiers were in Korea, when the actual number was 400,000. Ridgway ordered aggressive patrolling to capture prisoners and gain intelligence. He announced that any soldier who abandoned equipment without good cause would be court-martialed. And the general ordered winter clothing for 8th Army.

Ridgeway introduced a simple method of fighting, the "Meat Grinder": take the high ground, employ artillery effectively, create far stronger defensive positions, and fight better at night by using massive numbers of flares. All firepower, including aircraft, artillery, and tanks, was to concentrate on killing Chinese. And American losses were to be minimized, even at the expense of losing real estate.

When Ridgway requested 30,000 Korean laborers to build fortifications for the 8th Army, South Korean president Syngman Rhee approved, and an army of workers arrived the next day. They began construction of broad belts of defensive redoubts on the north and south sides of the Han River. These workers became the basis for the Civil Transport Corps, an invaluable labor source for transporting supplies to the front lines.[12]

Ridgway expressed concerns about the weaknesses of the Republic of Korea (ROK) divisions fighting in the 8th Army. He ordered General Edward Almond's X Corps to the center sector of Line B to back up the ROK divisions and the US Army's 2nd Division. Ridgway did not like Almond but decided to keep him as commander, though on a tight leash. The 1st Marine Division had already been detached from X Corps, and Ridgway left it in reserve at Masan.[13]

While Ridgway prepared for the Chinese offensive, MacArthur kept up his predictions of disaster and his litany of demands. In response, the JCS told him that Korea was not the place to fight a major war and that the United States could not commit additional forces in the event of a possible general war. They directed MacArthur to maintain defensive positions and inflict as many enemy casualties as possible, supporting Ridgway's new strategy.

MacArthur responded on December 29 by proposing an immediate and all-out war with China. He called for a blockade of China and the destruction of its industrial capacity by US/UN air and naval forces and suggested having Chang Kai-shek's garrison on Taiwan take diversionary actions against the Chinese mainland. Unless these measures were taken, MacArthur warned, the 8th Army would inevitably have to evacuate Korea.

MacArthur's response infuriated Washington. Secretary of defense Omar Bradley thought that the Chinese had wounded MacArthur's pride, making "a fool of the infallible 'military genius.'" In Bradley's estimation, MacArthur saw his only path to recovery as inflicting an overwhelming defeat on the Chinese generals who had previously beaten him. MacArthur was willing to go to war with China to redeem himself. While Washington considered a proper response to MacArthur, events in Korea quickly took a dramatic turn.

The long-expected Chinese offensive began on January 1, 1951, hitting ROK divisions in the central sector of the US/UN line. The South Koreans disintegrated in panic, and the 8th Army had to pull back from Line B. Ridgway evacuated Seoul on January 4 and set up a new defensive line 40 miles to the south—275 miles south of the Army's advance positions when the Home by Christmas offensive began in November 1950. The Chinese captured Seoul for the second time but again exhausted their supplies and had to stop their offensive.

General Ridgway was not happy with the 8th Army's performance during the retreat. Too many soldiers still rode trucks and pulled back instead of setting up defensive barriers and fighting. Ridgway told Rhee that the ROK divisions needed better leadership and threatened to withhold arms and supplies unless the South Korean soldiers improved.

Ridgway recognized that he needed to get the Marines back on the front line. Meeting with General Smith, who was eager to get the division back in combat, Ridgway outlined his plan to maximize enemy losses.

The Marines were given a new zone of operation, north of the old Pusan Perimeter area, about 1,600 square miles of mountainous terrain teeming with North Korean guerrillas. The Marines were to maintain control of a seventy-five-mile stretch of the main supply route from Pohang to Andong. Smith reported his lack of confidence in Almond to Ridgway, who offered assurances that as long as he commanded the 8th Army, "the 1st Marine Division would never again be placed under command of the X Corps."[14]

The Marines moved north from Masan and began sending out four-man Rice Paddy Patrols in search of the enemy. The patrols went out for days at a time, covering secondary roads and mountain trails. Supplied by helicopter drops, they were alert to sniper fire and enemy ambushes. The patrols provided excellent training for replacements, and suffered only light casualties. By January 27, the enemy began withdrawing from the zone.[15]

While Marines were clearing areas to the north, Ridgway sent two "reconnaissance in force" operations that revealed only small Chinese elements north of the 8th Army line. Believing the Chinese to be temporarily exhausted, Ridgway launched Operation Thunderbolt on January 28. Army units moved slowly northward, and with air cover from the Air Force, Navy, and Marines, Chinese resistance collapsed by February 9.

With strong air support, General Almond's X Corps shattered three Chinese divisions in the February 14 "Wonju Shoot," leaving more than 5,000 enemy dead on the battleground. Ridgway nevertheless chewed out Almond over the heavy US/UN casualties: 9,800 South Koreans, 1,900 Americans, and 100 Dutch soldiers. Ridgway ordered an investigation, which ultimately blamed the losses on the flight of the Korean soldiers and the failure of their "commanders to advise or alert US units of their departure." The report vindicated Almond, though Ridgway still faulted the general for the tremendous losses.[16]

The 8th Army now had the initiative. The 1st Marine Division moved up to Chungju to provide support to IX Corps and became part of two successive offenses. Marines were the centerpiece of Operation Killer, which began on February 21. The operation included eight infantry divisions—more than 100,000 men—backed by five tank battalions, twenty-two artillery battalions, and Air Force and Marine air support.

General MacArthur flew to Suwon on the eve of the offensive and drove to Wonju, where he held a press conference to praise Ridgway and the 8th Army. His remarks included thinly veiled criticisms of the Truman administration and complaints about the enemy's "sanctuary." MacArthur hinted that Operation Killer was his idea and expressed support for crossing the 38th Parallel, again flirting with insubordination.

Operation Killer did not live up to its name. Unseasonably warm weather brought heavy rains. Ice on the Han and other rivers melted, causing flooding and destroying pontoon bridges. Few enemy soldiers were killed. However, the operation restored the US/UN line in the central sector where the Chinese had breached it, and Army engineers gained valuable experience with the Korean weather. US/UN forces recaptured Inchon and Kimpo airfield, but Seoul remained in enemy hands.

Ridgway stressed coordinated movement against the enemy during Killer, avoiding gaps in the offensive line to prevent enemy breakthroughs. The 1st Marine Division moved north with strong air cover and pushed the North Koreans out of Hoengsong. On February 24, General Bryant Moore died from injuries suffered in a helicopter accident, and Smith became acting IX Corps commander, the third time in US military history that a Marine general had commanded an Army unit. General Puller stepped up to division command until Smith returned on March 4.

The Marines overcame weather-related logistical challenges with the help of the Korean civilians in the recently formed Civil Transport Corps. The US Army fed, clothed, and paid members of the corps, who were organized into companies and carried supplies to advancing units using A-frames, a centuries-old Korean means of carrying burdens that enabled as much as 120 pounds of cargo to be transported over rough terrain inaccessible to jeeps and trucks.[17]

The soldiers of the 8th Army showed improved morale during Operation Killer, in part because the Army introduced a rest and recuperation (R&R) program that provided combat officers and enlisted men with five days of leave. After experiencing loneliness, exhaustion, and danger in Korea, soldiers could now look forward to a break in Japan. Marines in Korea were not eligible for R&R until late in the war.[18] After Killer, Ridgway decided to throw the entire 8th Army into a peninsula-wide offensive, Operation Ripper, that sought to reach the 38th Parallel. Officials in Washington again debated whether to stop at the parallel or cross into North Korea in keeping with the moral commitment that the United States and United Nations had made to create a "unified, independent and democratic Korea. US/UN forces had suffered heavy casualties and to settle for less than a total ground victory would show weakness and moral irresponsibility." To stop at the 38th would also leave the Army in poor defensive positions and vulnerable to a counterattack.

Those who favored stopping at the 38th Parallel argued that the Chinese might be on the verge of agreeing to negotiations and might settle for the status quo ante bellum. If the US/UN Army crossed the parallel, the Chinese would lose face and refuse to negotiate. America's allies opposed crossing the line, and the American public was divided on the question.

While the Truman administration considered its options, Ridgway continued his planning. He wanted to inflict maximum punishment on the Chinese and disrupt their preparations for another offensive. Ridgway also wanted to retake Seoul. He ordered all units to have a "base load" of ammunition plus a five-day surplus.

Ridgway and Smith met on the eve of Operation Ripper. Smith renewed his request for Marine air cover as the Marine division began the operation, but Ridgway answered, "I'm sorry, but I don't command Fifth Air Force."[19] Smith would be undertaking a major mission without full control of his "flying artillery."

Operation Ripper started at 5:45 a.m. on March 7. The 1st Marine Division led the attack along a fifty-mile front in the central sector. Enemy resistance was weak, but the advance was slow—no more than a mile or two per day. Moving into the terrain where the Wonju Shoot had taken place, the Marines saw hundreds of American bodies and found a few live Americans still hiding from the enemy. Marines tagged the area Massacre Valley and put up a sign: "Massacre Valley—Scene of Harry S. Truman's Police Action—Nice Going Harry." They did not think of the president as a friend.

General MacArthur issued a review of the campaign's military strategy that Washington considered indiscreet and wholly unnecessary. The press seized on two of MacArthur's phrases in particular—"savage slaughter" and "theoretical military stalemate"—and labeled them "Die for a Tie," an idea that had an unsettling and demoralizing impact on the 8th Army.

For the third time in three weeks, MacArthur had violated the Truman administration's restrictions on public statements. Moreover, by flying to Korea, MacArthur had alerted the enemy that an offensive was imminent.

General Ridgway was with the Marines on March 12 when he held a press conference to respond to MacArthur's "Die for a Tie" statement.

Ridgeway announced that reaching the parallel would constitute "a tremendous victory" for the US/UN forces. MacArthur fired back by ridiculing positional warfare on a line, yet another violation of Truman's directive on public statements.

The Marines reached Line Albany and captured the city of Hongchon on March 14. To the east of the Marines, Almond's X Corps moved more slowly through muddy terrain. To the west, South Korean forces reached Seoul and found it unoccupied. For the fourth time in the war, the Korean capital changed hands.

Operation Ripper was a success. Ridgway appeared on the cover of *Time* and received congratulatory letters from Omar Bradley and Dwight Eisenhower. The State Department asked Ridgway to refrain from using such punitive names as *Killer* and *Ripper* for his operations; Ridgway laughed but changed *Ripper* to *Courageous*.

While Operation Courageous moved forward, General MacArthur again flew to Korea, meeting with Ridgway at Wonju, now the Marine command post. MacArthur wanted to see a Marine battalion in a combat area, so he, Ridgway, and Smith traveled by jeep over mountain passes and met with Marines on the line. MacArthur was pleased with the visit.

By April 1, the 8th Army was at or north of the 38th Parallel in more secure defensive positions, and South Korea had been cleared of invaders for the second time. The Chinese controlled 475,000 troops in North Korea, including 197,000 North Koreans, with another 478,000 Chinese in reserve in Manchuria. The Chinese also had eight hundred aircraft dispersed among ninety North Korean airfields. According to intelligence reports, a new offensive was coming, and Ridgway suspected that the Chinese would challenge the United States for control of the air.

Ridgway developed a plan for advancing into North Korea and won support from the JCS and ultimately from President Truman. The US/UN forces would move forward on a series of phase lines—Kansas, Utah, and Wyoming—to Line Quantico. Located a few miles north of the parallel, Kansas constituted the best defensive position Ridgway could find in the area. Utah was a minor extension of Kansas, while Wyoming was a larger extension, a hump in the line that brought the US/UN forces as far north as the Iron Triangle, a level area of central Korea bounded by the cities of Kumhwa, Chorwon, and Pyongyang that the Chinese used as a staging area. Line Quantico, the objective, lay between Line Kansas and the Iron

Triangle. Ridgway wanted to prevent a buildup of Chinese forces there and disrupt their preparation for a new offensive. The general was moving offensively while thinking defensively.[20]

On April 3, the 8th Army crossed the parallel to Line Kansas, beginning Operation Rugged. On that day, General Almond was in Japan with his family and probably expected to meet with MacArthur, but the general flew to Korea to review ROK units on the east side of the front. During his five hours on the ground, his jeep convoy crossed the parallel. Five days later, the 1st Marine Division crossed the parallel and advanced to Line Kansas, where the Marines were to relieve the 1st Cavalry Division and prepare for an attack north to Line Quantico.[21] And three days after that, President Truman relieved General MacArthur of his command of all US forces in East Asia and UN forces in Korea.

Harry S. Truman and Douglas MacArthur had contrasting backgrounds and temperaments that doomed their relationship from the beginning. Truman was a common man, a haberdasher from Missouri whose ties to the Pendergrass political machine had won him a seat in the US Senate. He was added to the presidential ticket in 1944 because his less-than-luminous Senate record would not detract from the failing President Franklin D. Roosevelt, who died just five months after the election. Truman surrounded himself with capable advisers and listened to what they recommended, and although he at times acted foolishly, he also could rise to international challenges with the courage and wisdom of a great leader.

MacArthur, in contrast, was born to command. The son of an Army general and graduate of the US Military Academy, he rose to brigadier general during World War I. After serving as superintendent at West Point, MacArthur became chief of staff of the Army and led American forces to victory in the Pacific theater during World War II. As an absolute ruler in postwar Japan, he acted with both ceremony and compassion and was exceedingly popular with the Japanese people.

MacArthur occupied a unique position on the American scene. Officially he was the military commander in East Asia, but MacArthur was also much more. An active soldier for more than half a century, he was far senior to those above him at the Pentagon, and they treated him with deference, especially after the success at Inchon, where he had been right and they were wrong. MacArthur's roles also muddied the waters between what was military and what was political.

MacArthur's dismissal constituted one of the most controversial and politically explosive decisions of the Truman presidency. But faced with a rebellious military commander who opposed and often tried to neutralize the administration's military and diplomatic policies, Truman really had no choice. Bad behavior meant that a beloved military hero had to be removed from his command.

The October 1950 meeting at Wake Island was the only time that the two men encountered each other in person. Truman, who had served as captain of an artillery battery in World War I, was in awe of the five-star general and thought he had all the answers. The president listened to MacArthur's thoughts on Chinese intervention in Korea rather than relying on assessments by the Central Intelligence Agency and other intelligence-gathering offices. MacArthur, for his part, was amused by Truman's belief in his knowledge of history, which the general thought superficial at best.

In early January 1951, Truman wrote to MacArthur a letter congratulating him on his seventy-first birthday and complimenting his military leadership. The president then reviewed the military situation and restated US policy before concluding, "The entire nation is grateful for your splendid leadership in the difficult struggle in Korea and for the superb performance of your forces under the most difficult circumstances."[22]

Truman's conciliatory efforts had little effect. On January 13, when the UN General Assembly voted 50–7 in favor of a peace plan that offered China UN membership in exchange for a satisfactory Korean settlement, MacArthur joined members of the US Congress in accusing the United Nations of selling out Taiwan.[23]

On March 20, MacArthur received a letter from House minority leader Joseph Martin, a Republican and a critic of the administration's refusal to use Chinese Nationalists against the Chinese Communists. In response, MacArthur wrote that "there was no substitute for victory." Also on March 20, MacArthur received a "top secret—priority" cable in which the JCS said that diplomatic efforts toward a Korean settlement should be made before any major advance across the 38th Parallel and asked for MacArthur's thoughts on a proposed presidential announcement on the new diplomacy. MacArthur responded that "no further military restrictions should be imposed upon the United Nations Command in Korea."[24]

MacArthur realized that he was losing the policy battle over Korea. The administration would not support expanding the war to China itself. There would be no naval blockade or bombing of mainland China, nor would Chiang Kai-shek be allowed to invade. MacArthur decided to preempt the president with an announcement that would pull the rug out from under the proposed diplomatic move. On March 24, MacArthur issued a public statement that taunted the Chinese, inferring that they were a defeated army and reminding the world that China lacked the industrial base necessary for modern warfare. If the restrictions imposed on him were lifted, he contended, he could strike the Chinese immediately and bring the war to an end. MacArthur offered to meet with the Chinese commander to discuss a cease-fire. In addition to insulting the Chinese, MacArthur's statement was a slap in the face to the president, short-circuiting the proposed peace initiative.[25]

MacArthur's statement coincided with another visit to Korea. His cable reached Washington around 10:00 p.m. on March 23 and led Acheson to convene a meeting of shocked and angry State Department officials, several of whom demanded the general's immediate removal from command.[26]

Acheson and members of his staff met with military leaders the next morning and composed a message to the ambassadors of all UN countries fighting in Korea that described MacArthur's statement as "unauthor-ized and unexpected." The State Department officials later met with the president, who shared their anger, declaring that "MacArthur thought he was proconsul for the government of the United States and could do anything he damned pleased."[27]

Nevertheless, political considerations led Truman to refrain from fir-ing MacArthur. The president wanted the support of secretary of defense George Marshall and Omar Bradley, chief of the JCS. Under military law, MacArthur could request a legal hearing or a board of inquiry if he were removed from command. An acquittal from such a board would be politically disastrous. Truman did not want to dismiss MacArthur until there was no question that he had been insubordinate.

Moreover, in light of MacArthur's statement inviting the commander of the Chinese army to confer with him in "an earnest effort" to achieve a cease-fire, firing the general might send the wrong signal to the Chinese. Though Truman was privately determined to fire MacArthur, the president had Bradley send a mild reprimand directing MacArthur's attention to the president's December 5 directive.

On April 5, however, Martin released the March 20 letter in which MacArthur had criticized administration policy.[28] The general had done the unthinkable: he had used the leader of the House opposition to publicly attack the administration.

Truman met with his closest diplomatic and military advisers the next day. General Bradley recommended calling MacArthur home for "consultation," but Acheson warned that "the effect of MacArthur's histrionic abilities on civilians and of his prestige upon the military had been often enough demonstrated. To get him back in Washington in the full panoply of his commands and with his future the issue of the day would gravely impair the President's freedom of decision." The JCS then agreed to dismiss MacArthur on military grounds: the general's past actions and public statements meant that he simply could not be trusted. General Collins, the Army chief of staff, was out of town but would be returning to Washington that weekend. No final decision would be made until Collins was present.[29]

On Sunday, April 8, the full JCS met and unanimously agreed that MacArthur should be fired. They wanted to avoid using insubordination as the reason for his dismissal and chose instead to cite his failure to comply with the president's directive on clearing public statements. The JCS affirmed that the military had to be controlled by civilian authority and that MacArthur's actions jeopardized that authority. Ultimately, MacArthur's dismissal resulted from his failure to submit his statements for clearance in accordance with the December 5 directive, his repeated challenges to the president's role as the nation's spokesperson on foreign policy, and his public opposition to the administration's decision to limit the conflict to Korea.[30]

After an April 9 cabinet meeting, Truman met with Acheson, Marshall, and Bradley, all of whom agreed that MacArthur should be relieved. On the advice of Bradley and Marshall, Truman approved General Ridgway as MacArthur's successor as commander in chief in East Asia and General James Van Fleet as Ridgway's replacement as head of 8th Army in Korea. Uncertain about how the Chinese would react to MacArthur's firing, the president authorized an immediate attack on air bases in China if they were used to launch an air attack on US/UN forces in Korea, though

MacArthur was not told of the authorization lest he try to use it for his own political reasons.[31]

The JCS then set up the machinery for dismissing MacArthur. Truman wanted the move carried out with utmost courtesy and dignity. Marshall decided to have secretary of the Army Frank Pace, who was already en route to Asia, call on MacArthur in Japan to deliver the notification. To avoid having the news leak prematurely, Pace's instructions and documents would be encoded and sent via State Department channels to the US ambassador to Korea, who was in Pusan. After receiving the materials there, Pace would proceed to Tokyo. Before traveling to Pusan, however, Pace was scheduled to visit Tokyo, where he was received with appropriate honors by General MacArthur on April 9.[32]

MacArthur realized that something was up. A day earlier, he had admitted, "I have been politically involved and may be relieved by the president." And after business hours on April 9, MacArthur learned that a cable from Marshall to Pace had been received at headquarters.[33]

The cable instructed Pace to proceed to Korea and remain there until he heard from Marshall. Pace arrived in Taegu on the morning of April 10 and was met by a beaming Ridgway. Operation Rugged was a success, and Operation Dauntless, the attack on the Iron Triangle, was set to begin the next day. After spending the night in Taegu, Pace spent April 11 with Ridgway, awaiting further instructions.[34]

On the morning of April 10, President Truman told staffers that he had fired MacArthur the previous day. That afternoon, with the White House buzzing over the news, Truman signed the documents and instructions to be transmitted to Pace.[35]

At around the same time, newspaper correspondents called the Pentagon and Truman's press secretary for comment on the rumor that MacArthur was about to be fired. White House staffers assumed that MacArthur had learned of his pending dismissal and had decided to resign, achieving a public relations coup and placing the administration on the defensive. Marshall, Acheson, Bradley, and presidential adviser Averell Harriman met hurriedly at the White House. The military leaders wanted to follow the original announcement plan, but Harriman argued that the president should be contacted at once. They called Truman around 10:00 p.m.; thirty minutes later, the president authorized an official White House release of the documents, allegedly declaring, "The son of a bitch isn't going to resign on me. I want him fired." At an extraordinary press conference held at 1:00 a.m. on April 11 in Washington (2:00 p.m. on April 12 in Japan and Korea), MacArthur's dismissal was announced.[36]

Bradley cabled MacArthur with the news, while Marshall directed Pace to disregard the previous instructions, remain at Taegu, and advise General Ridgway that he was replacing MacArthur as supreme commander in the Pacific. But MacArthur's dismissal was announced on Tokyo radio before the official cables reached Asia. The general and his wife, Jean, were hosting a luncheon at the embassy when an aide told Jean MacArthur the news. She told the general, who calmly responded, "Jeanie, we're going home at last." MacArthur received the cable before leaving the embassy that afternoon.[37]

Marshall's cable to Pace was delayed even longer. He and Ridgway were in Seoul when a reporter approached and asked if Ridgway were due congratulations. Ridgway did not know what the reporter was talking about. Pace subsequently received an urgent telephone call from General Lev Allen, a MacArthur staff member in Tokyo, who read aloud Marshall's cable. Only then did Ridgway learn that he was now supreme commander.

President Truman explained MacArthur's dismissal to the nation on the evening of April 11: the general had to go to eliminate any confusion regarding the real aims of American policy, which above all included preventing a third world war. Truman did not mention any specific incidents or the constitutional need to maintain civilian control over the military. His speech left many Americans puzzled: How did going to war equate with preventing a world war? Truman later offered a blunter explanation for MacArthur's dismissal: "I fired him because he wouldn't respect the authority of the President. That's the answer to that. I didn't fire him because he was a dumb son of a bitch, although he was, but that's not against the law for generals."

The Truman administration had failed to carry out MacArthur's dismissal with the "utmost courtesy and dignity." The fact that MacArthur learned of his firing from a radio report generated sympathy for the general, and his supporters took the opportunity to assail the president. Congressional Republicans began a campaign to discredit the Truman administration, inviting MacArthur to address Congress and calling for an investigation of US policy in East Asia and even for the president's impeachment.[38]

MacArthur's departure from Japan was emotional. At least half a million people standing ten deep lined his route to the airport, bowing as his motorcade passed, waving small American and Japanese flags, and holding banners with messages such as "We Love You, MacArthur" and "We Are Grateful to the General." Jets streaked overhead, and MacArthur received a nineteen-gun salute.[39]

General Ridgway was instructed to follow MacArthur's policies on the occupation of Japan and to provide reassurance regarding America's good intentions. After MacArthur's plane became airborne, the new supreme commander returned to his headquarters and terminated General Almond as chief of staff, though he remained in command of X Corps in Korea.

When Ridgway took over the Far East Command, Washington had at last decided just what it wanted to achieve in Korea and how far it was willing to go to do so. National Security Council Report 48/4, dated May 4, 1951, declared that the United States wanted a unified, independent Korea attained by political means. The United States now sought an armistice, security for South Korea on a defensible line north of the 38th Parallel, the withdrawal of all non-Korean forces, and a buildup of ROK forces to a level where they could defend themselves.[40] What MacArthur viewed as a Munich-style defeat the administration saw as the only sane, middle-of-the-road course, and Ridgway accepted it.

MacArthur received a tremendous welcome when he returned to the United States after a fifteen-year absence. Despite strong pressure from Republicans, Congress's Democratic majority only agreed to have him address a "joint meeting" rather than the more formal and prestigious "joint session." Neither Truman nor his cabinet attended, but the president was among the thirty million Americans who watched the April 29 speech on television, the largest audience in American history up to that time.

MacArthur received a standing ovation when he entered the House chamber. He offered a general assessment of the situation in East Asia and argued in favor of going all out to unify Korea. He ended by saying that after fifty-five years of military service, "I now close my military career and just fade away, an old soldier who tried to do his duty as God gave him the light to see that duty. Good-bye."[41]

The emotional thirty-four-minute speech brought many of those who heard it to tears. Said Congressman Dewey Short, a Republican from Missouri, "We heard God speak here today, God in the flesh, the voice of God." Truman, however, dismissed the speech as "a bunch of damn bullshit."[42] After receiving another enthusiastic welcome in New York City, MacArthur traveled up the Hudson River to speak to the Corps of Cadets at West Point. His speech there again made headlines and raised further questions about the administration's treatment of the general. Republicans urged MacArthur to run for president in 1952, but the general retired to New York's Waldorf-Astoria hotel to write his memoirs.

Beginning on May 3, 1951, the Senate Foreign Relations and Armed Services Committees held joint hearings regarding MacArthur's dismissal. The first witness was the general himself, who testified for three days and repeated his long-standing complaints about the administration and its war-related policies, again declaring, "There is no substitute for victory."[43]

By the time the MacArthur Hearings concluded on June 25, Acheson had spent eight days on the stand, Marshall seven, Bradley six, and service chiefs Collins, Hoyt Vandenberg, and Forrest Sherman two days each. They responded to MacArthur's charges point by point, with Bradley explaining that "in the opinion of the Joint Chiefs of Staff," widening the war to China "would involve us in the wrong war, at the wrong place, at the wrong time, and with the wrong enemy." Many Americans thought those words were appropriate for Korea as well.

The hearings ultimately discredited MacArthur and vindicated the Truman administration and its policies. The two committees voted along party lines with the Republicans issuing a minority report critical of US policy in East Asia.[44]

In *The Truman-MacArthur Controversy*, John Spanier summed up the rationale for General MacArthur's firing: "Military men seem sometimes to forget that they are servants of the state and that they will not be judged by the nature of the policies they implement, only by how well they implement these policies. Their civilian superiors are responsible for the actual formulation of political strategy, not they. It is not their function to take their disagreements into the public forum for national debate."[45]

When Frank Pace was later asked what he would have done if the firing had gone according to plan and the cable from Bradley had arrived while Pace was in Korea, he replied, "No problem. Presidential orders. I'd command the first plane and fly to Tokyo. Being after hours, I would have gone immediately to General MacArthur's quarters. I'd have taken the order, rang the doorbell, shoved it under the door and run like hell."[46]

Joe Albritton with
the bodies of Chinese
soldiers, Morae Kagae
Pass, May 18, 1951.
Courtesy of the family of
Peggy Albritton Sharp.

5th Marines rifle platoon
near the Punchbowl,
1951. RG 127, General
Photograph File of the
US Marine Corps,
National Archives,
College Park, Maryland;
Local ID 127-GR-155-A8868.

Marines overlooking the Punchbowl, 1951. RG 127, General Photograph File of the US Marine Corps, National Archives, College Park, Maryland; Local ID 127-N-A155066.

Dead North Korean/Chinese soldier killed by the 7th Marines, Hill 673, August 1951. RG 111, National Archives, College Park, Maryland; Local ID 111-SC380918.

Operation Blackbird, first night helicopter troop movement behind Chinese lines, September 27, 1951. Photo by Waller King; courtesy of Clay King.

Waller King during Operation Blackbird, September 27, 1951. Photo courtesy of Clay King.

Trucks crossing the Imjin River, September 1951. Photo by Joe Albritton; courtesy of the family of Peggy Albritton Sharp.

Marines carrying a Chinese soldier west of the Hwachon Reservoir, April 23, 1951. Photo by Joe Albritton; courtesy of the family of Peggy Albritton Sharp.

Refugee child, Korea, 1951. Photo by Joe Albritton; courtesy of the family of Peggy Albritton Sharp.

Marines "going up," spring 1951. Photo by Joe Albritton; courtesy of the family of Peggy Albritton Sharp.

Marines traversing rugged terrain, 1951. Photo by Joe Albritton; courtesy of the family of Peggy Albritton Sharp.

3rd Platoon, G Company, a few days before Homer Ainsworth was killed, June 1951. Photo by Joe Albritton; courtesy of the family of Peggy Albritton Sharp.

7th Marines on patrol, Chunchon, May 1951. Photo by Joe Albritton; courtesy of the family of Peggy Albritton Sharp.

Hand grenade, 1951. Photo by Joe Albritton; courtesy of the family of Peggy Albritton Sharp.

Joe's feet - on a Helicopter Jumping the Chinese Lines

Joe Albritton's feet hanging out of a helicopter, probably Operation Bumblebee, October 1951. Photo by Joe Albritton; courtesy of the family of Peggy Albritton Sharp.

Peggy Cain Albritton and Joe Albritton, Clinton, Mississippi, spring 1952. Courtesy of the family of Peggy Albritton Sharp.

Fallen Comrade. Photo by James D. McBrayer.

Chapter 7

FALLEN COMRADE, APRIL–JUNE 1951

What to the historian is a nameless little company-sized fight, is to the
participant the place where his best friend got killed, or he himself got
wounded, or some incident happened that is forever engraved on his memory.
—James Stokesbury, *A Short History of the Korean War*

American soldiers, sailors, and Marines learned of Douglas MacArthur's
dismissal via the Armed Forces Network, a mobile radio broadcasting
operation in Korea, or from the Army's *Stars and Stripes* newspaper. Waller
King, Joe Albritton, and Homer Ainsworth were en route to Korea when
the general was relieved of his command and did not learn of the firing
until after they reached their destination.

The three men had returned to Camp Pendleton after their Christmas
leave to complete the final twelve weeks of training. They spent part of
that time in cold-weather training in the mountainous Pickle Meadows
area near Bishop, California. Base camp was at six thousand feet, and
they climbed as high as nine thousand feet in temperatures that reached
thirty-four degrees below zero. Pickle Meadows was also located on the
38th Parallel.

Writing about the training in a February 7, 1951, letter to Ralph Marston,
a high school friend serving in the Air Force, Homer reported that the
weather was so cold that "one of Joe's balls froze off (I don't know what he

is going to do)." More seriously, Homer added, "I see a lot of fellows fall out every day & guess they just can't take it, but the boys from Mississippi have not or will not be stopped."[1]

Folks back home in Clinton were experiencing the coldest winter in memory. In February, pipes had frozen, shutting down the water department and forcing residents to draw water from the nineteenth-century "town spring" until the pipes thawed. When fire broke out at the Hillman apartments on Leake Street, there was no water to extinguish the blaze, and the building was destroyed.[2]

Homer wrote another letter to his parents that was printed in the *Clinton News* in mid-February. He described the mountain experience as "the hardest part of our training. Joe and I stayed about ten miles back in the mountains last night on a night problem. We only had a blanket roll. Oh boy! Was it cold? We didn't get much time to sleep anyway."[3]

Waller wrote to his older brother, John, who was in the Air Force at Lackland Airfield, Texas, at around the same time. While on a weekend pass to Los Angeles, Waller had been sightseeing on Hollywood Boulevard when someone shoved him from behind. He turned and saw Peggy Cain and Joe Albritton, who told him that they had married. He had no idea that they were a couple.[4]

During their last weeks of combat training, Homer, Joe, and Waller served as extras in *Flying Leathernecks*, a John Wayne movie filmed at Camp Pendleton. Joe used his Leica camera to photograph Homer and John Wayne, ignoring orders not to fraternize with the movie stars. Homer took one of Joe and the Duke. In March, Homer's parents spent a week in California visiting the three young men.[5]

In early January 1951, Bill Smith, still suffering from frostbite, was transferred to the naval hospital on Treasure Island in San Francisco Bay. He recovered enough to take a thirty-day leave in April, returning to Clinton and meeting his infant son, Buster. Bill's next assignment was Camp Lejeune, North Carolina, and Betty Jo and Buster accompanied him there.[6]

George Sharp arrived in Korea in January 1951. He was assigned to Dog Company, 2nd Battalion, 5th Marine Regiment, and had his baptism of fire in General Matthew Ridgway's January Thunderbolt offensive. Herbert Pearce rotated home from the Bean Patch at Musan in January and after enjoying leave in Clinton was assigned to the Memphis Naval Air Station.

Homer, Joe, and Waller completed their training at Camp Pendleton in March, unaware of General MacArthur's spiral toward dismissal. Homer and Joe were part of the seventh Marine replacement draft. After an uneventful two-week voyage across the Pacific aboard a Navy troop transport, the ship stopped at Yokohama, Japan, where the Marines exchanged their American dollars for military pay scrip and received weapons and combat equipment. They sailed on to Pusan, Korea, arriving on April 5.

Waller King's voyage across the Pacific was eventful. His transport had equipment problems and floundered at sea for three days before repairs put the ship back on course. The Navy crew ran low on food near the end of the voyage, but Waller and his Marine comrades knew where Navy food stores were kept and liberated what they needed. After a layover in Japan, the ship reached Pusan on April 12.[7]

Homer and Joe were assigned to the 1st Squad, 3rd Platoon, George Company, 3rd Battalion, 7th Marine Regiment. They moved north on a small Korean train and traveled by truck to division headquarters, where they dropped their bags at regimental headquarters. The two joined a so-called G--k Train (as the Marines referred to the Korean laborers who used A-frame racks to carry supplies to units) for the last leg of their journey. Snow was still on the ground when Homer and Joe joined G Company. They were assigned to the same squad and shared the same tent, just as they had since their call-up eight months earlier.

G Company was a Marine rifle company commanded by First Lieutenant W. G. Airheart. At full strength, the company had 7 officers and 221 enlisted men, divided into three rifle platoons, a mortar section, and a machine-gun section. Each rifle platoon had 40 men—four squads of 10. A first or second lieutenant commanded each platoon, and sergeants led each of the four squads.

The rifle platoon's structure was based on the Marine belief that in a firefight no one man could be expected to effectively control and direct more than three other Marines and still be aware of the enemy. Sergeants were trained to maintain contact with platoon leaders, who issued orders to the four squad sergeants not to 40 men. Each sergeant, in turn, commanded three three-man fire teams, each directed by a leader, usually a corporal. Each fire team was built around a Browning automatic rifle (BAR), a steady, fast-firing, fully accurate weapon with a range of more than five thousand yards that fired the same cartridge as an M-1 rifle. Each

Marine rifle platoon had twelve BAR gunners giving a platoon leader a great deal of firepower. Homer and Joe served in the same fire team; Joe made corporal during his tour and was a BAR gunner leading a team.[8]

Waller was assigned to the 1st Marine Regiment and was flown north from Pusan to the Marine combat zone before traveling by truck to Hongchon, where the regiment was in reserve. Waller's draft included several men with the surname *King*, and confusion over assignments left Waller in the Headquarters and Services Company at regimental headquarters.[9] It was a choice assignment, but Waller knew he would not be there long.

Waller shared a tent with veterans of the Chosin Reservoir fighting and heard gruesome stories about the operation. One day while his unit was still in reserve, he investigated a hole on the side of a hill and found the decomposing bodies of four American soldiers. Waller reported the discovery to his sergeant, who said that Waller would see a lot of that in Korea. Veterans seemed indifferent to death.[10]

When Homer, Joe, and Waller arrived in Korea, the Chinese had been driven north of the 38th Parallel and Operation Rugged was just beginning. Homer and Joe arrived in Korea on April 5, two days after Rugged started, and joined their company in the advance past Line Kansas to Line Quantico on April 21, meeting little resistance.

Homer and Joe's 7th Regiment was on the left side of the Marine line, George Sharp's 5th was in the middle, and the Korean Marine Corps regiment was on the right. Waller's regiment was initially in reserve. Captain Charles McAtee, 3rd Platoon leader, George Company, led the platoon up through Wonju, Hongchon, and Chunchon and across the 38th Parallel to the Kansas Line. During March and early April, the platoon fortified positions, built bunkers reinforced with logs and sandbags, and covered the perimeter with mines, trip flares, and concertina wire. Heavy ground artillery and air support put the Marines in a good defensive position.[11] Lieutenant General James Van Fleet, Ridgway's replacement at the head of the 8th Army, arrived in Korea on April 20.

The Chinese had been backtracking during the early weeks of Rugged, but on April 22, 90,000 Chinese and North Korean troops poured out of the Iron Triangle staging area, launching their spring offensive by attacking the IX Corps sector. The Marine division, positioned directly in front of the Chinese attack, weathered the initial assault, but when the ROK 6th Division on the Marines' left flank collapsed, they suddenly had a ten-mile gap in their line from the extreme right flank of I Corps's 24th Infantry Division to the Marines' 7th Regiment. Both units had to bend back from the Chinese attack but did not break.[12]

The offensive gave Homer and Joe their first taste of the Chinese penchant for announcing the attack with green flares and bugles, followed by smothering mortar barrages and hordes of swarming troops. G Company's small-arms fire helped, but Marine artillery, mortars, and automatic weapons cut down the attackers by the hundreds. Fighting continued through the night, and although the Marines gave up ground, no major breakthroughs occurred.

The Chinese took advantage of the break between the ROK 6th Division and the Marines' 7th Regiment, forcing General Oliver Smith to move two battalions from the 1st Regiment to reinforce the line. Waller King was in this fight as his battalion took Hill 902. Homer and Joe's 3rd Battalion of the 7th Marines (3/7) moved to the bottom of Horseshoe Ridge, just north of the hill and less than a mile from Waller's battalion (1/1). The Marines stabilized their line for the expected Chinese night attack.[13]

Marine Corsairs and Panthers flew more than two hundred sorties on April 23 in support of the Marines, but when night came and air cover was lost, the Chinese attacked again, coming in waves against Hill 902 and Horseshoe Ridge. The 3/7 pulled back, with the Chinese following closely until air cover returned the following morning. The 3/7 had support from the British 29th Brigade, brought in to fill the ROK gap, forcing the Chinese to splinter the attack to counter the British. All three Marine regiments were ordered to pull back to Line Kansas.[14]

The Chinese carried out probing actions during the next two nights as the Marines continued withdrawing south of a modified Line Kansas toward Chunchon, a major road junction in central Korea that both the 8th Army and the Chinese sought to control. This retrograde allowed the Chinese to regain control of the strategic Hwachon Reservoir and threaten Marine positions by flooding the area below it. The Navy sent six dive bombers from the carrier *Princeton* to damage the reservoir and prevent the Chinese from unleashing the water, the first time the Navy used torpedoes to attack a dam.[15]

The Marine division withdrew to Chunchon and took up defensive positions on the south bank of the Pukhon River. The 7th Regiment went into reserve, but Joe and Homer's 3rd Battalion was sent back to

Chunchon and attached to the 1st Marines on the left flank. The enemy continued probing the Marine lines for three nights, without success. Homer and Joe were fighting in the same combat zone as Waller King but were unaware of their proximity

During this lull in IX Corps's sector, the Chinese sought to capture Seoul by May 1, a worldwide Communist holiday. American air strikes and the threat of naval bombardment discouraged enemy advances, and 8th Army ground forces held the capital. By April 29, the first phase of the Chinese spring offensive came to an end. The enemy had attacked with numerical superiority and gained territory, especially in the central sector, but suffered an estimated 120,000 casualties.[16]

General Van Fleet organized US/UN forces along the No Name Line, which ran from a point above Seoul through Sabangu and then along a line slightly north of the 38th Parallel to the Sea of Japan. Van Fleet decided to return the 1st Marine Division to X Corps and position those troops at the center of the Corps's sector next to the Army's 2nd Infantry Division.

Homer and Joe had been in Korea for seventeen days when the Chinese spring offensive began. On May 1, Joe described the April 21–29 fighting in a letter to his parents that appeared in the *Clinton News* on May 25. As was common among Americans fighting in Korea, Joe referred to enemy soldiers using racist and dehumanizing terms.

> We dug in on a high ridge about ten o'clock that night [April 21], and were all tired and hungry from climbing up and down mountains. We had about four hours sleep that night because we always had to stand about a 50 percent watch and at six o'clock the next morning we started out again. About 3:30 that afternoon we started hitting the enemy in large numbers about a mile south of the Quantico line.
>
> We got there about ten o'clock that night [April 22]. By then our casualties were very high and we were unorganized because we had lost so many, and it was dark. The enemy was heavily dug in on the ridge that was called the Quantico line, and it would have been suicide for us to try to take it that night, so we moved in at the bottom of the hill and tried to hold there that night. From then on it was a steady bloody battle that raged all night and until about 7:40 the next morning. We didn't have time to dig fox holes or anything.[17]

G Company had been attached to the 1st Battalion, 7th Marines, and was dug in on a ridgeline west of the Hwachon Reservoir. According to McAtee, at midnight on April 22, waves of Chinese attacked with mortars while making noises with whistles, shouting, and singing. They came over the ridgeline "into the pocket of death" and were mowed down by machine guns, M-1s, and BARs. The Chinese paid a heavy price: "Pictures taken the next morning by Joe Albritton, a BAR man from my 1st Squad, confirm that statement and reflected the heavy enemy casualties inflicted that night."[18]

At first light on April 23, the entire left flank of the Marine division lay exposed to the Chinese, who poured into the gap left by the collapse of the ROK 7th Division. The Marines received orders from IX Corps to fall back to Line Pendleton, an 8th Army defensive line below Line Quantico where Major Maurice Roach, the 3/7 battalion commander, had G Company about a thousand yards to the northeast of Horseshoe Ridge. Waller's 1st Battalion as well as the 3rd Battalion of the 1st Regiment took positions to the southeast of Roach's troops, forming a defensive line facing west and north.[19]

According to Joe,

We just hid behind rocks or whatever we could get behind. They came down the hill in large numbers and overran some of our positions. Homer and I were by a machine gun trying to protect it, but the g--ks wiped out part of our unit and began coming in on our left flank and a bit to our rear. We had the machine gun set up behind a rock that was about the size of a 50 gallon drum.

The gunner grabbed the gun and we ran back about twenty feet and got behind a sort of rock wall. There was a small knoll on our left flank about forty feet, and we could see them coming over it two or three at a time. We kept killing them as fast as we could, but they kept coming. We were running low on ammunition and the battle was only started good. One of our machine gun positions that was overrun had five out of seven killed and the other two wounded. Our platoon sergeant was killed about eleven o'clock that night. The g--ks and Chinese kept getting closer and closer until they were within fifteen feet of us.

We were never so thankful in all our lives to have hand grenades. We threw hand grenades in the middle of them time after time trying to hold them back. We knew they were going to try to overrun us. We were firing like mad at them point blank. We could hear the guys that were wounded calling for the corpsmen and it made chills run up and down your back.

At four o'clock [a.m.] on the dot [on April 24] we froze when a loud horn that sounded like a deer horn blew on top of the hill. We knew what that meant. It was their well-known signal for their usual four o'clock attack. When it started blowing nearly all the firing stopped for a minute and it sounded as though it had hypnotized everyone, and your head felt as though you had a rubber band on it that was slipping off. You know what I mean.

Then it all broke loose again, and they opened up on us with machine guns. There was a big rock about fifty yards in front of us that they set a machine gun on and we could see them as day-break came. They were climbing all over the rocks. We shot them off like clay pigeons. They kept us pinned down for a while with machine gun fire, but we finally knocked it out.

It was getting lighter and lighter, and they began to pull back. However, there were still some right behind a pile of rock in front of us. A grenade went off about six feet behind me and I was standing up, but not a piece hit me. Homer and I were together behind the wall, along with Taylor. Just as it got where you could see fairly good seven Ch--ks jumped up in front of us and started to run up the hill. All three of us cut loose on them and no one made it.

About seven o'clock our planes came in and strafed and bombed them for about half an hour. By 7:40 the Ch--ks had withdrawn to the other side of the ridge. We stayed low until about 8:00 o'clock and then five of us went out among the dead and wounded Ch--ks to take prisoners and collect all their weapons. Any of them that made any wrong move we shot, because we have been tricked so many times by the Ch--ks. Ninety percent of their weapons were our own weapons they had captured. We counted 67 dead.

We had as many casualties ourselves, and as soon as possible helicopters were brought in to carry out the dead and wounded. We held the Ch--ks back until all the dead and wounded could be taken out. One company had 65 percent casualties. Doctors were operating and giving blood transfusions at the bottom of the hill. After they had all been carried out, what was left of our Company withdrew to a high ridge opposite the ridge the Ch--ks were on, and served as a rear guard while the other Companies withdrew, then we began to withdraw toward the Kansas line as fast as possible.

The ROKs were supposed to have been on our flanks, but they had pulled out and let the Ch--ks behind us. They were about to trap us and we marched a forced march all that day. That night our Company got lost. We wandered around trying to find some of the other Companies in our battalion.

We didn't know where the Ch--ks were, and neither did anyone else, but we knew they were all around us. We hadn't had any food or sleep in two days and had been traveling or fighting nearly all the time. Some of the men just couldn't go any further so we climbed up on the side of a hill and started to just lie down and sleep until morning.

We had been there about five minutes when artillery started dropping on us. We were all so exhausted by then that we just didn't care hardly what happened to us, but what was left of us practically ran down the hill.

It was one of our own artillery barrages, and the hill we had started to sleep on had over 4,000 Ch--ks on it. Our platoon Lieutenant and I were together when the Ch--ks heard us in the valley below them and fired some flares over our heads that lit us up like day. I heard our Lieutenant say, "Well, I guess this is it." We all thought it was the end for us this time and we were expecting them to open fire on us any time, but just as everything was up . . . one of our Companies on the opposite ridge that we had no idea was there, spotted us and recognized us as Marines.

They opened up on the Ch--ks with all they had and kept them pinned down until we could get out of the valley. By this time we had lost a lot of men. Some had just disappeared in the night and we don't know what happened to them all. It was getting daylight by this time, and we climbed to the ridge and joined the Company that had saved our lives.

At six o'clock [a.m. on April 26] we lay down for two hours rest, and then started out again. The two Companies of us stuck together from then on, to protect each other in our withdrawal to the Kansas line. We were all so tired by then that we couldn't go over fifty yards at a time without having to stop and rest. We got to the Kansas line about four o'clock that evening and that was where the Regiment was assembling to begin the withdrawal.

All that day while on our way there we were fired at from the ridges all around us, and sometimes we would have to turn around and go another way because they would have us blocked off, and we were in no condition to fight. We found out that we had gone through the Ch--k lines three times that night we were lost.

When we reached the Kansas line the Ch--ks were within one-half mile from it and moving fast that way. We were left behind as a rear guard again and given ammunition, etc. along with two other Companies. When all the rest had gotten out we withdrew and started on another long march with tanks behind us to blast the hills and ridges as we moved out. As soon as we left, the Ch--ks swarmed into our position that we had left about ten minutes before.

We were on the road going south. There was a double line of troops that was about ten miles long. After we had walked about fourteen miles we were picked up by trucks and taken about four miles. Then we got out and slept from 3:45 a.m. until 6:00 o'clock [on April 27], then got on trucks and went back north and crossed the river to fill in a gap in the line where Ch--ks had broken through.

After we crossed the river by amphibious trucks we marched eight miles back in the mountains and dug in on a high ridge. We held there for that night and until about five o'clock the next afternoon. We received a lot of mortar and artillery fire from the Ch--ks that were using some of our own artillery on us that they had captured.

It seems as though our Company was always left behind as the rear guard. Our Company, along with "D" Company were left until about 12:30 a.m. as a rear guard while the others pulled out and got across the river. We lost radio contact with "D" Company, and they pulled out about two hours before us. We were reported to have been wiped out, and by the time we got to the river all the amphibious trucks were gone, and there were no bridges to cross on.

It was about 150 yards wide but fairly shallow. We threw away all our ammunition, etc. The water was ice cold, but we waded across in a shallow place, which, in a few spots, was over our heads. It was about neck deep. By this time our Company was scattered all over the place. Homer and I just started walking south.

We met up with an army outfit that was left behind to destroy equipment and blow up ammunition dumps so the Ch--ks wouldn't get it, and got a ride with them until about 5:15 that morning [April 29]. There were six of us together from our Company. When we got off the truck we built a big fire and stood around it trying to dry our clothes. The Army fed us later that day and we rejoined our Company and are still withdrawing.

Today is May 1st and we have not taken off our clothes since April 5th. We are now set up on a ridge protecting an artillery unit until they pull out and then we will pull out.

Homer and I are in good health and fairly well rested. We had our first good sleep last night and there has been no action today. We are taking advantage of it. Yesterday we marched 15½ miles with all our equipment in seven hours. Tomorrow we will pull another fifteen miles.[20]

Jim Nicholson, a 3/7 BAR gunner, recalled that "Lonesome George Company once again seems to have been left for 'last man out, turn off the light.'" Moving above the cliffs along the river as fast as possible to catch the last trucks headed south, they had to rappel thirty feet down a cliff to the riverbank. A long rope was stretched across the river to guide them through the swift, cold water. Before going over the cliff, Nicholson took his BAR back down the trail to head off any Chinese who might make contact before the men could cross the river. At the last minute, he made it back to the cliff and across the river to the trucks. Joe and Homer may have gotten separated from the rest of G Company in the roadblock on the cliffs and missed the last truck.[21] Waller's battalion also had to withdraw, first to Line Kansas and then to Chunchon. Soon, however, withdrawal from Chunchon also became necessary, and Waller's company was the last unit to leave. He later recalled that the

regiment went back to Chunchon and waited to see if we could stop the attack. We did stop them, but only after losing Chunchon again for the third time. My squad, still part of the Regimental Headquarters, was ordered to burn what was left in Chunchon which might be useful to the enemy.

Chunchon was a real town—about the size of Brookhaven, Mississippi, my birth place. Even though mostly destroyed by the ravages of war, it was still a beautiful place. Very Modern.

One of the truly tragic things about war is the effect on innocent civilians who may be caught up—unable to escape. This was especially true of what happened to me in Chunchon. My squad was ordered to destroy anything of value to the enemy in that town. That meant burning with flame throwers and phosphorus grenades any standing structure. I went through many of the houses in Chunchon—ordered to destroy everything.

The civilian population had fled southward long ago as this was our third foray through their almost destroyed town. All except two old Korean women, maybe too old or weak to make the escape southward. They were on different sides of town. One had a western style house and when my squad walked by, she was arranging broken chairs and sweeping her floor. She knew we were there but she took no notice of us. We left! We went through all sorts of patios, houses, and workshops. Not much left anyway.

The other woman I spoke about—she was just sitting in the doorway of her house. There was no back of the house—just the shell of a front wall and she was sitting in the doorway. Her home had been blown away. She never moved. I felt like a heel going through what was left of the houses. We kicked in doors of empty houses and continued to break up anything of value to the Chinese who were coming into the outskirts of the town. We left nothing of value for them.

Surely, it must be against the rules of the Geneva Convention to do what we did, but we had broken just about all of the rules anyway. That is an openly admitted truth. Just think, if this was my hometown in this condition and I had foreigners rummaging through my home. Oh! God! Save my people from war. Why does there have to be War anyway? Give to us, your Blessings, Oh God! Yet how can you bless such underhanded dealings with which we have to put up with!

We left Chunchon in flames. I watched as 2,000 Chinese crossed the River. We were going out the other side of the town. I was one of the last out of the town. My squad had gotten into a six-by which had been left for us. I boarded and we followed our retreating troops southward.[22]

Waller King found himself in a war doing things he would never have done in civilian life. He was in a strange, unfamiliar land that war had turned into an evil landscape. There were demons on the battlefield, and Waller felt he had opened a gate to hell.

During the withdrawal, Waller's company rode through the retreating Marine columns and set up a defensive position, holding until they were almost overwhelmed by the advancing Chinese, a process repeated over the next twenty-four miles until a static line of defense was formed. After a week of rest, Waller's battalion then went back to Hongchon for three weeks of reserve on May 15. While in reserve, Waller got a hot steak dinner, took a shower, and had his first change of clothing since his arrival in Korea a month earlier.[23]

On April 24, with the Chinese offensive at its most threatening, General Smith turned over the division to Major General Gerald C. Thomas, a change of command that had been scheduled weeks earlier. Shortly thereafter, the 1st Marine Division was returned to X Corps and a delighted General Edward Almond, who later wrote that Smith's departure "was a relief to all of us at X Corps headquarters."[24]

Heading the 8th Army during the Chinese 1951 spring offensive was Van Fleet's first experience commanding a Marine division. He was impressed by the Marines' performance and especially their use of helicopters, and he requested that the Joint Chiefs of Staff (JCS) provide helicopters for the Army.[25]

Early May was a time of watchful waiting for the next enemy attack. The Marines improved their defensive positions and patrolled to maintain contact with the enemy. Each battalion sent a company forward to establish a patrol base that would serve as a screen for the battalion's position on the main line of resistance (MLR). The base was an outpost line of resistance that could give warning of an impending attack and delay the enemy's advance. Homer and Joe's G Company set up a patrol base operation on May 4, occupying the what was left of Chunchon after Waller's unit had departed.[26]

Van Fleet expected the next Chinese offensive to be directed against Seoul. The enemy, however, moved several divisions to X Corps's sector. The Chinese started their second-phase offensive on the night of May 16, attacking all along the front but concentrating on X Corps and particularly on two ROK divisions east of the Hwachon Reservoir. The South Korean soldiers panicked and withdrew, allowing the Chinese to drive thirty miles to the south and opening a gap in the line that threatened the Army's 2nd Infantry Division, which was next to the Marine division.[27]

Homer and Joe's G Company sent out patrols north of Chunchon on the night of the Chinese attack and came under enemy fire. The firefight lasted until 7:00 that night, when the Chinese disengaged and the company returned to the battalion position. G Company repulsed the Chinese north of Chunchon, but the enemy moved forward elsewhere along the sector line.[28]

The Marine division was not directly in the path of the enemy spearhead, but the Chinese made probing attacks along the Marine line. On May 16, the 3/7 was ordered to Morae Kagae Pass, south of Chunchon, to defend it while the rest of the 7th Regiment passed through to the rear of the 1st Marine MLR. The 3/7 arrived late at night and dug in on a steep hillside. At 2:45 a.m. on May 17, a Chinese infantry regiment stumbled onto the battalion in the darkness, and a bloody fight began. Supported by I Company, mortars, artillery, and a tank platoon, the 3/7 stopped the Chinese at the pass and inflicted more than 900 casualties. Jim Nicholson said, "We killed them all—there is no second prize in warfare." A photograph taken the next morning shows Albritton standing among hundreds of dead enemy soldiers.[29]

General Van Fleet decided to go on the offensive all along the MLR, attacking the rear of the retreating Chinese. Operation Detonate began on May 20 with the goal of regaining the old Line Kansas and possibly the Iron Triangle. In the X Corps sector, the Marines' 7th Regiment was deployed on the right flank on May 23, while the other two regiments advanced three miles against little enemy resistance. The next day, Homer and Joe's 3/7 encountered heavy enemy mortar and machine-gun fire. Artillery and air support were called in, and the enemy withdrew. The battalion received orders to set up a blocking position along the division's main supply route, where they engaged in a firefight with a regiment-size Chinese force. Tank fire and air support forced the Chinese to withdraw. The 7th Regiment then moved to the center of the division zone, reaching the southern bank of the Soyang River by nightfall on May 26.[30]

It was apparent by this time that the second phase of the Chinese offensive had failed. Chinese casualties between May 15 and May 31 were estimated at 105,000, including 17,000 counted dead and more than 10,000 prisoners. The Marine division inflicted 1,870 dead and captured 593 enemy soldiers while losing 83 men and 731 wounded, a more favorable ratio of killed to wounded than was usual. The Marines had learned to take cover quickly and avoid needless risk.[31]

The 3/7's May 1951 summary report noted that the enemy continued to supply its forward elements by animal pack train, had expanded the use of 60-, 82-, and 120-millimeter mortars, and possessed an ample supply of mortar ammunition. In the battalion's sector, the enemy dead included 388 counted KIA and another 546 estimated KIA, while the battalion had lost 14 men and 106 wounded. The battalion's combat efficiency was excellent in light of the fact that it had been fighting for sixty days, and "morale was excellent throughout the period."[32]

The fight had been taken out of the enemy. Chinese soldiers were surrendering in unprecedented numbers, many starving and weakened by disease. The Chinese had again overextended their lines, gaining territory at a tremendous loss of soldiers. The 200,000 casualties the Chinese had suffered meant that they were now too weak to mount an offensive. The men from Clinton—Homer, Joe, Waller, and George Sharp—had survived the Chinese spring offensives and knew that the enemy was in retreat but had no idea what US generals and officials in Washington were considering.

General Van Fleet considered another Marine amphibious landing, this time on the east coast forty miles north of the US/UN line. General Ridgway rejected the proposal and recommended to the JCS that the MLR be moved north to better defensive positions that would reduce American casualties while preventing future Chinese advances. He wanted the MLR to extend from north of the zone that included Seoul, Inchon, and Kimpo airfield, which was south of the 38th Parallel but protected by mountains, to the Iron Triangle area north of the parallel. The line would then continue east to a dead volcanic crater known as the Punchbowl and from there to the east coast. Located about twenty miles north of the 38th Parallel, the Punchbowl is an oval flatland measuring four to five miles in diameter with the longer axis running north to south. Though the Punchbowl itself had no military significance, the surrounding granite ridges enabled the North Korean forces to control a vast area.[33]

The Truman administration was looking for a way to bring the war to a close. Presidential advisers reasoned that the Chinese should be receptive to negotiations after suffering such heavy casualties in their spring offensives. The threat of Soviet intervention in Korea had subsided, and Washington believed that Moscow might help bring the war to an end. Secretary of state Dean Acheson had explicitly stated that the United States would accept a peace based on the status quo ante bellum, an idea endorsed by the UN secretary-general. Ending the escalating war became more important than the political goal of uniting all of Korea.

Ridgway disagreed with the possibility of accepting the status quo ante bellum. He argued through the JCS and won Washington to his idea of the battle line being the western sector of the Kansas-Wyoming Line moving east through the Hwachon Reservoir sector to the Sea of Japan. Ridgway's plan required each side to withdraw ten miles from this battle line, placing the Chinese forty-five miles north of the 38th Parallel. The US/UN line on May 23 was about thirty-five miles south of that portion of Line Kansas that ran from the Iron Triangle to the Punchbowl, which remained in enemy hands.

Ridgway launched Operation Pile Driver to take control of Line Kansas. The 1st and 5th Marine Regiments, with the Korean Marines in between, moved forward on May 23. The 7th Regiment, deployed on the Marines' right flank, reached the banks of the Hwachon Reservoir on May 31. Tanks led the assault, and by nightfall the 3/7 occupied nearby Yanggu. The battalion continued toward Line Kansas, facing stiff enemy resistance, and by June 2 had reached an extended ridge near the southern tip of the Punchbowl.[34]

That day, Waller's 1st Regiment relieved the 7th, which went into reserve for the first time since Homer and Joe had joined the regiment almost exactly two months earlier. The two men and their comrades enjoyed hot showers in tents set up over a dry stream bed with shower nozzles attached to hoses hung from crossbeams, discarding their filthy clothing in favor of clean underwear, sweatshirts, pants, and sweat socks before reclaiming their boots, weapons, web belts and packs. They had not changed clothes in more than fifty days.[35]

While the 7th was in reserve, the 1st and 5th Regiments continued the assault toward Line Kansas. Any gains were met by enemy counterattacks, though air and artillery support pushed the North Koreans out of their defensive positions. On June 10, the Korean Marine Corps launched a night attack, catching the enemy by surprise and capturing Hill 1316 overlooking the Punchbowl.[36]

Waller's 1/1 fought north of the Hwachon Reservoir, about ten miles above of the 38th Parallel and just southeast of the Iron Triangle. Between June 6 and June 8, the regiment made moderate gains in clearing out the ridges where the enemy was entrenched. By June 14, it had reached Line Brown, an advance position north of Line Kansas. The Marine 5th and the Korean Marine regiment joined the 1st southwest of the Punchbowl.[37]

After the Marines suffered heavy casualties, General Thomas called out the 1st and 2nd Battalions of the 7th Regiment on June 8 and the 3rd Battalion on June 18. Homer and Joe returned to combat against an

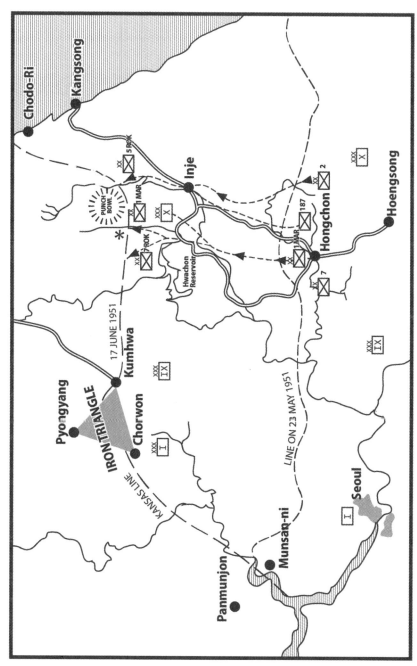

Marine Operations, May–June 1951. *Site where Homer Ainsworth was killed, June 19.

enemy prepared to make an all-out effort to defend the ridges in and around the Punchbowl.[38]

The 3/7 moved into a defensive position southwest of the Punchbowl along the steep east-west ridge marking Line Brown. The terrain made maneuvering impossible and prevented all but a frontal assault. The enemy employed reverse slope defenses, sweeping each crest of the ridge with fire and carrying out sudden assaults against the Marines. Homer and Joe thought they were fighting Chinese, but North Koreans had been placed in the sector with orders to "hold until death." Jim Nicholson described the ensuing fight as "the day our 1st Squad died . . . attempting to take another senseless hill in another senseless battle."[39]

G Company moved up the ridge at 4:00 a.m. on June 19 and had advanced within a hundred yards of the crest when the enemy counterattacked. Bushels of grenades, machine guns firing right and left, and deadly accurate mortars kept G Company pinned down near the top of the ridge. According to the battalion's daily action report, "'G' Company attacked objective #11 five times, but was forced to withdraw each time because of heavy enemy fire. Between the fourth and fifth attacks the enemy launched a counter-attack which failed to dislodge 'G' Company. The fifth attack by 'G' Company took place at 2030 and shortly thereafter the enemy again counterattacked but was repulsed by 2120." An estimated 60 enemy soldiers had been killed and 110 wounded. Thirteen members of the 3rd Battalion had been killed, among them Homer Ainsworth.[40]

Nicholson's 3rd Squad had moved further up the steep slope when Homer and Joe's 1st Squad moved in behind for support. They were pinned down, shooting almost straight up to the ridgeline, when "a short round of supporting American artillery fell into the midst of our 1st Squad in the area we had just vacated. They were blown to pieces." "Short rounds" were not uncommon in Korea and were frequently caused by unexpected wind, miscalculations by gunners, or mistakes by forward observers who could not see over ridgelines. The one that killed Homer Ainsworth and his fellow Marines came from a 155mm Howitzer, and Nicholson was stunned that any of the 3/7 had survived.[41]

Joe subsequently wrote to his parents,

> You remember in the last letter I wrote you on the 19th [18th] of June I put a P.S. saying we were moving out the next morning. Well we did and

went back to the east-central front where the [Korean Marines] were having trouble taking three hills. We were in position to attack that night and moved out into the attack at 4:00 o'clock before daylight.

We received a very large amount of artillery and mortar fire. We fought from about 4:30 a.m. until 11:05 p.m. trying to take hills 10, 11, and 12. Homer and I were still O.K. at 5:30 p.m. although we had had some mighty close calls.

Homer and I, along with the remaining members of our squad were by a machine gun the Ch--ks were trying to knock out. Machine gun fire came sweeping through us and one of the guys got up to run. When he did a bullet hit my helmet, glanced off and hit him (the guy who tried to run) in the stomach. He died within 10 minutes. The Ch--ks got our squad blocked off and started to move on us. A grenade hit by my left side. I rolled away from it as fast as I could before it exploded. When it went off a piece went through my jacket and only slightly burned me.

They then started to zero us in with artillery. At first were hitting a little short and then a little too far. I told Homer we were going to have to move fast because the next ones would be right in the middle of us but the Ch--ks kept us pinned down so we couldn't move. One of the guys in the squad got back to get ammunition and earlier one had run off. I guess you couldn't blame him though. He has a wife and two kids. He is now up for court martial.

Up until then we had had three killed and one wounded in our squad that day, but then it happened. The next shells hit right in the middle of us. After that I was just so shocked. I hardly remember what happened. It killed the rest of the squad instantly and wounded the gunner. I don't know why I was spared but God has a reason. I know, or I wouldn't be here today. My pack and sleeping bag were blown off my back. My helmet went about twenty feet. Now there are only three of us left in our squad. The doctor said he didn't think my ear drum was burst, however. I can hold my watch to my left ear and can't hear it running. That night a concussion grenade went off near my left side and also could have had something to do with it.

I have seen many men killed since I have been over here but it really hurts to the limit to see someone as close as Homer and I were in friendship taken. We couldn't take any of the bodies off the hill until after dark. I got another guy to help me take Homer's body down which was the saddest thing I have ever had to do or ever hope to do. We took the rest of the hill the next morning just after daylight.

We are now set up in a defensive position on the east-central front and the only action is patrol action. There has been lots of talk about cease fire and peace talks.

The Ch--ks seem to have pulled way back but the North Koreans are about 2500 yards from our front. Our company commander has volunteered to go out and meet the North Korean officer in charge of the ones in front of us when the cease fire order comes out. I have volunteered to go with him as one of his aides. I don't know yet whether I'll be able to go or not. I hope so. Each day the action seems to be decreasing. There is a large valley to our direct front with a river running through it. We plan to meet at a big water wheel at the river.

It is such a pity Homer had to be taken this late in the game because I believe this thing will be over very soon. I certainly feel sorry for the Ainsworth family. . . .

I wrote the Ainsworths and tried to express my feelings although it was a very hard thing to do.[42]

It is a Marine tradition that the wounded or dead are not left behind if it is possible to recover a fallen comrade. Joe's retrieval of Homer's body was more than tradition. Homer had been Joe's friend and comrade since childhood, and he did not think of his own safety. Homer and Mary Ainsworth received notification of their son's death on June 27. The entire Clinton community mourned. It was a parent's worst nightmare, the loss of a child. Homer was nineteen years old. His death was devastating to his family and a shock to the community.

Wrote Bea Quisenberry in the Clinton News on June 29,

The tragic news of Homer Ainsworth's death has just come in. It suddenly becomes impossible to write of the little everyday things in the face of such a loss. I remember Homer as such a fine boy with small children. When Billy [Quisenberry] decided to learn to swim in the College Pool he was so very afraid of the depth of the pool. He couldn't find the bottom and the water was over his head. I remember it was Homer who persuaded him to try. And it was only Homer that Billy would go into the water with. He had such faith and confidence in him.[43]

Sergeant Gerald H. Vaughn, a Marine in George Company from Lowndes County, Mississippi, wrote to Homer's parents, "He was a fine young man and he died bravely, fighting for his country. . . . Homer didn't have to suffer. He never knew what happened. We took the hill he died on."[44]

On Sunday, July 22, a memorial service took place at the Clinton Baptist Church, with the Reverend Nolan Kennedy officiating. He was assisted by Hendon Harris, whose son had been killed in Korea a year earlier. The service included the reading of Joe Albritton's letter to the Ainsworth family:

> Sometimes things happen that we can't understand but God always knows what he is doing. I have lost the best friend I ever had or will ever have on earth but he is in a far better place than any of us left on earth.
>
> God has a time for each of his followers to come and be with him in that wonderful place forever and when that time comes no matter where we are or what we are doing we cannot disobey His command to come and be with Him forever. I want you to know that Homer did not suffer. It is very good to know that he was fully prepared to meet the Lord. It may be a while before we see him again or it may be tomorrow, we just don't know, but we all know that we will see him again in a far better place than here on earth.[45]

Homer and the other Marines killed that day were temporarily buried at the UN Cemetery in Tanggok, south of the 38th Parallel, on June 30, 1951. His remains were later disinterred and shipped home, arriving in New York City in late October. His father escorted the body back to Mississippi by train, stopping in Magee, Homer's birthplace, before reaching Clinton, where he was buried on November 11. Boy Scouts from Clinton's Troop 12 provided an honor guard. The American Legion and Marines from the reserve base in Jackson performed the military service. Dr. Howard Spell, dean of Mississippi College and family friend, officiated at the graveside as Homer's mother and sisters wept. For years, Rev. Ainsworth clung to the hope that the body in the closed coffin was not Homer's and prayed that his son was missing in action and perhaps being held prisoner.[46]

Chapter 8

THE FIGHT FOR HILL 749, JUNE–NOVEMBER 1951

It's a big hill, and we spread out across it—three platoons abreast, bayonets fixed. We start up. The artillery and big mortars have finished. Now the heavy machine guns are firing just in front of us and our company; 60mm mortars are landing about fifty yards out and moving ahead as we advance. On this hill it works. Before we get to the top, everyone is firing, moving on up to the hill and over enemy positions. . . .

[W]e roll over the top. It may be anticlimactic, but Hill 749 is finally ours.

—**John Nolan,** Lieutenant, 3rd Battalion, 1st Marine Regiment

Homer Ainsworth's death came exactly 359 days after North Korea invaded South Korea. He was one of 21,625 Americans killed during that year. The United States also accounted for 78,000 of the estimated 250,000 US/UN casualties. More than 1,000,000 Chinese and North Korean soldiers were also killed or wounded. An estimated 2,000,000 civilians fell victim to privation, violence, and disease, with another 3,000,000 having lost their homes and become refugees. The 8th Army occupied twenty-one hundred square miles of North Korean territory on June 25, 1951, and the country's industrial base was in ruins. It was time to talk peace.[1]

The first overtures toward negotiations had come shortly after the invasion, with the United States making unofficial contact with the Soviet Union. Neither power wanted a general war, and backchannel talks continued into 1951. The 8th Army's May 1951 offensive inflicted serious losses, and by June, the Chinese and North Korean armies were soundly defeated and demoralized. The Chinese were ready to talk.

On June 22, Jacob Malik, the Soviet ambassador to the United Nations, gave a speech in which he hinted that his country was willing to engage in talks to end the fighting, though he cloaked his overtures in a tirade against American imperialism in Korea. US State Department officials responded by contacting the Soviet foreign office to determine whether peace talks were possible. The Soviets answered that a military armistice was possible if it was carried out by military negotiators and limited to military matters.[2]

President Harry S. Truman replied with an attack on Malik and the Soviet Union as "absolute tyrants" who were trying to conquer the world, though the president added, "We are ready to join in a peaceful settlement in Korea now, just as we have always been. But it must be a real settlement which fully ends the aggression and restores peace and security to the area and to the gallant people of Korea."[3]

The United Nations and those countries fighting under the UN banner supported Truman's statement, even though South Korean president Syngman Rhee opposed any negotiations and demanded the surrender of Chinese and North Korean forces and a unified Korea with him in charge of the government. But Rhee had no voice in the matter.

Two days after Malik's speech, China expressed a willingness to talk. General James Van Fleet and other military leaders believed that China's position reflected military necessity—a truce would enable its army to recover from the military setbacks—rather than any genuine desire for peace. The Chinese eventually agreed to meet in July at Kaesong, the old imperial capital, located between the opposing lines in western Korea below the 38th Parallel.[4]

US/UN forces controlled their most favorable line since the January 1951 beginning of the Chinese offensive. General Matthew Ridgeway's troops occupied the area around Seoul, Inchon, and the Kimpo airfield and the main line of resistance (MLR) extended east across the 38th Parallel to the Sea of Japan. The 8th Army had a strong defensive position that could be held while negotiations ensued.

In late June 1951, Waller King left Headquarters & Services Company at the regimental headquarters and moved to Weapons Company, 2nd Battalion. He had met Marines from the 2nd Battalion while in reserve and been impressed by the battalion chaplain. When he joined his new company, Waller was surprised to find that the members of his squad included his boot camp nemesis, Eddie Gomez, whom Waller greeted cautiously.[5]

Shortly after Waller joined the unit, the company commander warned that anyone throwing a hand grenade to celebrate the July 4 holiday would be court-martialed. Waller ran afoul of the regulation but swore he had only done so accidentally:

> I heard this noise,—I slipped my finger through the pin on one of my grenades—and then it happened! The parapet above my hole collapsed on me. I threw the grenade straight up. I knew I had been had. I am surprised that I did not get blown away from my own grenade. Here comes the Lieutenant—just a cussing. I don't know how I got out of that one, but I did.[6]

The regiment continued patrolling its sector of Line Kansas in early July. After two weeks with no enemy contact, patrols became more aggressive, moving directly forward where the enemy was supposed to be on what the Marines called suicide missions. Before Waller's squad went on patrol, he gave his high school class ring, watch, and wallet to a buddy so that the enemy would not get his possessions if he were killed or captured. He later recalled,

> We moved out around 8 o'clock—moved through our mine field without incident. My squad with 11 men, the Lieutenant and his radio man, and one "gung-ho" Corporal (I don't remember his name but he volunteered for every patrol). He had keen eyes and could spot trip wires or newly dug earth which could be a cleverly planted "Bouncing Betty" mine—Those horrid things would be tripped by the man in front of you—and it would explode about four feet off the ground, wounding or killing everybody.
>
> Since I had drawn the "short" straw, my fire team went on ahead. I was uneasy—downright scared as we came to where we had been told that the Chinese had hit the fire team the day before. I was thankful for my long legs—I could get across open ground very fast. The Lieutenant had a radio message to hold up so our artillery could plaster the ridge immediately in front of us. They did their job well and we moved out slowly. Certain that we had been seen because we could hear a Ch--k soldier in the valley below

shout out the warning that we were coming. He was an outpost—we never saw him, but we certainly could hear him shouting.

We were approaching our final objective when the order came over the radio that we were to come back quickly. A couple of the guys argued that we were so close that we needed to go on—the others of us wanted to go back. (I just wanted to sit down and dig a hole).

The Lieutenant had his orders, so we returned without incident. I learned later that the two successive patrols before us had been ambushed. Many things could have gone wrong—my main worry was the mines. That is something you cannot fight unless you have X-ray eyes. Some, like the Corporal, had even developed those.[7]

On July 8, General Edward Almond, still commander of X Corps, ordered an attack on Taeu-san (Hill 1179), a strategic four-thousand-foot peak on the Punchbowl rim that anchored the main defensive position of three heavily fortified North Korean divisions. Almond did not think the North Koreans would fight for the hill. General Gerald C. Thomas initially opposed the order and then assigned the mission to the Korean Marine regiment. The Korean Marines spent five days unsuccessfully attacking the hill, suffering heavy casualties, until an American military adviser demanded that the attack be called off before the regiment was destroyed. The American press ignored the Taeu-san Affair because the lives lost were Korean, and Thomas, like his predecessor General Oliver Smith, began to question nearly all of Almond's orders. Almond's departure from Korea was imminent, and Thomas believed that the situation would improve.[8]

Negotiations started at Kaesong on July 10. Vice Admiral C. Turner Joy headed the US/UN delegation, while Lieutenant General Nam Il represented the North Korean People's Army. Observers initially thought that a cease-fire agreement could be reached within six weeks, but the talks dragged on for two years as the North Koreans haggled over every issue and delayed decisions as long as possible.[9]

Preliminary meetings produced an agenda on July 26, with the belligerents agreeing to discussions in four areas: (1) the establishment of a military demarcation line and a demilitarized zone; (2) cease-fire and inspection arrangements; (3) the disposition of prisoners of war; and

(4) recommendations to the governments of both sides. Joy insisted that the military demarcation line be north of the Line Kansas-Wyoming and refused to budge in the face of Communist demands that the 38th Parallel be the line. Issues relating to the cease-fire and inspections dominated the early talks.[10]

Many Marines greeted the beginning of negotiations with optimism. As Waller remembered, "The Top Sergeant came around for a talk with me before nightfall. He said that this was our last time on the line—that the Russians were working out a 'peace plan' and that we were going home." But almost three months later, "the 'peace talks' are far from being settled—maybe not even started."[11]

The Marine division went into reserve on July 17, 1951, with three locations in the Hongchon area serving as tent cities for the 25,000 Marines who were far enough behind the MLR they could enjoy fires and lights and movies. During this time, Waller recalled,

> I got word in a letter from Dad that Homer Ainsworth had been killed. He was killed on June 19th, the very day I had left my unit to go over to the 7th Marines, George Company, to see Homer and Joe Albritton. They were supposed to be in reserve, but guys don't get killed in reserves.
>
> I felt bad—I did not know what to do or say. I grew up with these two guys—best friends. What could I do? I only wish that Homer had known that I was in a line company too.[12]

Soon thereafter, Waller wrote to his brother, John,

> I don't know if you know about Homer being killed or not. Dad wrote me today telling me. I wrote to Joe and asked him about it. He'll tell me. They have been together since September & were really close.
>
> It's a tragic thing to happen to someone who was our close buddy. I'm glad he was a Christian and I feel sure he's happy in Heaven. His folks must be pretty broken up over it, but they too understand it must have been God's plan.
>
> That's going to start Mom & Dad, as well as Mrs. Sharp & Mr. & Mrs. Albritton, to worrying like the devil. I wrote the folks & tried to tell them I'm pretty safe, but I know they won't believe me.[13]

During this time, Waller was aware of the ongoing peace talks but knew little of the results. He visited Joe and George Sharp and began hoping that he would be rotated home before Christmas under the mistaken belief that his one year of service had started when he began training in September 1950 rather than when he arrived in Korea in April 1951. Waller also received a promotion to corporal in May 1951 and transferred to the Weapons Company, 2nd Battalion, 1st Marines in June 1951. He continued his duty on the front lines alongside Easy Company.[14]

On August 9, 1951, Joe transferred to the Headquarters and Service (H&S) Company of the 3rd Battalion, 7th Marine Regiment. H&S Company, one of five in the 3rd Battalion (H&S, Weapons, G, H, and I), was primarily an administrative and logistical support group that included the command officers, executive staff, and medical, intelligence, and communications personnel. Usually located on the field closely behind the frontline companies, H&S was not always directly engaged in fighting; however, Joe retained his rifleman classification after the transfer and continued to fight on the front line. Joe was promoted to corporal in December 1951 and remained in H&S until he returned to the States.[15] While in reserve, the Marines maintained a structured daily schedule that included equipment maintenance and military training intended to keep them ready to return to battle. Every morning started with physical training, with veteran Marines working with new arrivals to prepare them for integration into combat-ready units.[16]

The Marine Command took the opportunity to evaluate the division's performance over the past year. The war's foremost tactical innovation was undoubtedly the use of helicopters, primarily to evacuate casualties. Over the first year of the war, 1,926 wounded Marines had been flown out of combat zones, with 701 flights taking place between April 1 and June 30, 1951.[17]

The US/UN Command suspended the peace negotiations on August 5 because armed enemy troops had entered the neutral zone. The troops were withdrawn, but on August 22 the Communist side broke off talks, charging that a UN aircraft had violated the neutrality zone. Though the UN Command apologized for the incident, the North Koreans denounced the "imperialists" and refused to return to Kaesong.[18]

General Ridgway responded by ordering ground and air action against the Chinese and North Koreans to apply military pressure while strengthening the UN position at the negotiating table. The offensive targeted Bloody and Heartbreak Ridges southwest of the Punchbowl, where Army and ROK units led the attack, and Yoke and Konmubong Ridges north of the Punchbowl, where the 1st Marine Division carried out the assault.[19]

Regiments from the Army's 2nd Division and the South Korean 7th Division started the attack on August 24. All of the attacks met stiff enemy resistance, and after four days of combat, one of the desolate hills on the west side of Yoke Ridge remained in enemy hands. The fighting continued at Bloody and Heartbreak Ridges until Heartbreak was fully occupied on October 10. The American and ROK regiments suffered more than 6,000 casualties.[20]

On August 26, Major General Clovis Byers, who had replaced Almond as X Corps commander while the Marines were in reserve, alerted the division to prepare for offensive operations on the north side of the Punchbowl. The Marines' 5th and 7th Regiments moved forward to relieve Army units on Line Kansas, while the 1st Regiment remained in reserve. The Marines sought control of the east side of Yoke Ridge and then Konmubong Ridge, about a thousand yards to the north. Konmubong, ran seven miles west to east and had five major hills (1030, 1052, 980, 812, 749), with two additional hills (680 and 673) on southern spurs of the ridge, all above the Hays Line, a defense line running east-west above the Punchbowl. If the Marines could gain control of the two ridgelines, X Corps's sector would be strengthened and officials believed that the Communists would return to the truce talks.[21]

For three weeks beginning on August 31, the division slugged it out with two North Korean divisions for control of the two ridges. Joe Albritton's 3/7 and two Korean Marine battalions started the offensive, moving up from the eastern edge of the Punchbowl toward Yoke Ridge, where Army and ROK regiments were still engaged on the western side. Despite heavy rain and enemy minefields, the Marines occupied the southeast end of the ridge by nightfall on August 31. The 3/7 faced heavy fire as it moved north to its objective, the ridgeline between Hill 924 and Hill 702. The 3/7 repulsed North Korean attacks from Hill 602 with the support of air strikes and artillery from the 11th Marines. On September 2, George Company marched out toward Hill 602 with the 3rd Platoon in the lead, although the 1st Platoon soon moved to the point. Still under heavy fire,

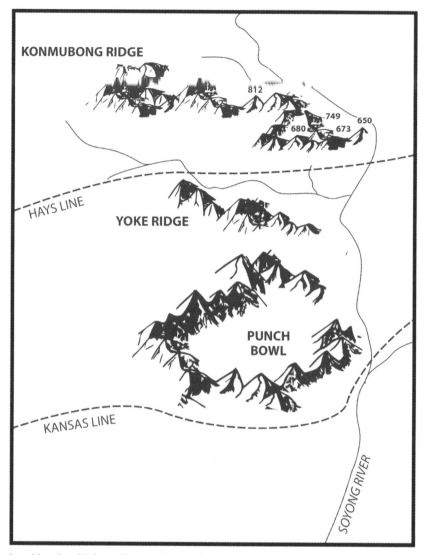

Punchbowl and Yoke and Konmubong Ridges, August–September 1951.

the 3/7 fended off four enemy counterattacks and within two hours took Hill 602, though Jim Nicholson was seriously wounded in the fighting. Pinned down and exposed in a shallow crater, he defiantly flipped the bird to the enemy and was instantly hit in the back by shrapnel. By September 5, all of Yoke Ridge was under UN control, and the Hays Line had become the main line of resistance north of the Punchbowl.[22]

The next Marine objective, Konmubong Ridge, had a network of well-built and heavily fortified bunkers connected by tunnels. Hills 680 and 673 were close enough to each other that enemy defenders could fire mortar and artillery on Marines advancing on either hill. The same was true for Hills 650 and 749. Only Hill 812 stood at a distance from the others. Hill 749 was the anchor of the enemy's defensive position on the Punchbowl. Its bunkers were deep and solidly built of massive logs under several feet of earth, able to withstand anything except a direct hit. If the Marines got close, the defenders could call in mortar fire on their own positions. The surrounding ridges meant that it was nearly impossible to get more than one infantry squad in position to attack, and the main ridgeline leading to the hill was crossed by another wooded ridgeline at a right angle. Marines moving up the leg of the T would come under deadly crossfire from mortars and machine guns on the crossbar.

During the fight for Hill 749, Waller King, Joe Albritton, and George Sharp were located on the same five-mile front, but although they must have passed each other going up and down the hill, they were never aware of each other's presence.

The offensive against Konmubong Ridge began on September 11 with the 7th Marines moving from the Hays Line through a narrow valley and across a tributary of the Soyang River and uphill toward Hills 680, 673, and 749. Enemy fire slowed their advance, and Joe's 3/7 stopped for the night some three hundred feet south of the summit of Hill 680. The advance of the 1/7 was stopped on Hill 673. The 2/7 moved behind Hill 673 during the night and drove the enemy off before moving up to Hill 749.

The 3/7 made the initial assault on Hill 749 the next morning. According to the battalion's daily action report,

> G Company moved on the attack at 0500. Employing a double envelopment the G Company Commander maneuvered his company up the last 500 meters in a fast moving attack that never lost its momentum. Expertly moving fire teams and squads quickly reduced seven active bunkers by the use of organic weapons and hand grenades. At 0900 the lead fire team of the left platoon successfully assaulted the top machine gun position on the first pinnacle of the objective. That platoon immediately reorganized on that hill prepared to meet a counterattack. As the right flank platoon quickly passed through the position the order was given for H Company and I Company

to assault the main ridge line from the east, or right side. The combined effort of the three companies was sufficient to seize the top of the objective. By 1028 all three companies had made physical contact on the objective. At 1100 the enemy made a futile counterattack against G Company's left that was quickly repulsed. By 1115 all of objective #1 had been secured and all enemy defenders either destroyed or driven from the hill.[23]

The enemy still held several nearby bunkers and called in heavy artillery fire on the Marines. On the night of September 13, the 3/7 was relieved by the 3/1 and sent into reserve. Forty-one members of the 3/7 had died in the fighting on Yoke Ridge and the assaults on Hills 673 and 749, with another 334 wounded. One Navy corpsman had been killed and 9 others wounded. Among the members of the 7th Regiment who were killed in the fighting for Hill 749 were Second Lieutenant George H. Ramer, I Company, 3rd Battalion, and Sergeant Frederick W. Mausert III, B Company, 1st Battalion, both of whom received the Congressional Medal of Honor.[24]

Waller and the 1st Regiment moved forward to relieve the 1/7 and 3/7 near Hill 673. According to his account,

> We had reports of heavy fighting that the 7th Marines were encountering and we were to relieve them immediately. The 7th Marines were taking a series of peaks on a long ridge line. Hill 673, Hill 749 and Hill 812—All in Hell's playground! We were there now—feeling sort of confident as we went over that area. . . .
>
> Then we came upon the wounded and dead of the 7th Marines. In just one day they had been decimated. The survivors were dirty, tired, had that far-away look—a starkly stare. We heard their story. We searched their faces for buddies,—asking about a good buddy who we did not see. This was truly war!
>
> We launched immediately into the attack. We set up the mortars at the base of a peak and dug in best we could. It was raining. We were tired and were afraid of our future. After 2 hours of digging my foxhole, I crawled into it and pulled a piece of supply parachute over me.
>
> We dug in—I remember the difficulty with many rocks—getting dark. But I finished and was getting ready to spend the night in my new hole. No sooner had I stretched out than the word came to move out. There were a few grumbles—but it made no difference to anyone, too tired to care.

I started up the slope. Then whistle and an explosion, more whistles and more explosions. They say you don't hear the one which gets you. I heard these, so I guess I'm still here.

How little and helpless you feel against the mortars and 76mm fire. The Ch--ks had blasted our positions that we had just left. It was dark now, but I was sure that one of the shells had landed in my hole. I never went back to look. We were pinned down for 45 minutes before the order to continue to move forward. I had a shield of ammo on my breast and a thick pack on my back. Should stop any shrapnel. None came. . . .

I found a shell hole to sleep in. We had had so little sleep. We dug in that day. Fortunately, we moved no more. Some of the 7th still passed us—going back,—the walking wounded. . . .

Reports of the action were given to us by our wounded coming past the first day. We were carrying the wounded the next day, from then on. We wondered who was doing the fighting. I know that I thought at least one Division of wounded had already come past. These were my buddies. I carried some on stretchers, others in ponchos.[25]

The next day Waller's battalion (2/1) was ordered to attack Hill 749 and then Hill 812. The attack was delayed because of a shortage of ammunition. The Marines used transport helicopters to deliver tons of supplies and ammunition—the first operational use of helicopters in combat. In a single day, fifteen HRS-1 Sikorsky helicopters conducted twenty-eight flights carrying nineteen thousand pounds of supplies and evacuated seventy-four casualties. Marine artillery laid down smoke shells to conceal the helicopters. Operation Windmill was a success and was repeated two days later.[26]

The 2/1 began its attack on Hill 749 at 9:00 a.m. on September 13 and reached the summit by 3:00 p.m., but it took another five hours to relieve the 2/7 on the reverse slope. The North Koreans had hidden bunkers among the trees in and around the hill and would not give up. The fight for Hill 749 continued on September 14. The 3/1 joined the 2/1, but the advance bogged down as a consequence of frontal and flanking fire from Hill 751. Eddie Lopez and Waller were together during the assault on Hill 751:

The last time I saw Eddie, he and I were each carrying two boxes of 30 caliber machine gun ammunition up to a forward machine gun which was about to be overrun. He was in the lead as we crossed open space on the ridge. Sniper fire from the valley below stopped me but Eddie kept running. I tried to get behind this 4 foot stump of a pine tree then I realized that the sniper had me zeroed in and that stump offered no protection.

It did not take this ole boy long to realize that I had to keep going. I left that stump and dove into a shell hole which was made by a 16 inch shell fired from the offshore Battleship Wisconsin. I stayed in that hole for a while, until the sniper lost interest or went for another target. I then continued running with my boxes of ammo in each hand—running faster than I ever had before.

When I got to the trench on the top of the ridge, the fire fight had already stopped. I went back over the ridge to my mortar without carrying any wounded. Eddie got it on this Hill. I understand he threw himself on a g--k grenade. Later, I heard that he had been recommended for the Congressional Medal of Honor.[27]

The 2nd and 3rd Battalions continued the attacks in and around Hills 749 and 751 on September 15, but repeated counterattacks by the enemy forced both battalions to withdraw to their earlier positions. Within twenty-four hours of Eddie Lopez's death, another 2nd Battalion Marine, Corporal Joseph Vittori of Fox Company, was recommended for the Congressional Medal of Honor. Under heavy shellfire, Vittori rushed through a retreating platoon to lead a counterattack. Throughout the night, "he leaped from one foxhole to another," firing machine guns and replenishing ammunition. He was killed in the last few minutes of the fight.[28]

Enemy attacks on the Marine positions on Hill 749 ended the following day, but the attacks on positions on Hill 751 continued. During the four-day fight for Hill 749, the Marines suffered 90 KIA, 714 wounded, and 1 MIA. US/UN forces counted 771 enemy dead and estimated that another 750 had been killed. Eighty-one enemy prisoners were taken.[29]

The lack of close air support contributed significantly to the Marines' heavy casualties. The Air Force controlled all air operations and diverted Marine aircraft for use in Operation Strangle, the interdiction of all supply lines in North Korea.[30]

The 5th Marine Regiment, with George Sharp in Dog Company, 2nd Battalion, moved forward to relieve the 1st Marines on September 16 and attacked Hill 812. Sharp described the fighting in a letter to his mother that was printed in the *Clinton News*.

As we were going up to relieve the 1st, we met a train of Korean stretcher bearers coming down with the dead and wounded. It was the most or largest amount of Marine blood any of us had ever seen, and it wasn't at all comforting. Knowing that a lot of us would be riding down the hill just like that before long.

As luck would have it "Dog" co. didn't participate in the actual assault, but laid down covering fire for "Fox" and "Easy" companies while they went up. They got about half way up the first day when they got pinned down by "g--k" Machine guns. They dug in for the night while the artillery softened them up. I might add that the enemy was doing some softening up too.[31]

Fox and Easy companies attacked again and reached the top of the ridge, suffering 177 casualties (among them 7 killed). The two companies exchanged rifle fire and grenades with the enemy over the next two days before the North Korean defenders launched a counterattack and took two hundred yards of the ridgeline. The Marines drove them off the next morning.[32] After Sharp's company replaced Fox and Easy Companies on the ridgeline,

I was out there five days and not once in that five days did I sleep more than just a short cat nap in the day time. No one out there dare close an eye during the night. I have heard all my life how the Indians could slip around without making noises, but they could take lessons from these g--ks. They practically live on garlic and most of the time the only way you know they're around is when you can smell their breath, then they're too close. I think the only after affects I will have from this mess, is, if I ever smell garlic on anyone, the first thing I will think of is to kill them. . . .

The second night I was out with the 3rd platoon, I was on watch from 10 to 2. Around 11:30 I was standing there thinking of everything pleasant that I could think of, when I got the strongest whiff of garlic. In about 30 seconds the air was full of grenades and I would swear by all that's "Holy" that there hadn't been a sound in the last hour—just that sickening odor of garlic. Anyway, in that little raid, they killed two machine gunners, wounded five more and the guy next to me got a concussion. We got one of them.

During the next two weeks we were up there, they would attempt these little probing attacks somewhere each night. But as soon as we could, we strung barbed wire and laid mines and that just about put a quietus on that.

But that wouldn't keep out the mortars and artillery, which accounted for the majority of our casualties, the total being in the neighborhood of 100.[33]

As of September 18, the enemy still held Hills 980 and 1052 and could look down on the Marines on Hill 812. The 2/5 needed sandbags, barbed wire, and mines to fortify its position and requested helicopter support. The following day, Operation Windmill II brought in 12,800 pounds of supplies in about an hour.

According to the 2nd Battalion's daily action report for September 18,

No enemy was encountered by elements of the 2nd Battalion during the night, except for a light probing attack suffered by Dog Company (attached to the 3rd Battalion) at approximately 0230. An undetermined number of enemy had crawled to within a short distance from the 3rd Platoon's positions and threw hand grenades into the platoon CP [command post] and into foxhole and bunker positions of defending Marines. Several marines became casualties.

The enemy continued to press forward fiercely screaming and shouting to buoy up their spirits (and possibly to help maintain contact with one another) as they attempted to strike terror into the hearts of the Marines. So fanatic and with such speed was the assault conducted, that the platoon was forced to withdrew eastward to positions held by the 3rd Platoon, Easy Company.[34]

A prominent feature near Hill 812 was the Rock, a granite knob about seven hundred yards to the west that the Marines won, lost, and then retook. Also called Luke the G--k's Castle, the Rock was "weird and forbidden, particularly after dark, and effectively obscures from sight a considerable area." On November 8, G Company sent two squads from the 3rd Platoon and a fire team to take out an estimated 25 to 30 Chinese who were emplaced in bunkers and trenches with three machine guns, grenades, and booby traps. The approach to the Rock was covered with land mines. Lieutenant Robert McIntosh, the leader of the 3rd Platoon, ordered the two squads to assault the Rock as the fire team furnished cover. Employing flamethrowers and satchel charges, G Company destroyed the bunkers during the two-hour raid, killing about two dozen Chinese, losing one man, and suffering 32 wounded. Fighting for the Rock was unfortunately symbolic: it had little tactical value in the last phase of the battle for Konmubong Ridge.[35]

The North Koreans changed their defense strategy during the fighting for Yoke and Konmubong Ridges. North Korean troops had previously used an elastic defense, bending and stretching their lines as needed, but they now fought fiercely for every piece of land and counterattacked to regain every position lost. Chinese officers directed the North Koreans to fight to the last man, and they complied.[36]

General Van Fleet concluded that the Marines were suffering too many casualties in trying to control what his staff considered the obscure terrain of Yoke and Konmubong Ridges. He ordered the X Corps commander to "firm up his line by 20 September and plan no further offensives after that date, as it was unprofitable to continue the bitter operations." That day marked the end of warfare of movement in Korea and the beginning of warfare by position.[37]

Van Fleet directed the Marine division to relieve the ROK 8th Division on its sector of the Hays Line, including strategic Hill 884, which dominated enemy-held territory to the northeast. The move added two miles to the Marine front, which now stretched for more than thirteen miles. To avoid having the Marines endure a fifteen-hour march to the hill, which was not accessible by vehicles, General Thomas decided to bring in the troops via helicopter, the first use of rotary-wing aircraft in this manner. Two landing sites were selected and cleared during the night of September 20–21, and at 10:00 a.m. the next day, Operation Summit began. Over the next four hours, 224 Marines from the division's reconnaissance company, including a heavy machine-gun platoon from 2/7, as well as 17,772 pounds of cargo were airlifted fourteen miles from the helicopter base to Hill 884. North Korean troops watched but did not interfere with the operation.[38]

Summit's success brought accolades from General Lemuel Shepherd, commanding general of Fleet Marine Pacific, who saw the troop lift as "a bright new chapter in the employment of helicopters by Marines." Major General Byers, commander of X Corps, believed that the "imaginative experiment with this kind of transport is certain to be of lasting value to all the services." General Omar Bradley, chair of the Joint Chiefs of Staff and an old foe of the Marine Corps, told his staff and journalists that the Marines had discovered an operational technique that might change the conduct of land warfare. General Thomas commended his troops for their "outstanding success," declaring "To all who took part, well done!"[39]

By the last week of September, the Marine division's right (east) flank was well protected by rugged terrain. The left flank, just northeast of the Punchbowl, was divided by high mountains with no roads, making it difficult to move reserves to meet any enemy threat. Military leaders decided to bring in Marines via helicopter at night on September 27, when the moon would be waning. In Operation Blackbird, the war's first and only large-scale night lift of combat troops, 200 Marines of 2/1, including Waller King, were airlifted to a sector near the Punchbowl.[40] According to Waller,

> A never-before-tactic was given to us. We were to "jump" over the entrenched Chinese regiment before us. We were on separate spurs of 749, under heavy attack, so some of us went into the river bed below and boarded the new 10 place "choppers" and flew two ridges behind the Chinese. Twelve choppers & 228 Marines—success!
>
> These Sikorsky helicopters would carry from 6 to 8 men with full combat equipment. It took 28 flights to get all of us behind the Chinese. We lost only one man to a land mine.[41]

The intense fighting around the Punchbowl seemed to have taken the spirit out of the enemy. Army and ROK units had complete control of Bloody and Heartbreak Ridges by October 15, and the Marines were entrenched in their sector of the MLR. The North Koreans and Chinese finally agreed to return to the negotiating table, this time at Panmunjom, a deserted mud-hut village on the Munsan-Kaesong road.[42]

Beginning on October 25, the delegates focused on a cease-fire based on a line of demarcation. Both sides had already agreed to accept a line two thousand yards forward of the current UN MLR. The Communists wanted Kaesong, which was below the 38th Parallel, to be north of that line, but General Ridgway refused to cede the ancient capital and its accompanying propaganda and political value. The press and the Truman administration questioned Ridgway's intransigence on the issue, and he was eventually overruled. The North Koreans apparently learned of the decision before Admiral Joy, because he and his team found themselves confronted by "cocky" Communist negotiators who "knew something" that the Americans did not. Only later did Ridgway instruct Joy to cede Kaesong.[43]

Marguerite Higgins and other Western reporters had returned to Korea to cover the talks at Panmunjom. The correspondents complained that American military briefings were often incomplete and that North Korean and Chinese sources provided more detailed and accurate information.[44]

Despite the resumption of the peace negotiations, the 8th Army Command cautioned all units that hostilities would continue until an armistice agreement was signed. However, all units would reduce operations to those essential to maintaining present positions. Counterattacks to regain key terrain lost to an enemy assault were authorized, but "every effort will be made to prevent unnecessary casualties."[45]

Between late August and October 1951, the Chinese and North Koreans suffered an estimated 234,000 casualties, compared to 60,000 for the US/UN forces. Of that number, 22,000 were Americans, bringing the total to about 100,000. The American public viewed these losses as resulting from fighting for inconsequential ridges and increasingly turned against the war. An October 1951 poll indicated that two-thirds of the country saw the conflict in Korea as "an utterly useless war."[46]

The new positional nature of the war in Korea was reminiscent of conditions during World War I. Marines and UN soldiers constructed bunkers on the reverse slopes of the steep hills while the enemy dug tunnels into the hillsides. Patrol actions and small attacks dominated the next twenty-two months of the conflict, when the Marine Corps suffered 40 percent of its total casualties in Korea.

The Marine division used the month of October to organize, construct, and defend its position. Patrolling forward of the MLR and screening rear areas, the Marines found little enemy presence. During the last two weeks of the month, foot patrols ranged farther into enemy territory and company-strength tank-infantry raids supported by air and artillery, were launched at every opportunity.[47]

Defensive warfare limited contact with the enemy, and the Marine division stopped offering day-by-day summaries of events. Line Minnesota, which ran parallel to Line Hayes, became the new MLR.[48]

October also saw the Marines expand their use of helicopters. Two company-size helicopter lifts had taken place since Operation Summit, and division leaders pondered whether an entire battalion could be transported with comparable speed. At 10:00 a.m. on October 11, Operation Bumblebee began as Joe Albritton's 3/7 was transported fifteen miles.

Over the next five hours and fifty minutes, twelve helicopters moved 958 combat-equipped Marines weighing an average of 240 pounds each, with each flight lasting between ten and twelve minutes.[49]

On October 22, the 1/1 carried out a helicopter sweep of an area suspected of harboring North Korean and Chinese guerrillas who were ambushing Marines in the rear of the MLR. Ten helicopters, each carrying 6 Marines, conducted thirty-six flights.[50]

Waller's 2/1 was in regimental reserve during the first days of October. When the battalion returned to the line on Konmubong Ridge, it carried out patrols, improved defensive positions, and carefully dealt with the mines in the area. Of the period, he wrote, "We went back up on October 16th. Most action had stopped and a wide river separated us from the Chinese. We were on Hill 812 now. Here a month of easy life was spent. It was getting cold now and action had slackened up. We had our first ice on October 23rd and the first snow on October 25th. This snow stayed with us on through the winter."[51]

Joe Albritton's 3/7 was also in reserve until it was airlifted to Hill 673, a spur on the southeastern side of Konmubong Ridge, on October 11 in Operation Bumblebee. Company-size squads carried out patrols for the rest of the month, salvaging equipment and weapons lost during the September fight for the ridge. Though the patrols were considered routine, the battalion suffered 2 KIA and 5 wounded in action.[52]

George Sharp's Dog Company, 2/5, was located west of Hill 812 at the beginning of October, although his battalion's other companies went into reserve. Dog Company received almost daily enemy mortar and artillery fire from the hills to the northwest, causing casualties, until it joined the rest of the battalion in reserve on October 11.[53]

November differed little from October. The Marines improved their bunkers, cleared lines of fire, and patrolled their assigned sectors of Line Minnesota. Ambushes, outposts, and observation posts were maintained to safeguard against enemy probes and attacks. Reserve offered periodic respites from the tedium of trench warfare. In preparation for the winter, warming bunkers and tents were erected behind the MLR and stoves were installed.[54]

The division celebrated the Marine Corps birthday on November 10 by having all troops fire one round on enemy positions at a designated time. Eighty-three aircraft carried out a birthday air strike on enemy positions in the Marines' sector and dropped leaflets inviting enemy soldiers to the Marine birthday dinner. The cruiser USS *Los Angeles* fired salvos on enemy positions at the designated times, adding a tremendous thunderclap to the celebration.[55]

On November 28, Marines from the 3/7 got an interpreter to use a loudspeaker to ask some North Korean troops about one hundred yards away for their thoughts about the cease-fire. The North Koreans invited the Americans to meet, and the two groups sent representatives carrying white flags to talk over the situation. Nothing is known of what they discussed, but both sides returned safely to their own lines. Lieutenant John Nolan, an intelligence officer for the 1/1, described the meeting as "one of the remarkable moments in a long, nasty war."[56]

George Sharp returned from sick leave on November 8 and transferred to the Division headquarters on November 12, thus seeing no further frontline action. On November 11, his former unit, the 2/5, was airlifted to relieve Waller King's 2/1 on the front line. Helicopters also provided supply support on Thanksgiving Day, when each man on the front lines received a hearty meal.[57] General Ridgway ordered the 8th Army to cease major offensive action on November 12 and to confine its forces to an active defense of the MLR. General Van Fleet restricted attacks to battalion-size or smaller. The Communists agreed to Ridgway's limited cease-fire, and on November 27 the "Little Armistice" went into effect. Ridgway then launched Operation Ratkiller, designed to eliminate the guerrillas who were harassing the UN Command's rear and supply lines from the mountains of South Korea. The operation resulted in the death or capture of more than 20,000 enemy guerrillas and bandits. The Marine division finished the month in the same position on the MLR it had held on November 1.

Both the 8th Army and the enemy engaged in psychological warfare during the Little Armistice. The US/UN dropped leaflets encouraging Chinese and North Korean soldiers to defect. The Communists used loudspeakers to appeal to South Korean soldiers to surrender and scattered "safe conduct" passes over the UN lines, encouraging Americans and their allies to defect. Waller collected more than eighty such passes and brought them home as souvenirs.

Joe Albritton had come to Korea armed not only with an M-1 rifle but also with a 35mm Leica camera and twenty rolls of film. During Operation

Rugged, he photographed the Marines in action—firing at the enemy, on the march, fording rivers, crawling through woods, and climbing ridges. Jim Nicholson did not always know when Joe was taking pictures and was surprised that the camera and photographs survived at all "given the hard-scrabble life we were living." The pictures are amazing considering that first and foremost, Joe was a combat Marine. Some of these pictures were in 'hot zones' and all were in very dangerous territory."[58] When he had used up his film, he mailed the rolls home and bought more from the mobile post exchanges behind the lines. Back in Mississippi, Joe's father had the film developed at Standard Photo in Jackson and then mailed the prints back to Korea, where Joe selected a hundred that he thought were the most representative of the war and then offered prints to other Marines at a cost of ten dollars per set. He sent an initial order for 176 sets to his father, along with $1,760 in money orders and his customers' home addresses, and Dick Albritton obtained and mailed out the prints.

More orders followed, with business accelerating while the Marine division was in reserve. However, the substantial money orders caught the attention of military authorities on the lookout for gambling activity. Joe was summoned to regimental headquarters, where Colonel John Wermuth, the regimental commander, began asking if the source of the money was gambling. When Joe explained about the photographs and showed the colonel a set of prints, and he ordered a set.

Joe left a set of prints with a sergeant at battalion headquarters who then began taking orders, and the next money order Dick Albritton received covered 760 sets. Joe's brother, Dick Jr., visited their parents and found every surface in the house covered with stacks of photographs. Dick pitched in with the mailing and received a set of photos in return for his help. Peggy Albritton was living with her parents in Natchez but helped with the business whenever she was in Clinton. By the time Joe returned to the United States, he had sold more than 1,250 sets of prints and was planning to use the money he had earned to buy a car.[59]

Chapter 9

THE ARMISTICE, DECEMBER 1951–JULY 1953

The Communists, as Admiral [C. Turner] Joy and his team were slowly and brutally learning, looked upon the conference room as an extension of the battlefield. It provided not only the machinery for ending the fighting but, just as important, an opportunity to claim what had been lost, or could not be won, by forces in the field.
–Harry J. Middleton, *The Compact History of the Korean War*

By December 1951 Joe Albritton and Waller King thought of themselves as short-timers, though they still had four months to serve. George Sharp expected to be rotated before the year was out but learned that his time in Korea would continue into February. Their regiments held most of Konmubong Ridge, and the main line of resistance (MLR) was Line Minnesota, above the 38th Parallel. The Marines settled in for the winter.

Christmas was celebrated with a hot turkey dinner with all the trimmings. The Chinese marked the occasion by showering the MLR with thousands of attractively colored cards with a simple message:

Greetings from the Chinese People's Volunteers.
Whoever the colour, race or creed, All plain folks are brothers indeed.
Both you and we want life and peace, if you go home the war will cease.
Demand Peace! Stop War![1]

December 1951 was a troubling month for the Marines. Even though not a single large-scale operation took place, 24 Marines were killed and 149 wounded in patrol actions. The enemy also captured 8 Marines. For their part, the Marines counted 246 North Koreans killed and took fifty-six prisoners.[2]

The Marines rang in 1952 with an artillery salvo against enemy positions along the MLR. On January 11, Major General John T. Selden relieved Gerald C. Thomas as commander of the Marine division, which remained in the same position it had defended for the preceding four months. Most of the twelve-plus miles of the Marine sector was good defensive ground, strengthened by an elaborate system of trenches and bunkers behind miles of barbed wire. The enemy still held the area west of Hill 812. The opposing lines were separated by between 50 and 150 yards.

Joe and Waller's last months in Korea were tedious, and they focused most of their thoughts on survival—getting through each day without harm. Patrolling day and night on their assigned sector of Line Minnesota, they frequently interrupted enemy movement. George Sharp transferred to the 1st Marine Division headquarters mail service in Pusan in November 1951, "riding shotgun on the north bound mail flight to a little half-pint strip near Inje." In December he moved from Pusan to K-50, the northernmost airstrip controlled by the United Nations, where he transported mail by truck convoy. Sharp enjoyed good chow, movies, a post exchange, showers, and two stoves in his tent, but he also looked forward to returning home.[3] In early January, Sharp's former unit, 2/5, took part in Operation Guerrilla, a four-day attempt to block the escape of some 250 Communist guerrillas. The Little Armistice expired on December 27, but both sides continued to observe it.

Marine tanks played a critical role in defending the MLR during this phase of the war. Tanks cleared minefields, destroyed enemy bunkers, and wiped out enemy machine-gun nests and mortar positions. Waller recalled watching

> a duel between a Chinese anti-tank weapon and one of our bunker-busting tanks. We had a 50 caliber machine gun loaded with tracer bullets. We could see the Chinese bunker from which they were firing at the tank. The tank gunner could not see the Chinese emplacement at all. Our 50 caliber machine gun would fire one round at a time until the tank gunner could

see the bunker. The Chinese had by that time scored 11 out of 15 shots on our tank. Our tank needed only one shot to settle the problem. Usually we did not have tank support. Only on "flat" ground—and none around here—but when we held a static line, they would somehow get the tanks up on top of the hills where they were dug in to give us heavy firepower.[4]

Waller, who had been promoted to sergeant, and the rest of the 2/1 remained in regimental reserve for most of February, and although he was "comfortable," he just "wanted to go back home to the U.S.A. and see my family. I count the days now."[5]

Joe and the 3/7 continued occupying a defensive position on Line Minnesota. The battalion maintained ambush outposts and listening posts at night for security reasons as well as to capture enemy prisoners. Daily reconnaissance patrols were sent north of the MLR, and daily patrols and outposts maintained security in the rear. Joe lost his camera in the snow while on patrol in February, but with less than a month before he was slated to go home, the loss was not critical.

In March 1952, the Marine Corps introduced the armored vest, a "zippered, vest-type, sleeveless jacket constructed of water-resistant nylon incorporating two types of armor. One a flexible pad of basket-weave nylon, covers the upper chest and shoulder girdle; the other, overlapping curved Doron plates, covers the lower chest, back and abdomen [and consists of] several layers of fiber glass cloth bonded or laminated together with a resin."[6] The vests proved effective in their initial combat trials.

While the war was in a lull, General James Van Fleet ordered a realignment of 8th Army forces along the MLR to strengthen the defenses around Seoul, Inchon, and the Kimpo airfield in what was dubbed Operation Mixmaster, which took place during a ten-day stretch in late March, while snow remained on the ground. Van Fleet could not allow any loss of ground in the western sector that would endanger the Seoul area. Losing territory in the mountainous east was acceptable since it had no major strategic value, but a loss of ground in the western sector would endanger the area around the South Korean capital. Van Fleet selected the Marine division to defend the historic invasion route to Seoul.

By the time Operation Mixmaster began, Joe and Waller were already on their way home. Joe turned twenty-one on March 4, while Waller turned twenty on March 9. Their families got ready to celebrate.

Negotiations at Panmunjom

While the Little Armistice continued in effect, negotiators at Panmunjom took up the issue of the cease-fire and inspection arrangements. General Matthew Ridgway wanted joint observers to conduct free inspections throughout Korea during a cease-fire to prevent the Communists from secretly bringing in reinforcements and building up their military. The Joint Chiefs of Staff (JCS) disagreed with Ridgway, opposing anything that would disrupt negotiations and favoring a UN statement that punitive action would be taken if a major violation of the armistice occurred.

The Communists accepted the inspection proposal on December 3 but added the requirement that both sides could not introduce any additional military forces, prohibiting the United Nations from rotating troops or allowing leave to Japan. The UN countered by proposing routine one-for-one replacements. Another point of contention was the UN position that the Communists could not rebuild air bases in North Korea, an unrealistic proposal because the United Nations had airfields all over South Korea. In January 1952, the negotiators decided to set aside the airfield issue and deal with prisoners of war, next on the negotiators' agenda.

That topic became the most controversial issue the negotiators faced and delayed any final agreement for more than eighteen months. The United States wanted to prevent the Communists from keeping thousands of American POWs in slave-labor camps as the Soviets had done with German POWs after World War II. In addition, the US/UN POW camps held more than 100,000 Chinese and North Korean prisoners, but neutral observers had determined that about 70,000 of these men preferred not to be repatriated, and the United States opposed involuntary repatriation on moral grounds.[7]

Negotiators began discussing POWs on December 11, and Admiral Joy asked that lists be prepared for review. The Communists objected, arguing that lists did not need to be prepared because all prisoners would be exchanged after an armistice agreement had been reached. The UN team refused to budge, and prisoner lists were exchanged on December 18. The UN list included 95,531 North Koreans, 20,700 Chinese, and 16,243 South Korean residents who had been impressed into the North Korean army. The United Nations did not include another 44,000 South Koreans who had voluntarily fought for the Communists; those names had been sent to the International Red Cross. The Communists then accused the United Nations of failing to report those 44,000 people.

The UN Command in turn questioned the accuracy of the POW lists submitted by the Communists, who claimed to hold only 11,559 POWs (3,198 Americans, 7,142 South Koreans, and the remainder from UN countries). UN records showed 11,500 Americans (including 61 Marines and 2 Navy corpsmen) and 88,000 South Koreans missing, and the Communists were believed to hold a much larger number of prisoners. The size of the numbers reported by the Communists indicated that many American POWs had died in captivity.

Admiral Joy made a special radio broadcast to the American people on January 1, 1952, admitting that negotiations with the enemy had been "painfully slow . . . but in dealing with the Communists there is no other way." The next day he officially proposed that all POWs be allowed to repatriate voluntarily and that none be forced to return to their countries. The Chinese called it a "shameful proposition" that went against the Geneva Convention (which they had not signed).

On February 18, Chinese and North Koreans at a POW camp rioted over the conditions under which they were being held. American troops suppressed the disorders, resulting in 77 dead prisoners and another 140 wounded, along with 1 American soldier killed and 38 wounded. The riot attracted worldwide attention to the UN POW camps, with the Communists charging that Americans and their allies were holding prisoners under inhumane conditions and torturing those who resisted.[8]

Another embarrassing incident occurred on May 7, when POWs at the Geoje camp seized the commander, General Francis T. Dodd, and held him hostage until officials agreed to sign a statement admitting that UN troops had been responsible for bloodshed in the camps. The result was a public relations coup for the Communists. General Mark W. Clark replaced Ridgway as commander of US/UN forces in East Asia immediately after Dodd's release and ordered an immediate cleanup of the POW compounds. A regiment of American paratroopers and a squad of tanks began a two-hour battle for control of the Geoje camp that ended with 31 POWs and 1 American paratrooper killed and many more wounded. American guards seized massive stores of spears, Molotov cocktails, and knives. The surviving prisoners were distributed among other POW camps, where disturbances continued.[9]

To convince the Communists to negotiate in earnest, General Clark ordered a series of bombing attacks on North Korea, initially targeting power-generating plants on the Yalu River near the Supung Dam. US/UN planes destroyed the power plants on June 23, causing a national catastrophe for North Korea but having little effect on the negotiations. On July 11, twelve hundred US/UN bombers turned their attention to Pyongyang, destroying factories, warehouses, railroad yards, military barracks, and airfields, but this attack and another in August similarly failed to move the Communist negotiators.[10]

Clark also sought to influence the armistice talks by throwing the Communists off-balance. With JCS approval, he unilaterally called a three-day recess on June 7, and Admiral Joy subsequently staged periodic three- and four-day walkouts, confusing the Chinese and North Koreans.[11]

Marines on the Western Front

In the wake of Operation Mixmaster, the 1st Marine Division moved from the eastern sector (X Corps) to the western sector (I Corps), where its mission was to defend the invasion route to Seoul. Most observers believed that Van Fleet wanted the most reliable division in his command to defend the South Korean capital.

Some Marines were relocated by ship to Inchon, while most moved overland with equipment, artillery, and vehicles. The Marines were now on the Jamestown Line, a thirty-five-mile stretch of the MLR starting on the Kimpo Peninsula, crossing the Han and Imjin Rivers, and running to the west bank of the Samichon River. The terrain was mostly coastal lowlands, with hills and valleys to the northeast. The Korean Marine Regiment held the left sector of the line; two US Marine regiments were placed in the center and right sections, with the third in reserve. Aligned with the Korean Marines, the US Marines' 1st Armored Amphibian Battalion used its capabilities to patrol, cross, and defend the Han and Imjin Rivers. The 11th Artillery Regiment positioned its four battalions behind the three infantry regiments to shore up the men on the ground. The Marine tank battalion divided into four companies, with one assigned to each of the four regiments.[12]

The Marines found themselves in an uncomfortable situation. Though they had been trained to maneuver and attack, there would be no more

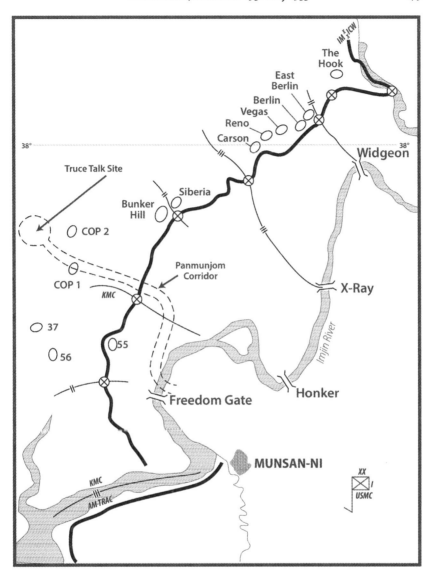

Western Korean Front, 1952–53.

chases up and down the Korean peninsula. The Marines now had to improve and learn how to fight under stalemate conditions. Gains would be measured in yards rather than miles.

Great Britain's 1st Commonwealth Division was positioned on the US Marines' right flank. The British were considered the most effective unit in I Corps. The commander, Major General A. J. H. Cassels, a Scot, had little confidence in the US Army, but with the Marines on his left flank, he was confident in the UN forces' ability to hold I Corps's sector of the Jamestown Line. The Marine sector was a long trench line of machine-gun positions, fighting holes, and tank slots with heavily sandbagged bunkers serving as living quarters, first-aid stations, and command posts. Concertina wire was strung in front of the trench line to discourage and slow any Chinese advance.

In front of the trenches, in a no-man's-land between the Chinese lines and the MLR, the Marines set up the outpost line of resistance, the first line of defense. Outposts were set up to give early warnings of an enemy attack and delay any enemy advance. Squads or platoons on full alert occupied the outposts for up to twenty-four hours but were expected to fall back to the Jamestown Line when under attack.

US/UN forces were now fighting positional warfare. Their defensive mission meant that the Marines could patrol the no-man's-land but were not to attack the enemy's main line. If an outpost fell, a counterattack was authorized. Over time, the outposts were moved closer to the Jamestown Line, becoming observation points to detect enemy movements and providing safe haven for Marines withdrawing from enemy fire.

Outposts were initially assigned individual identifying numbers and later received names. Hill 190 became Outpost Chicago and then Outpost Elmer. Some outposts took on names based on their identifying characteristics on a topographical map—Boot, Hook, Arrowhead, and Three Fingers. Others were named for Hollywood women: Marilyn, Ingrid, Hedy, and Dagmar. Carson, Reno, and Vegas got their names because Marine commanders considered holding them a gamble.

The Marine division faced two Chinese armies with about 80,000 soldiers. Each army had three divisions of well-trained, well-equipped, and combat-experienced men. Like the Marines, the Chinese had observation posts to warn of an attack and to delay any advance.

General Clark served as commander of the US/UN forces for the remainder of the war. He avoided major policy issues with his superiors but argued for an increasingly forceful approach against the enemy, even recommending use of Nationalist Chinese troops in Korea and the bombing of Manchuria. Like his predecessors MacArthur and Ridgway, fighting a limited war soon frustrated Clark. Fighting from hilltop to hilltop continued along the Jamestown Line during the summer of 1952.

No end was in sight for the war, and the only thing Marines had to look forward to was being rotated back to the States. These doldrums ended on August 9 when a Chinese attack on Outpost Siberia forced a squad of Marines to pull back to the MLR, setting off a chain of events that led to the Marines' first major engagement since Operation Mixmaster.

Outpost Siberia had strategic value because it was close to the division's main supply route. When the Chinese attacked, the Marines responded with their full arsenal of weapons—artillery, tank fire, and air strikes. Siberia changed hands six times during the three-day fight, with heavy casualties on both sides. The 7th Regimental Command recognized that nearby Hill 122, which the Marines called Bunker Hill, was the key to controlling the area. Occupying the hill would give the Marines a better post for surveying territory behind the enemy's main line and provide better control of Outpost Siberia.

One company from the 7th Regiment, supported by tank and artillery fire, began an assault on Bunker Hill on August 11. Jet fighters launched dozens of air strikes over the next week, but the Chinese held out until August 17 before withdrawing. They tried to regain Bunker Hill but were driven back by hand-to-hand fighting. Bunker Hill had cost the Marines 50 dead and 313 wounded, and the JCS and the general staff debated whether the hill was worth such a steep price. However, the Chinese toll was much higher—an estimated 3,200 casualties. During August, the Marine division lost 144 KIA, 1,243 wounded, and 15 missing, resulting in a shortage of fighters. Five hundred men from the 3rd Marine Division at Camp Pendleton were airlifted to Korea.[13]

The Marines engaged in a second major battle with the Chinese in October at the Hook, a vital—and extremely vulnerable—part of the MLR that could not be fully protected by outpost defenses. Outposts Seattle and Ronson were located some five hundred yards to the west of the Hook, with Outpost Warsaw about a half mile to the north. The Marines' 7th Regiment protected the Hook and the six-mile front around it, with a forty-five-man platoon garrisoning Warsaw and a fire team of five occupying Seattle. The 7th was overextended, with only one company in reserve.

On the night of October 2, Chinese troops overran Outposts Seattle and Warsaw, but the Marines counterattacked and drove the attackers back. Regimental command pulled its reserve battalion with the exception of one company to the front to reinforce the outposts because losing the

Hook would have forced the Marines to withdraw more than two miles to reestablish a defensive line. After heavy artillery fire on October 6, the Chinese attacked Outposts Warsaw, Detroit, Frisco, and Reno as well as other Marine positions on the MLR. Squad- and platoon-size units defended Detroit, Frisco, and Reno, but they were overrun. The Marines counterattacked, retaking all of outposts except Detroit.

The Chinese tried again on October 23, firing thousands of shells at Outposts Warsaw and Ronson as well as at the Hook in a three-day barrage that leveled Marine trenches and gun emplacements and destroyed bunkers. At dusk on October 26, the Chinese attacked Ronson and Warsaw. Ronson fell in less than thirty minutes, with all of its Marine defenders killed. After hand-to-hand combat against superior enemy numbers, the Marines at Warsaw also succumbed. After overnight fighting on October 26–27, the Chinese had control of a small sector of the MLR and turned their attention to Hill 146, the high ground behind the Hook. Units from the Marines' 1st and 7th Regiments launched a counterattack on the Hook at 5:00 a.m. Ground forces were supported by continuous air strikes all day. Tons of bombs and napalm dropped on advancing Chinese reinforcements, coupled with heavy artillery fire, drove the enemy from the Hook by dawn on October 28, and the Marines were again in control.[14]

The thirty-six hours of fighting for the Hook constituted the most intense combat of the Korean War. It was the first time that enemy troops breached the Marine MLR and held it for any period of time. The Marines suffered 70 KIA, nearly 400 wounded, and 39 missing, 27 of whom were later confirmed captured. The Chinese lost an estimated 494 killed and 370 wounded. In November, the Marine sector of the MLR was shortened, and the 1st Commonwealth Division assumed responsibility for the Hook.[15] Operations had been hampered by a shortage of artillery, mortar, and rifle ammunition that restricted Marines' ability to fire.

With the Korean War mired in a stalemate, the conflict became an issue in the November 1952 US presidential election. President Harry S. Truman had decided not to run for another term, leaving the Democratic nominee, former Illinois governor Adlai Stevenson, to defend the administration's policies. The Republican candidate, General Dwight D. Eisenhower, who had served as commander of the Allied forces in Europe during World War II, promised to go to Korea if elected. Most political historians believe that the Korean War decided the election, in which Eisenhower swept to victory.[16]

Less than four weeks later, on November 29, Eisenhower flew to Korea under heavy security. The trip was a political gesture. Ike met with Syngman Rhee and listened as the South Korean president lobbied for the US/UN forces to begin a drive to the Yalu River. The president-elect put on field gear and talked with line commanders and troops, but General Clark never had a chance to share his plans to win the war. Eisenhower left Seoul on December 5, admitting to the press that he had "no panaceas, no tricks" to end the war.[17]

Enemy attacks on the outposts continued in November and December, slowed somewhat by the intense winter cold. The temperature on the Jamestown Line dropped into single digits and occasionally below zero. On December 16, the Marines attacked Outpost Frisco, which the Chinese had captured in October, but failed to retake it. Three days later, two reinforced squads of How Company, 3/1, carried out a raid on a Chinese trench line north of Outpost East Berlin, using tank fighting lights to illuminate the enemy's line and give support fire. The maneuver kept the Chinese soldiers in their trenches while fire teams burned two hundred yards of enemy trenches with napalm canisters.

On December 3, the Indian government introduced a UN resolution declaring that "force shall not be used" against POWs in the Korean War. A repatriations commission composed of Czechoslovakia, Poland, Sweden, and Switzerland would take charge of the prisoners for 120 days, during which the prisoners would have their rights explained and be permitted to choose freely where to go. Although fifty-four nations accepted the plan, the Soviet Union and China rejected it. The Indian government then introduced a resolution in the League of Red Cross Societies in Switzerland that called for sick and wounded prisoners to be exchanged in advance of a cease-fire, and this proposal eventually led to the armistice.[18]

On January 9, 1953, just prior to leaving office, the Truman administration launched air attacks on North Korea. B-29 bombers blasted transportation targets on the west coast, where three major railway lines from Manchuria converged. The aerial assault continued for five days as US/UN aircraft flew a total of 2,292 combat sorties and knocked out all bridges in the targeted area. The bombings constituted only a temporary setback, however, as makeshift pontoon bridges were in place at all critical crossings less than a week after the bombing stopped.

After Eisenhower's inauguration on January 20, the Chinese government announced that it was "ready for an immediate cease-fire on the basis of the agreement already reached at Panmunjom." Accepting this offer would have required the United States to yield on the issue of voluntary repatriation, and Washington refused to do so. The State Department and the JCS instructed General Clark to suggest an exchange of sick and wounded prisoners, but the Communists did not reply.

Eisenhower did not intend to enlarge the war or seek a conflict directly with China or the Soviet Union, but he wanted to confuse the enemy. The United States began shipping atomic artillery to East Asia and dropped hints that if no cease-fire were achieved by the summer of 1953, the United States/United Nations would launch an all-out offensive to drive the Chinese out of Korea.

In February, General Maxwell Taylor replaced Van Fleet as commander of 8th Army. The Chinese refusal to consider an exchange of sick and wounded prisoners gave the appearance that the Communists preferred to continue sacrificing lives and turned world opinion against them. In the face of increasing outside pressure, problems within China such as the failure of the spring crop, the repercussions of the March death of Soviet leader Joseph Stalin, and the threat that atomic weapons would be used, the Chinese modified their position on the exchange of prisoners. On March 29, Communist commanders in Korea surprised American leaders by accepting Clark's proposal for the prisoner exchange, and within five days, the two sides had agreed on an "all for all" exchange.

At the same time, however, the heaviest fighting to date broke out in the Marine Corps sector of the MLR as the Chinese launched a general assault. On March 23, fearing another US/UN offensive, the Chinese converged from three directions on Outposts Carson, Reno, and Vegas. Vegas fell the first night, but the Marines held Carson and Reno. Air support the next morning pounded enemy positions on and around the outposts, and over the next week, both sides sent in reinforcements as the outposts repeatedly changed hands. The Chinese finally withdrew on March 30, but by that time they had inflicted 1,015 Marine casualties, including 116 killed—63 percent of the division's total for the month. Chinese losses were estimated at 2,221, with 536 confirmed killed. Marine air power was decisive in the fight for Reno, Carson, and Vegas. The air wing flew 218 missions and dropped more than 426 tons of bombs despite rain and snow that restricted visibility. The failure to capture and hold the three outposts probably motivated the Chinese high command's change of heart regarding the POW exchange.

The exchange of sick and wounded, Little Switch, began on April 20. Over the next two weeks, the UN Command returned 6,670 captives to the Communists and in return received a total of 684 prisoners (471 South Koreans, 149 Americans, 32 British, and 32 of other nationalities). Those repatriated reported that about 60 percent of those interned in Communist prison camps had died and that prisoners had been indoctrinated in Communist ideology.[19]

On April 16, President Eisenhower delivered a speech, "The Chance for Peace," in which he called on the new Soviet leadership to work with the free world by ending Communist aggression in Indochina and Malaya; supporting a free, united Germany; and allowing an "honorable armistice" in Korea. America and Western Europe hoped progress would follow at Panmunjom, where talks resumed on April 26.

The Communist delegates, however, sought to require all POWs who sought political asylum to spend six months in a neutral country, where agents from their governments would attempt to persuade the prisoners to come home. Those who still refused repatriation would be turned over to a joint political conference, which would make final decisions. On May 7, after the US/UN delegation had rejected the proposal, the Communists proposed that prisoners be screened in Korea.

The 1st Marine Division went into I Corps reserve at Camp Casey on May 5, replaced by the Army's 25th Infantry Division. Marine air, artillery, and tanks continued their support of the I Corps front. Turkish units took over the defense of the Carson, Vegas, and Elko outposts, which fell to the Chinese during a two-day fight at the end of the month. On May 22, the United States/United Nations declared a willingness to allow all North Koreans and Chinese who did not wish to be repatriated to be interned in camps in the demilitarized zone (DMZ), where they would be guarded by Indian soldiers and subjected to no more than six months screening and persuasion. The Eisenhower administration was losing patience with the Communists and sought India's assistance in bringing about an armistice, telling Indian officials that "if the armistice negotiations collapsed, the United States would probably make a stronger rather than a lesser military exertion, and that this might well extend the area of conflict." This message, delivered personally by secretary of state John Foster Dulles, hinted at the use of atomic weapons, and US leaders assumed that India's Jawaharlal Nehru would relay the threat to China.[20]

The final US/UN POW proposal was presented at Panmunjom on May 25. On June 4, the Communists asked for minor changes, and an agreement was signed four days later. All POWs would be turned over to Indian troops of a Neutral Nation Repatriation Commission as soon as the armistice was signed. POWs would have two months to decide on repatriation, all governments involved would have ninety days to try to change prisoners' minds, and then those who still wanted political asylum would revert to civilian status and be released. Though the POW agreement might have seemed to signal a new, more conciliatory position by the Communists, on June 10 they launched a series of attacks along the MLR. The heaviest Communist offensive in two years, it targeted South Korean forces along eight miles of the MLR between the Iron Triangle and the Punchbowl and pushed them back about three miles, forcing a realignment of the MLR. The South Korean divisions suffered 7,300 casualties, while the Communists lost an estimated 6,600 personnel.

Officials in Washington also worked to persuade Rhee to be more receptive to an armistice. The sixteen UN members with forces in Korea pledged to guarantee South Korea's security if the Communists broke the truce, while the United States agreed to fund the expansion of the South Korean army to twenty divisions and provide equipment to maintain an adequate defense. The United States would also give the Republic of Korea $1 billion for reconstruction and economic rehabilitation and make every effort to secure the withdrawal of Communist Chinese forces from the Korean peninsula and bring about its unification.[21]

Rhee responded by withdrawing his representative at Panmunjom, writing to Eisenhower that the armistice terms constituted a "death sentence for Korea." In a final attempt to disrupt the peace negotiations, Rhee ordered the June 18 release of 25,000 anti-Communist North Korean POWs, who quickly melted into the South Korean civilian population or joined the country's army.[22]

This violation of the pending truce arrangements forced General Clark to apologize to the Chinese and North Korean commanders for Rhee's defiant act while cautioning recapturing those released would be difficult, just "as it would be for your side to recover the 50,000 South Korean prisoners 'released' by your side during the hostilities." Washington considered whether to remove Rhee from office or make another attempt to gain his cooperation. On June 25, the third anniversary of the invasion, Walter Robinson, assistant secretary of state for Far Eastern affairs, arrived in Korea to negotiate with Rhee. Robinson spent the next two weeks cajoling, flattering, arguing with, and threatening Rhee. When Robinson raised the specter that the United States would sign a separate peace and withdraw from Korea immediately, Rhee finally yielded.[23] Eisenhower then affirmed the earlier offer of military, reconstruction, and economic assistance after the armistice was concluded and agreed to a high-level political conference in Seoul to cement the US–South Korean relationship .On the battlefront, the 1st Marine Division reassumed operational control of its former MLR sector on July 7–8, relieving the Army's 25th Infantry Division. The tactical situation had deteriorated since the Marines last occupied the area. Chinese troops now controlled Outposts Carson, Vegas, and Elko and threatened Outposts Berlin and East Berlin, both of which were located about 325 yards from the MLR. Taking advantage of the confusion caused by the change in personnel, the Chinese attacked Berlin and East Berlin on July 7. After a day of savage fighting, the Chinese had taken East Berlin. Four Marine F9F aircraft assisted the Marines in retaking East Berlin on the afternoon of July 8. For the next ten days, the two Marine regiments carried out patrols, making intermittent contact with the Chinese. Heavy rains made movement of troops and vehicles difficult. A firefight on the night of July 16–17 resulted in 6 Marines dead and 1 missing as well as 22 Chinese casualties. The Chinese sought to maintain military pressure while the delegations at Panmunjom completed negotiations.

On July 19, the negotiators reached final agreement on all points. The fighting would end twelve hours after US general William Harrison and North Korean general Nam Il signed the armistice. Each side would then withdraw two kilometers from its positions to create the DMZ. Once the armistice was in effect, neither side could increase the number of non-Korean troops. A military armistice commission made up of five UN Command nations and five Communist nations would supervise implementation of the agreement. Further negotiations to unify all of Korea would be transferred to a different commission that would meet at a later date. The POWs would be screened by a neutral commission and either returned or not, as they chose.

On the night of July 19–20, the Chinese again stormed Outposts Berlin and East Berlin, overrunning both within three hours. Chinese artillery fire was matched by Marine, Turkish, and US Army artillery batteries that fired thousands of rounds at the enemy. General Randolph Pate, the Marine divisional commander, opted not to attempt to retake the two outposts, calculating that with an armistice near, the cost in Marine lives was not worth it. Pate reinforced the sector across from the outposts to prevent any Chinese attack on the MLR itself.

The Marines saw Hill 119, known as Boulder City, as the next Chinese target and sent in reinforcements, setting the stage for the Corps's last battle of the Korean War. The Chinese staged a diversionary move against Outposts Hedy and Dagmar on July 21 before launching a regiment-sized attack on Boulder City two evenings later. The 3/1 defended the hill and its nearby outposts with help from Marine air power and M-46 tanks. By dawn on July 26, the enemy attacks abated and the Marines still held Boulder City. During July, the Marines suffered 1,611 casualties, the most losses since October 1952. Chinese losses for the month in the Marine sector exceeded 3,100, but they had gained ground at several key strategic locations.

On July 23, staff members of the two delegations at Panmunjom finished charting the position of the cease-fire line and the contours of the DMZ. At 10:00 a.m. on July 27, less than twenty-four hours after the Chinese gave up trying to capture Boulder City, Generals Harrison and Nam began signing copies of the armistice agreement in English, Chinese, and Korean. Eleven minutes later, their task accomplished, the two men left the hall without having spoken a word to each other.[24]

At 10:00 p.m. on July 27, 1953—three years, one month, and two days after the North Korean invasion of South Korea and two years and seventeen days after truce talks began—the armistice went into effect.

Each army drew back two kilometers from its battle line, leaving a dark and blasted neutral zone. The Chinese and North Koreans pulled back to new fortifications. UN troops abandoned the hills for which they had fought and for which their comrades had died. The Hook and Bunker Hill; Marilyn, Ingrid, Hedy, and Dagmar; Carson, Reno, and Vegas; Berlin and

Armistice Line, July 27, 1953.

East Berlin—all were in the DMZ. No monuments would mark these battles or the heroism and sacrifices of the Marines who fought and died there.

South Korea gained 2,350 square miles north of the 38th Parallel, while North Korea gained 850 square miles south of that line. The cease-fire agreement and the DMZ did not really end the fighting. Both sides continued sending out patrols, and occasional clashes resulted during the uneasy armistice.

Operation Big Switch, the exchange of able-bodied POWs, took place between August 5 and December 23, 1953. The United Nations returned 75,823 POWs: 70,183 Koreans and 5,640 Chinese. The Communists repatriated 12,773 prisoners: 7,862 Koreans, 3,597 Americans, and just over 1,300 citizens of other UN members. Those who refused repatriation included

14,704 Chinese, 7,900 North Koreans, 23 Americans, 1 British, and 335 South Koreans.[25]

The Korean War ended in a draw. President Truman's doctrine of containment meant that the United States would not make a major military commitment to the struggle against Communism, and the United Nations demonstrated only a half-hearted willingness to battle Communist aggression. Both the United Nations and Truman's insistence on a limited war restricted military options and denied total victory to either side. The best the US/UN could hope to attain was the status quo. And that's what they got: borders that were roughly the same as they had been before the shooting started.

But the cost in human lives had been staggering. The US Defense Department estimated that the Chinese had lost 900,000 dead and wounded, while North Korea had lost 520,000 dead and wounded. For the United States and the United Nations, those numbers were 345,000 dead and wounded. In addition, war, famine, and disease caused the deaths of nearly a million North and South Korean citizens, while the fighting uprooted hundreds of thousands more. The entire Korean peninsula lay devastated in 1953. Roads, rails, and bridges, factories, cities, and agricultural lands had been destroyed. Hunger and disease swept the countryside from the Yalu to Pusan.[26]

The Marine 1st Division maintained its sector of the DMZ until February 1955, when the final members of the Corps shipped out from Inchon and returned to Camp Pendleton.

AFTERWORD

For of all sad words of thought and pen,
the saddest are these:
it might have been
—**John Greenleaf Whittier,** "Maud Muller"

Going Home

After nearly twelve months in Korea, Waller King and Joe Albritton received orders to rotate back to the United States in March 1952. The two men traveled separately to Pusan, where they reunited aboard the *General Walker*, a troop transport vessel, on March 16.

Waller and Joe were going home, but the war hung over them like a dark cloud. Waller was in a reflective mood during the two-week voyage across the Pacific and wrote down his thoughts: "I don't want to forget Korea's action,—its ugliness,—its bitterness. It can and will happen again. I want to do my part to keep it from happening again. I pray to God that He will give us a common understanding with our fellow man and brothers; that we will be spared the foolish, ignorant method of settling our disputes."[1]

Waller and Joe didn't see much of each other during the voyage, but Waller did take a photograph of Joe hiding in a lifeboat to avoid a work detail. They landed in San Francisco and boarded a train to San Diego, where they would be discharged. They had a lot to talk about: their friend Homer Ainsworth and his tragic death; their proximity during certain battles, and the fight for Hill 749, which they agreed was one never to forget.

Waller was troubled by his experiences and was determined to leave Korea behind. In some ways, however, Korea had shown Joe at his best. Neither man worried about adjusting to civilian life.

The separation process at Camp Pendleton was slow, and Waller and Joe used some of their free time to visit a Pontiac dealer so that Joe could buy a new car. Waller watched as Joe peeled off twenty-one $100 bills in payment, money he had earned from his photo business. Joe received his discharge and raced home, probably driving straight through on Highway 80 from San Diego all the way to Clinton. The Albritton family welcomed Joe home with open arms. Dick Albritton was still filling orders for photographs and would do so for several more weeks. Joe and Peggy found an apartment in Clinton and started their marriage. Waller's discharge was delayed because his medical records had been lost; another two weeks passed before a Greyhound bus took him along the same route. Both of his parents were at work when he arrived, so he walked to his grandmother's house, carrying his seabag, and did not reunite with his parents until that evening. They were of course relieved that Waller had survived Korea and proud that he had been promoted to sergeant and had received medals for his service.

By the time Waller returned, Joe had already visited the Ainsworths, sharing details about Homer's last moments and crying with family members over their loss. Waller, too, went to see Homer Ainsworth Sr. and Mary Ainsworth, telling the bereaved father that the Marines would never have sent home a casket with the wrong body in it. Waller and Joe slowly caught up on the Clinton news. Herbert Pearce was still in the Navy, stationed at the Memphis Naval Air Station, and had married in January. Bill Smith spent his last months in uniform at North Carolina's Camp Lejeune and had received his discharge. He returned with his family to Clinton and went back to his job selling clothes at a store in Jackson. George Sharp had rotated two months earlier and was still enjoying his welcome home.

Clinton was growing at this time. The town that had measured one square mile in 1950 occupied more than twenty-nine square miles in 1990. In 1960, Clinton had a population of about three thousand, a number that doubled over each of the next three decades until it topped twenty thousand in the 1990 census. In 2020, Clinton had a population of 28,100.[2]

Waller and Joe shared their stories with church and civic groups. When they spoke to the Lions Club, audience members were supportive of the war and were still talking about General Douglas MacArthur's dismissal. Several people mentioned having read Joe's letters to his parents printed in the *Clinton News*.

Joe decided not to return to college. Instead, he and local mechanic Tom Mahoney rented a building and opened an auto repair shop in Clinton.

On Saturday, May 17, Joe was driving to Jackson when he sideswiped another vehicle that was attempting to make a U-turn on Highway 80 one mile west of the city. Joe's car rolled over several times, and he suffered a fractured leg and pelvis, back and internal injuries, and severe lacerations. He died on May 19, never having regained consciousness. He was twenty-one years old.

To die in an automobile accident at home after being in harm's way for twelve months in Korea was misfortune beyond belief. Joe had escaped injury when an enemy hand grenade exploded inches away and survived the mortar explosion that killed Homer Ainsworth. Being fatally injured in an automobile accident weeks after leaving Korea was unthinkable. His wife and parents were devastated.

Bea Quisenberry again paid tribute to one of the town's young men in the *Clinton News*: "Of those hundreds of friends whose prayers for the safe return of JOE ALBRITTON from the fighting lines of Korea, no less than to his family, the news of his accident and death came as a stunning blow, bringing a hush to the town."[3]

Jim Nicholson, who served in the same platoon as Joe, remembered him as a "really, really good Marine," a true "on the point infantryman" carrying a killer BAR. "Little Joe" had always been there when "it hit the fan."[4] Waller King and George Sharp were among Joe's pallbearers. The Reverend Homer Ainsworth; Herbert Pearce's father, Rex; and John King, Waller's father, served as honorary pallbearers. Joe was buried thirty feet from Homer, the only two graves in that sector of the cemetery at that time.

Civilian Life

The loss of two close friends under tragic circumstances gave new meaning to Waller's life, and the GI Bill meant that Waller could go to the college of his choice and no longer needed to depend on a football scholarship. He decided to enroll at Mississippi College.

Waller's family had strong ties to the college: his father, John, had been a football legend there, and Waller's older brother, John, was playing for the Choctaws. For the next two years, the Kings anchored the Mississippi College line, with Waller at left tackle and John at right tackle. Their coach was the legendary Robbie Robinson, who had coached with Baby John King in the 1920s.

Waller saw a number of familiar faces when school started in the fall of 1952. Mary Elizabeth Ainsworth, Homer's sister, a high school classmate, was now a junior at the college. Henry Lackey, a cousin of Joe's from Calhoun City, was a freshman in 1952 but did not meet Waller until some fifty years later.

Waller immersed himself in college life, majoring in chemistry under Dr. A. E. Wood, Clinton's longtime mayor, and Dr. Archie Germany, a young chemist who had worked at Oak Ridge, Tennessee, during World War II. Waller's time was consumed by football and by his studies, particularly the required freshman Bible courses.

Waller attended a dance at Belhaven College in Jackson, where Gwen Brake, a freshman from Memphis, caught Waller's eye. They began dating and married in August 1953. Gwen transferred to Mississippi College, and the two completed their sophomore year there in 1953–54. Waller then decided to give up and go to pharmacy school, so the couple moved to Memphis and Waller enrolled at the University of Tennessee Pharmacy School. He later transferred to Memphis State College and received his degree in chemistry in 1956. Waller and Gwen went on to have three sons and six grandchildren.

Memphis in the mid-1950s was the place to be for a young couple. Elvis Presley was making a name for himself, and Kemmons Wilson, a millionaire home builder, had started a small motel chain but had much bigger plans. Waller took a position with a company that sold cleaning chemicals to Wilson's six motels and soon recognized that the operation had no organized purchasing system. Waller presented Wilson with a plan for centralized purchasing that Waller said would save the company at least $25,000 a year. Waller walked away from their meeting with a job as a purchasing agent for the infant Holiday Inn chain. By 1968, the company operated a thousand motels, a number that had grown to fourteen hundred four years later, when Wilson appeared on the cover of *Time* magazine. Waller King was part of an international success story.

Waller's next idea was for Holiday Inn to form a chemical company that would manufacture supplies for the chain, but Wilson feared liability issues. Waller decided to start the chemical company himself and resigned from Holiday Inn. Wilson shook his hand and said that if Waller's prices were competitive, he could have all of Holiday Inn's business. Waller's new company, Chemical Specialties, had an exclusive contract with Holiday Inns nationwide for seventeen years.

Building a life founded on his religious faith, Waller devoted himself to family, church, civic affairs, and the Marine Corps League. His grandfather, George Riley, had been a Baptist preacher, Waller's parents were strong Baptists, and the Baptist Church had influenced his life since childhood. Waller served for thirty years as a deacon at Memphis's Kirby Woods Baptist Church and traveled to Israel and took part in biblical archaeology expeditions. During one of his seventeen trips to the Holy Land, he decided to stay an extra night so that he could watch the sunrise from Mount Hermon, Israel's highest mountain. It was a fortuitous decision: his original itinerary had him traveling from London to New York on December 21, 1988, via Pan-Am Flight 103. A bomb destroyed that plane over Lockerbie, Scotland, killing everyone onboard.

Waller King died on September 14, 2021. He is buried near Homer and Joe in the Clinton cemetery.

Other Lives

George Sharp and Peggy Cain Albritton married in January 1953 and lived in Jackson, where George worked as a salesman and foreman for Allen Builders Supply (later Allen Millwork Manufacturing) and continued to serve in the Marine Corps Reserve, receiving a promotion to sergeant. He accepted a job with Taylor Machine Works and moved to Georgia in 1967. The couple had three children. George died in 1987, and Peggy died in 2013.

Bill Smith and Betty Jo Connolly Smith settled in Clinton after his discharge in 1952, and he returned to his job at a Jackson clothing store. Bill became an active member of the Marine Corps League and as one of the Chosin Few took special pride in his wartime service. However, he was also haunted by the trauma of Korea and suffered from nightmares. He later took a sales position with Fox Manufacturing, serving furniture stores in Oklahoma for a few years before returning to Clinton in 1963. Bill and Betty Jo had three children prior to their 1967 divorce. Bill Smith died in 1986.

Herbert Pearce completed his Navy service and received a medical degree from the University of Mississippi School of Medicine. He practiced surgery in Jacksonville, Florida, for thirty years and was active in the Chosin Few and other military organizations. He died in 2011.[5]

Elwood Ratliff completed his studies at Mississippi State College in 1953 and spent four years in the Air Force. He served as a groomsman at Waller King's wedding. Ratliff completed his military service and married a woman from Jackson, Lowry Buie Westbrook, with whom he had two children. Ratliff worked for the state Cooperative Extension Service before returning to Clinton after his father's death and taking over operation of the family farm in the Tinnin community. He died in 2020.[6]

Dick Albritton Sr. and Martha Burson Albritton continued living in Clinton and remained active in the Baptist Church and in community activities. They took pride in the career of their surviving son, Dick Jr. After Dick Sr. died in 1984, Opal Burson Osborn, Martha Albritton's sister, came to Clinton to live with her. Martha died in 2003 at the age of ninety-five; Opal followed ten months later. They are buried with Joe in the Clinton cemetery.

Dick Albritton Jr. taught math and physics at Gulf Coast Military Academy for two years before receiving a master's degree in physics from Louisiana State University. He and his first wife, Barbara Lovell Albritton, had three children. Dick's work in the development and testing of missile weapons systems took the family to Maryland, where he worked at Johns Hopkins University's Applied Physics Lab, and to California, where he worked at the Stanford Research Institute. Dick was later employed by NASA in Huntsville, Alabama, before retiring and returning to Clinton, where he married Ann Overstreet Kitchings. He died in 2015.

Henry Lackey, Joe Albritton's cousin, received a degree in business administration from Mississippi College in 1956. He returned to Calhoun City to run the family's Ben Franklin store and married Helen Rose James, a music teacher. Lackey joined the Mississippi National Guard and was activated during the 1961 Berlin Crisis. He graduated from the University of Mississippi Law School in 1966 and was later elected Calhoun County prosecuting attorney before becoming the state's first public defender.

He was appointed circuit judge for the state's Third Judicial District in 1993 and served for seventeen years before taking senior status. In 2007, Lackey became a national hero when he refused to take a bribe from prominent attorney Dickie Scruggs, the "King of Torts." Lackey died in 2018.

Homer Ainsworth Sr. and Mary Lee Tullos Ainsworth remained in Clinton, where Rev. Ainsworth continued preaching and Mary Ainsworth continued her work with the college and produced two cookbooks for the Women's Missionary Union. In 1953, while serving as pastor at Branch Baptist Church in Scott County, Rev. Ainsworth led the construction of a new building, and the Ainsworths funded a mural in the baptistery in memory of their late son.[7] Mary died in 1983, and Homer Sr. followed the next year. Both are buried in the family plot alongside their son.

Mary Elizabeth Ainsworth, the elder of Homer's sisters, completed her studies at the college and married a ministerial student, Dan Hembree. The couple had four children before Mary died of cancer in 1966.

Billye Jean Ainsworth, Homer's younger sister, received a degree in business from Mississippi College but devoted herself to child care, helping with her sister's children and working in the Methodist and Baptist church nurseries. Late in life, she became known for her daily walks around Clinton, and at her death in 2003 at age sixty-seven, the *Clinton News* published a story on the "Walking Lady."[8]

John King Sr. and Mary Belle Riley King prospered after the Korean War. John worked for the Mississippi Red Cross, while Mary continued teaching, and both remained involved with church and community activities. In retirement, John served as sexton for the Clinton cemetery and gained local renown for his tomato crops. He died in 1985, and Mary died in 1992. Dr. Susan Riley, Waller's aunt, had a distinguished career as an educator and headed the American Association of University Women.

John King Jr. married *Bettye Ross Shores* in 1953. Both earned degrees from Mississippi College, and John went on to receive a master's degree from the University of Florida and a doctorate from Indiana University. He served as director of the Mississippi State Park System and as an adviser to the US National Park System. He and Bettye had two daughters and lived in Clinton, where they were active in church, community, and civic activities until their deaths in 2020 and 2021, respectively.

Jim Nicholson, from Dallas, Texas, arrived in Korea just weeks before Joe, Homer, and Waller. Known as "Nick the BARman," he served in the 3rd

Squad, 3rd Platoon, George Company, often fighting near Joe and Homer. He received a Silver Star for "outstanding courage and daring initiative" during the first Chinese offensive, and a Purple Heart for wounds received in battle at the Punchbowl. After the war, Jim worked his way through medical school and was a country doctor in Greenville, Texas, for over fifty years. He is the author of *G-3-7th Marines*, a collection of reminiscences that earned the Military Writers Society of America Gold Medal.

General Oliver P. Smith returned to Camp Pendleton, California, in May 1951 and became commander of the 3rd Marine Division until 1954, when he took command of the Atlantic Fleet Marine Force in Norfolk, Virginia. He retired in 1955 and lived in Los Altos, California, until his death in 1977.

General Gerald Thomas served as commander of the 1st Marine Division from April 1951 to February 1952. He subsequently returned to Marine Corps headquarters, received a promotion to lieutenant general, and became assistant commandant/chief of staff for General Lemuel Shepherd. Prior to his retirement in 1958, Thomas served as commandant of the Marine Corps schools at Quantico. After a career in private business in Washington, DC, Thomas died in 1984.

Marguerite Higgins returned to the United States and wrote *War in Korea: The Report of a Woman Combat Correspondent*, which became a best-seller. She was one of six correspondents—and the only woman— who received the 1951 Pulitzer Prize for their coverage of the war. Higgins subsequently covered the peace negotiations at Panmunjom and went on to cover the war in Vietnam in the early 1960s. While there, she contracted a rare tropical disease, and she died on January 3, 1966. She was buried in Arlington National Cemetery.

General Edward Almond returned to the United States in July 1952 to serve as commandant of the US Army War College at Carlisle Barracks, Pennsylvania, before retiring the following January. He lived in Anniston, Alabama, until his death in 1979.

General Lewis "Chesty" Puller returned to Camp Pendleton, California, in May 1951 to command the 3rd Marine Brigade. He was promoted to major general in 1953 when he took command of the 2nd Marine Division at Camp Lejeune, North Carolina. Puller later served as deputy camp commander until his retirement in 1955 with the rank of lieutenant general. He died in 1971.

Lieutenant Colonel Raymond L. Murray was promoted to the rank of full colonel in January 1951 in recognition of his stellar leadership during the Chosin operation. Murray rotated to the States in 1951 and served at the Marine Barracks in Washington, DC; in Quantico, Virginia; and at California's Camp Pendleton, where he was promoted to brigadier general in 1959. He was promoted to major general in 1967 when he became deputy commander of the 3rd Marine Amphibious Force in Vietnam. Murray retired in 1968 and died in 2004.

Colonel Homer Litzenberg won the Navy Cross for his leadership of the 7th Marine Regiment during the Chosin Reservoir operation. He returned to the Marine Corps headquarters in Washington, DC, in April 1951 and was promoted to brigadier general. Litzenberg later served as assistant commander of the 3rd Marine Division in Japan and in 1954 was named inspector general of the Marine Corps and promoted to major general. Litzenberg returned to Korea in 1957 as senior member of the UN Command component of the Military Armistice Commission at Panmunjom. He retired in 1959 with the rank of lieutenant general and died in 1963.

General Douglas MacArthur withdrew from public life after 1951 and spent the remainder of his life writing his memoirs, which he completed just before his death in April 1964.

Korea

Violations of the cease-fire began immediately after the armistice was signed in July 1953 and continued for years, with the North Koreans firing on UN patrols and staging raids across the demilitarized zone. The UN Command protested, but the Communists denied committing the violations, leaving the United Nations with the option of tolerating them or reopening the war.

The governments in Seoul and Pyongyang began the daunting task of rebuilding a land devastated by war. Syngman Rhee had been reelected to a four-year term as president of South Korea in 1952, and Kim Il-sung had a firm grip on power in North Korea. Both governments had outside assistance in their recoveries, the United States in the South and the Soviet Union and China in the North.

By 1960, American economic aid had totaled $3.2 billion, most of it spent on relief programs. Little was invested in the economy, and South Korea remained as poor as it had been before the conflict began. Its military budget hindered economic development. Maintaining a 500,000-strong army consumed most of the South Korean budget and drained the economy.

The Soviet Union and China provided North Korea with modern military weapons as well as material assistance, heavy equipment, and skilled technicians, allowing the country to concentrate on heavy industry and production. With North Korea's educational system training engineers and technicians, fuel, metal, machine, and chemical industries developed. By 1957, industrial output had returned to 1949 levels.

North Korea's weakness was food production. More people worked in manufacturing than in agriculture, and farmworkers were expected to operate like assembly-line operators and lived in much worse conditions. Farmworkers who failed to meet the quotas needed to feed the nation went hungry. The standard of living remained low. North Korea exported more than it imported and invested the profits to increase its capacity for growth, and new cities sprang up. But there was a lack of freedom. The state directed workers' lives, politics, and careers. The population remained stable at 10,000,000.

In 1956, Soviet leader Nikita Khrushchev began a de-Stalinization program, summoned Kim to Moscow, and denounced him for failing to conform to the new politics. Kim had already begun preparing to eliminate the Soviet and Chinese factions from his Workers' Congress, and he returned to Pyongyang and purged his opponents, playing the Soviet Union and China against each other to ensure his survival and maintain political stability. Chinese troops withdrew from North Korea in October 1958.

Rhee also began a purge after the armistice was concluded, targeting first those who had collaborated with the invaders and then his many political enemies. American leaders feared that Rhee was going too far, but he was a valuable ally and the United States did not interfere. He won another four-year term in 1956 and became even more autocratic. His people saw him as corrupt and out of touch.

At the time of the 1960 elections, South Korea's economy remained stagnant, and the people wanted change, but Rhee's government claimed to have received 90 percent of the vote. Students protesting the election fraud staged demonstrations in major cities, winning popular support,

and army commanders refused to follow orders to suppress the dissent-
ers. When the National Assembly turned against him, Rhee resigned and
fled to exile in Hawaii.

In 1961, after thirteen months of political instability, General Park
Chung-hee led a coup and took control of the South Korean government. Park emphasized technical education, and the country experienced a period of rapid export-led economic growth enforced by
political repression.

When the United States became involved in the Vietnam War, South
Korea sent 55,000 soldiers. Kim responded by calling for a "diversionary
attack" to help the North Vietnamese and by stepping up its propaganda
campaign with radio broadcasts aimed at South Korea and renewed
harassment of the UN Command along the DMZ.

In 1966, North Korea provoked about fifty incidents and truce violations, a number that topped six hundred over the following year. The
actions included firing across the DMZ, ambushing patrols, and sending
saboteurs south by land and sea. In January 1968, North Korean guerrillas
attacked the South Korean presidential palace in an attempt to assassinate
Park. Two Americans were killed and five wounded. The UN Command
ordered all its forces on full alert.

Three days after the assassination attempt, North Korea got a major
propaganda boost when the country's naval forces seized the USS *Pueblo*,
an intelligence-gathering vessel in international waters off the coast of
North Korea. The United States already had a half million troops in
Vietnam and wanted to avoid a new conflict in Korea. The United States
sent eighty jet planes to South Korea and increased US naval forces with
thirty-five additional ships. The nuclear aircraft carrier USS *Enterprise*
remained on patrol off the North Korean coast. On December 22, 1968,
after the United States signed a statement of guilt, the *Pueblo*'s eighty-
two surviving crewmen and the body of one killed during the seizure
were released.

For two decades after the armistice, North and South Korea did not
publicly seek to negotiate with each other. Secret, high-level contacts led
to a July 1972 North-South Joint Statement that established principles for
working toward peaceful reunification. The talks led nowhere, however,
and in 1973 South Korea, declared that the two Koreas should seek separate
memberships in international organizations.

In 1979, General Park was assassinated. General Chun Doo-hwan seized power, ruling until 1987, when Roh Tae-woo won election as president. The country's politics stabilized. In 1988, South Korea hosted the Olympic Games, providing a boost to the country's global image and economy. South Korea became a member of the United Nations in 1991.

In the late 1990s, President Kim Dae-jung initiated the Sunshine Policy for engagement with North Korea. The two countries held a summit in Pyongyang, and though nothing of note was achieved, Kim received the 2000 Nobel Peace Prize for his efforts.

South Korea's electronics and automobile industries prospered as the century drew to a close, helping the country become an economic power in Asia. North Korea, in contrast, began a period of economic decline and almost collapsed when the Soviet Union began its breakup in 1991. Kim Il-sung died in 1994 and was succeeded by his son, Kim Jong-il, who focused on strengthening the military. Foreign experts believed it was a strategy to discourage coup attempts. Flooding across North Korea in the mid-1990s deepened the economic crisis, and widespread famine resulted in more than 400,000 deaths, forcing the government to accept food assistance from the United Nations. Food shortages and threats of famine have continued over the next three decades.

In the mid-1990s, North Korea launched efforts to gain nuclear weapons, carrying out its first nuclear test in 2006. Kim Jong-un took the reins of power after his father's death in 2011 and has continued building North Korea's nuclear arsenal, making the country an outsider in international affairs and subjecting it to sanctions by both the United States and the United Nations.

The Marine Corps

When the armistice went into effect, the 1st Marine Division maintained its position on what was now the DMZ. The division remained in Korea until it returned to Camp Pendleton, California, in 1955. One battalion was deployed to Guantanamo Bay for two months during the 1962 Cuban Missile Crisis. The division did not return to combat until it was sent to Vietnam in March 1966. It remained there until 1971.

The 1st Division participated in various rescue and recovery operations before being sent to Saudi Arabia in 1990 to provide the ground force elements of the Marine Expeditionary Force against the Iraqi threat. It fought in Operation Desert Storm in 1991 and served during the wars in Iraq beginning in 2003 and in Afghanistan beginning in 2012.

In 1952, the secretary of defense agreed that the commandant of the Marine Corps would sit with the Joint Chiefs of Staff on all matters that involved the Corps.[9] In practice, the commandant participated in almost every meeting of the Joint Chiefs, and in 1977, under President Jimmy Carter, the commandant became a permanent member of the group.

Once a Marine

Many veterans of the Korean War suffered from what came to be known as posttraumatic stress disorder. Bill Smith, for example, spent the rest of his life haunted by terrible nightmares about Korea. But Waller King had much better memories of the war. He had received five battle stars, the Combat Action Ribbon, the United Nations Korean Service Medal with five stars, the National Defense Service Medal, the Republic of Korea War Service Medal, and the Presidential Unit Citation. In addition, Waller focused primarily on his family and his career.

Waller became active with the Marine Corps League in Memphis, becoming a charter member of Singleton Detachment #476 and serving as its commandant for eight years. In 2003 Waller helped Marine veteran Paul Savage finally receive the Purple Heart he had earned during the Chosin Reservoir operation but had refused to accept while recovering in a Tokyo hospital "because he wanted it presented by a Marine."[10]

Waller established contacts with the Korean community in Memphis and led the drive to fund a monument honoring the 144 Memphis men who died in Korea. As a result of those efforts, he was contacted by Thomas Sorensen, a Korean War veteran from Nebraska who was seeking information on Eddie Gomez because the Omaha school system was naming an elementary school after Gomez; a street had already been named in his honor.

The May 27, 2007, Korean War Memorial dedication at Memphis's Overton Park drew several hundred people. Retired Marine major general Al Harvey, native of Brandon, Mississippi, presided over the dedication; Lee Tae-sik, the Korean ambassador to the United States, made the acceptance speech; and John Keyes, Tennessee's veterans affairs commissioner, was the main speaker. Waller was recognized for his leadership in bringing about the monument. Waller subsequently remained active in area veterans' activities, receiving recognition from the US Marine Corps and the Marine Corps League and twice being honored as Tennessee's Marine of the Year. In 2011, he was inducted into the All-American Football Association for his outstanding play at Mississippi College.

Around this time Waller compiled a manuscript, "Marines in Korea," that included a twenty-eight-page narrative of his experiences in Korea that he wrote while traveling home in March 1952. He added photographs, newspaper clippings on Joe and Homer as well as letters they wrote home, combat statistics, and information on the Overton Park project. Waller made his "Marines in Korea" available to other veterans and to their friends and families. Judge Henry Lackey, Joe Albritton's cousin, received a copy.

Waller's support of the Marine Corps took a new direction when Sam Gore, an art professor at Mississippi College, proposed that Clinton erect a monument to honor veterans of all wars. The college had a stone marker commemorating the Mississippi College Rifles' service during the Civil War, but Clinton had no markers or monuments to celebrate the service of veterans in America's other wars. Gore was familiar with the story of how Joe Albritton retrieved Homer Ainsworth's body and suggested that he could create a sculpture of the two men that would epitomize "compassionate comradeship."[11]

About 2009, Gore created a fifteen-inch prototype and used it to persuade Clinton mayor Rosemary Aultman to back the idea. Gore's next stop was Jacqueline Tharp, the director of the Clinton Visitor Center off the Natchez Trace, where Gore proposed placing the sculpture. Tharp eventually embraced Gore's vision and recruited Aultman to serve as cochair of the monument project.[12]

Gore started work on a clay prototype of the sculpture, using two Army reservists, one carrying the other on his shoulder, as his models but making the faces generic to represent all veterans. Gore finished the clay figures in the summer of 2011.

John King Jr. put Gore in touch with Waller. Gore and Tharp delivered the clay model to the Lugar Bronze Foundry in Eads, Tennessee, in August 2011, and had their initial meeting with Waller, who lived nearby and watched the final steps in the bronze casting, thinking back to his childhood, high school, and boot camp days with Joe and Homer. *Fallen Comrade* was unveiled on Veterans Day 2012. Several hundred spectators gathered outdoors at the Visitor Center on a beautiful but chilly Sunday afternoon under a cloudless sky. Veterans of the Vietnam War, the Gulf War, and the operations in Afghanistan and Iraq attended in uniform. A small number of World War II and Korean War veterans were also present, as were US representative Tim Harper; Philip Gunn, Speaker of the Mississippi House of Representatives; and county and city officials. Dick Albritton Jr. and John King Jr. and Bettye King were also there.

Aultman presided over the ceremony, and Waller King gave a passionate presentation on the US military and the sacrifices of those who had given their lives for the country. Gore and his grandson, Sam Gearhart, who had helped create the sculpture, then removed the covering from *Fallen Comrade*.

Fallen Comrade provoked emotion among travelers who stopped at the Clinton Visitors Center, and Gore made replicas of the sculpture that were placed at Homer's and Joe's grave sites.

In 2014, Lackey visited the monument. Although Gore envisioned *Fallen Comrade* as an "interpretation of compassion and comradeship," Waller, Lackey, and many others saw it as Joe carrying Homer from the battlefield. Lackey described his reaction in a letter to Waller:

> There was no one else outside and I walked to the statue of Joe and Homer, reached up and caressed Joe's hand which held his weapon and the tears began to flow. Came home and re-read your tribute to Joe and your expression of love for him and our country, your sacrifice and their ultimate sacrifice and was again overwhelmed. When I remember Joe my mind is flooded with what an energetic, resourceful and fearless leader he was. Had he lived a normal lifetime I feel certain he would have been recognized for his accomplishments.[13]

Henry Lackey's sad thoughts and words are shared by everyone who has lost a loved one before their time and wondered what might have been.

ACKNOWLEDGMENTS

This book originated with a request from Stephanie Tracy of the *Clinton Courier* that I write an article on the two replicas of the *Fallen Comrade* monument that were being placed at Homer Ainsworth's and Joe Albritton's grave sites in the Clinton cemetery. While gathering background material on the two men, I contacted George Waller King, who shared tales about growing up with them. I realized that there was a story to tell about the three young men from Clinton who went to Korea in 1951, and Waller agreed.

Waller put me in contact with Homer and Joe's friends and families. Betty Jo Connolly Demoney, John King and Bettye Shores King, Bobby Hannah, Baylus Richard Albritton Jr., Tom McMahon, Henry Lackey, Elwood Ratliff, and Bill Barnett all shared memories through either interviews or emails. Waller also shared his unpublished account of his time overseas, "Marines in Korea," as well as letters he wrote while in Korea.

I offer special thanks to Waller's son, Clay King, and to Virginia Sharp Ganas, daughter of George Sharp and Peggy Albritton Sharp, for providing family photographs. Virginia Ganas provided additional information on her parents' lives after the war. I am grateful to Margaret Anne Black for the use of George Black's photographs; to James D. McBrayer for his photograph of the Fallen Comrade Memorial; to Judy Gore Gearhart for permission to use Dr. Samuel M. Gore's sketch of the memorial; to Lieutenant Colonel Cliff Rushing, USMC (Ret.), for assistance with Marine terminology and organization; and to Ben Ivey, Mississippi College Art Department, for drawing the maps.

Jim Nicholson's book, *George-3-7th Marines*, and interviews provided personal recollections and details about Joe Albritton and George Company. The book—a collection of personal, sometimes graphic reminiscences of men who served in George Company—is illustrated with many of Joe's photographs.

Reference librarians Nyma Blakersby of the Jackson-Hinds Library System and Hope Smith of the Mississippi College Library surmounted the challenges created by the COVID-19 pandemic, going the extra mile to ensure that I received the resources needed for this book.

At the University Press of Mississippi, Emily Bandy, Valerie Jones, Joey Brown, Michael Martella, and Ellen Goldlust provided guidance, assistance, and advice throughout the project.

Former Millsaps College librarian Tom Henderson assisted with photographs, editing, fact-checking, and preparing the final manuscript.

Finally, I thank my wife, Ann Howell, for her support and encouragement during three years of research and writing. She has been the essential presence in maintaining a happy home and keeping me on track, and since I suffered a stroke in 2021, Ann has been my guardian angel and caretaker.

—Walter Howell

NOTES

Chapter 1: The Backstory

1. For the history of the town of Clinton and Mississippi College from 1900 to 1950, see Howell, *Town and Gown*, 205–84.

2. *Jackson Clarion-Ledger*, August 14, 1940, p. 3.

3. Ratliff, interview.

4. Henry Lackey, email to author, January 14, 2016.

5. Demoney, interview; Waller King, interview; McMahon, interview.

6. Bettye Shores King, interview; Waller King, interview.

7. Demoney, interview.

8. George Waller King, interview.

9. Ratliff, interview, 2018.

10. George Waller King, interview.

11. George Waller King, interview.

12. Krulak, *First to Fight*, 34.

13. Truman, *Memoirs*, 2:47; Krulak, *First to Fight*, 31, 34.

14. Krulak, *First to Fight*, 35.

15. Bartlett and Sweetman, *Leathernecks*, 305.

16. Krulak, *First to Fight*, 49.

17. Bartlett and Sweetman, *Leathernecks*, 306.

18. Langley, *Inchon Landing*, 54; Krulak, *First to Fight*, 71.

19. Krulak, *First to Fight*, 121.

20. Krulak, *First to Fight*, 122.

21. Krulak, *First to Fight*, 122; "Marine Corps Fiscal Year End Strengths, 1798–2015," *Marine Corps University*, https://www.usmcu.edu/Research/Marine-Corps-History -Division/Research-Tools-Facts-and-Figures/End-Strengths/ (accessed October 22, 2023).

22. *Miami News*, September 10, 1950, p. 2D; *New York Daily News*, November 9, 1950, p. 87.

23. Bartlett and Sweetman, *Leathernecks*, 305.

24. Toland, *In Mortal Combat*, 15.

25. Bevin Alexander, *Korea*, 11.

26. Toland, *In Mortal Combat*, 16–17.

27. Oberdorfer, *Two Koreas*, 3–11

28. Bradley, interview.

29. Spanier, *Truman-MacArthur Controversy*, 24–25.

30. Toland, *In Mortal Combat*, 29.

31. Toland, *In Mortal Combat*, 29.

32. Toland, *In Mortal Combat*, 32.

33. Resolution in Tucker, *Encyclopedia*, 3:869; Tucker, *Encyclopedia*, 3:871.

Chapter 2: American Intervention, June–August 1950

1. Bevin Alexander, *Korea*, 42.

2. Toland, *In Mortal Combat*, 63.

3. Tucker, *Encyclopedia*, 3:874.

4. Quoted in Hastings, *Korean War*, 60.

5. Toland, *In Mortal Combat*, 52–53.

6. Krulak, *First to Fight*, 123–24.

7. Krulak, *First to Fight*, 125; Montross and Canzona, *Inchon-Seoul Operation*, 10.

8. Bevin Alexander, *Korea*, 55–56; Toland, *In Mortal Combat*, 77–85.

9. See, for example, *St. Louis Post-Dispatch*, June 13, 1951, p. 16C.

10. Bevin Alexander, *Korea*, 63–67.

11. Bevin Alexander, *Korea*, 69.

12. Bevin Alexander, *Korea*, 104–6; Blair, *Forgotten War*, 136–39; Dean, *General Dean's Story*, 33–52.

13. Bevin Alexander, *Korea*, 107.

14. Bevin Alexander, *Korea*, 108.

15. Bevin Alexander, *Korea*, 108–10.

16. Joseph Alexander, *Fellowship of Valor*, 255; Montross and Canzona, *Inchon-Seoul Operation*, 22, 25.

17. *Clinton News*, June 13, 1951, p. 1.

18. Chapin, *Fire Brigade*, 3, 13.

19. *Time*, August 14, 1950, p. 16.

20. Leckie, *Conflict*, 107–8.

21. Chapin, *Fire Brigade*, 35.

22. Bevin Alexander, *Korea*, 138–40; Chapin, *Fire Brigade*, 48.

23. Montross and Canzona, *Inchon-Seoul Operation*, 38–39.

24. Krulak, *First to Fight*, 133–34.

25. Chapin, *Fire Brigade*, 51.

26. Collins, *War in Peacetime*, 121–26.

27. Chapin, *Fire Brigade*, 52.

28. Chapin, *Fire Brigade*, 61.

29. Toland, *In Mortal Combat*, 150.

30. Toland, *In Mortal Combat*, 150.

31. Krulak, *First to Fight*, 56.

32. Krulak, *First to Fight*, 56–57; *Time*, September 18, 1950, p. 25.

33. Bevin Alexander, *Korea*, 164–65.

34. Blair, *Forgotten War*, 184.

35. Blair, *Forgotten War*, 185.

36. Blair, *Forgotten War*, 185–87.

37. Tucker, *Encyclopedia*, 3:886–87.

38. Bevin Alexander, *Korea*, 178

39. Bevin Alexander, *Korea*, 178–79.

40. *Jackson Clarion-Ledger*, August 10, 1950, p. 1.

41. *Jackson Clarion-Ledger*, September 2, 1950, p. 1.

42. George Waller King, interview.

Chapter 3: Inchon and Seoul, September–October 1950

1. Krulak, *First to Fight*, 160.

2. Waller King, "Marines in Korea" (unpublished manuscript, ca. 2015), 22.

3. *Clinton News*, January 5, 1951, p. 1.

4. Leckie, *Conflict*, 130–31.

5. *Time*, September 25, 1950, p. 31; Montross and Canzona, *Inchon-Seoul Operation*, 17–18.

6. Krulak, *First to Fight*, 135.

7. Krulak, *First to Fight*, 135.

8. Bevin Alexander, *Korea*, 196.

9. Krulak, *First to Fight*, 138.

10. Montross and Canzona, *Inchon-Seoul Operation*, 87–96.

11. Leckie, *Conflict*, 140–41.

12. Leckie, *Conflict*, 101–6.

13. Leckie, *Conflict*, 143–44.

14. Bevin Alexander, *Korea*, 204–5.

15. Joseph H. Alexander, *Fellowship of Valor*, 276; Montross and Canzona, *Inchon-Seoul Operation*, 152.

16. Bevin Alexander, *Korea*, 205.

17. Montross and Canzona, *Inchon-Seoul Operation*, 187–94.

18. Montross and Canzona, *Inchon-Seoul Operation*, 219; Cerasini, *Heroes*, 290–91; Joseph H. Alexander, *Fellowship of Valor*, 277.

19. Montross and Canzona, *Inchon-Seoul Operation*, 197–98.

20. Montross and Canzona, *Inchon-Seoul Operation*, 201.

21. Bevin Alexander, *Korea*, 219.

22. Bevin Alexander, *Korea*, 219–27.

23. Toland, *In Mortal Combat*, 215.

24. Blair, *Forgotten War*, 289–90; Toland, *In Mortal Combat*, 215–16; Halberstam, *Coldest Winter*, 427–30.

25. Halberstam, *Coldest Winter*, 531.

26. Collins, *War in Peacetime*, 140; Leckie, *Conflict*, 150.

27. Montross and Canzona, *Inchon-Seoul Operation*, 271 80.

28. Toland, *In Mortal Combat*, 225; Montross and Canzona, *Inchon-Seoul Operation*, 283–84.

29. Toland, *In Mortal Combat*, 227.

30. Toland, *In Mortal Combat*, 227–28.

31. Joseph Alexander, *Battle of the Barricades*, 46.

32. Leckie, *Conflict*, 152–53; Toland, *In Mortal Combat*, 230.

33. MacArthur, *Reminiscences*, 357.

34. Montross and Canzona, *Inchon-Seoul Operation*, 321, 333.

35. Rees, *Korea*, 96.

36. Bevin Alexander, *Korea*, 218.

37. Montross and Canzona, *Inchon-Seoul Operation*, 295–96.

38. Bevin Alexander, *Korea*, 230–35.

39. Bevin Alexander, *Korea*, 234–37.

40. Bevin Alexander, *Korea*, 237.

41. Bevin Alexander, *Korea*, 243.

42. Bevin Alexander, *Korea*, 243–44.

43. Spanier, *Truman-MacArthur Controversy*, 87–88.

44. Spanier, *Truman-MacArthur Controversy*, 107; Collins, *War in Peacetime*, 149–55; McCullough, *Truman*, 800–801.

45. Spanier, *Truman-MacArthur Controversy*, 106.

46. McCullough, *Truman*, 801–3.

47. McCullough, *Truman*, 803–6.

48. Quoted in Blair, *Forgotten War*, 348.

49. MacArthur, *Reminiscences*, 362–63.

50. Middleton, *Compact History*, 129.

Chapter 4: Chinese Intervention, October–November 1950

1. Stueck, *Korean War*, 106.

2. Blair, *Forgotten War*, 350.

3. Quoted in Blair, *Forgotten War*, 377.

4. Collins, *War in Peacetime*, 198–99; Blair, *Forgotten War*, 393.

5. Blair, *Forgotten War*, 394; Collins, *War in Peacetime*, 200–201.

6. MacArthur, *Reminiscences*, 420–21.

7. Blair, *Forgotten War*, 396

8. James, *Years of MacArthur*, 518–24.

9. James, *Years of MacArthur*, 525–26.

10. Collins, *War in Peacetime*, 211.

11. Collins, *War in Peacetime*, 212–13.

12. Montross and Canzona, *Chosin Reservoir Campaign*, 43–44; Blair, *Forgotten War*, 387–88.

13. Russ, *Breakout*, 17; Halberstam, *Coldest Winter*, 429.

14. Russ, *Breakout*, 59.

15. Russ, *Breakout*, 60.

16. Russ, *Breakout*, 25; Montross and Canzona, *Chosin Reservoir Campaign*, 98.

17. Montross and Canzona, *Chosin Reservoir Campaign*, 100–102.

18. Montross and Canzona, *Chosin Reservoir Campaign*, 103–6.

19. Montross and Canzona, *Chosin Reservoir Campaign*, 106–14,

20. Montross and Canzona, *Chosin Reservoir Campaign*, 119–20.

21. *Life*, December 11, 1950, p. 35; Blair, *Forgotten War*, 417–18.

22. Montross and Canzona, *Chosin Reservoir Campaign*, 121–23.

23. Montross and Canzona, *Chosin Reservoir Campaign*, 123–24.

24. Quoted in Russ, *Breakout*, 72; Halberstam, *Coldest Winter*, 433.

25. Russ, *Breakout*, 134.

26. Quoted in Russ, *Breakout*, 71; Halberstam, *Coldest Winter*, 433.

27. Halberstam, *Coldest Winter*, 434–35.

28. Demoney to the author, July 7, 2018; Montross and Canzona, *Chosin Reservoir Campaign*, 143–44; 11th Marine Regiment, Historical Diary, November 1950, RG 127: Records of the US Marine Corps, National Archives and Records Administration, College Park, MD. The historical diaries are available online at the Korean War Project, https://www.koreanwar.org/.

29. Blair, *Forgotten War*, 423.

30. Blair, *Forgotten War*, 473–81.

31. Blair, *Forgotten War*, 483–94.

32. Quoted in Collins, *War in Peacetime*, 220–21.

33. Blair, *Forgotten War*, 401–2.

34. Acheson, *Present at the Creation*, 466.

35. Halberstam, *Coldest Winter*, 478; Bevin Alexander, *Korea*, 371.

36. Blair, *Forgotten War*, 522–23.

37. Halberstam, *Coldest Winter*, 482–83.

38. Collins, *War in Peacetime*, 231–35.

Chapter 5: The Saga of the Chosin Reservoir, November–December 1950

1. Russ, *Breakout*, 85.

2. Halberstam, *Coldest Winter*, 438–39.

3. Halberstam, *Coldest Winter*, 437–38.

4. Russ, *Breakout*, 113–14.

5. Montross and Canzona, *Chosin Reservoir Campaign*, 154–75.

6. Fehrenbach, *This Kind of War*, 360.

7. Montross and Canzona, *Chosin Reservoir Campaign*, 180–82.

8. Montross and Canzona, *Chosin Reservoir Campaign*, 182–90.

9. Montross and Canzona, *Chosin Reservoir Campaign*, 190–92.

10. Montross and Canzona, *Chosin Reservoir Campaign*, 205–20.

11. Russ, *Breakout*, 196; Sandler, *Korean War*, 122; Halberstam, *Coldest Winter*, 439; Fehrenbach, *This Kind of War*, 360.

12. Russ, *Breakout*, 196; Halberstam, *Coldest Winter*, 780.

13. For the challenges Navy medics experienced because of the severe cold, see Bevin Alexander, *Korea*, 349.

14. *Life*, February 5, 1951, pp. 82–84.

15. Warren, *American Spartans*, 164.

16. Russ, *Breakout*, 166–67.

17. Russ, *Breakout*, 256.

18. Montross and Canzona, *Chosin Reservoir Campaign*, 226–32.

19. Russ, *Breakout*, 243; Montross and Canzona, *Chosin Reservoir Campaign*,, 232–34.

20. Blair, *Forgotten War*, 510–11.

21. Montross and Canzona, *Chosin Reservoir Campaign*, 249–54.

22. Montross and Canzona, *Chosin Reservoir Campaign*, 194–95.

23. Russ, *Breakout*, 259–60.

24. Montross and Canzona, *Chosin Reservoir Campaign*, 259–61.

25. Montross and Canzona, *Chosin Reservoir Campaign*, 245–46.

26. Russ, *Breakout*, 340.

27. Blair, *Forgotten War*, 514–15.

28. Blair, *Forgotten War*, 518–19.

29. Blair, *Forgotten War*, 515–18.

30. Blair, *Forgotten War*, 521.

31. Blair, *Forgotten War*, 519–20.

32. Demoney, interview.

33. Montorss and Canzona, *Chosin Reservoir Campaign*, 263–65.

34. Russ, *Breakout*, 320.

35. Montross and Canzona, *Chosin Reservoir Campaign*, 275.

36. Blair, *Forgotten War*, 534.

37. Montross and Canzona, *Chosin Reservoir Campaign*, 274–75, 278.

38. Montross and Canzona, *Chosin Reservoir Campaign*, 280–82, 322–23; Blair, *Forgotten War*, 537; Russ, *Breakout*, 355.

39. Montross and Canzona, *Chosin Reservoir Campaign*, 286–87; Jackson, *Air War over Korea*, 76.

40. Montross and Canzona, *Chosin Reservoir Campaign*, 301–3; Joseph H. Alexander, *Fellowship of Valor*, 283.

41. Montross and Canzona, *Chosin Reservoir Campaign*, 297–98.

42. Montross and Canzona, *Chosin Reservoir Campaign*, 303.

43. Russ, *Breakout*, 365.

44. Jackson, *Air War over Korea*, 75–76; Russ, *Breakout*, 257–59.

45. Montross and Canzona, *Chosin Reservoir Campaign*, 309–12.

46. Montross and Canzona, *Chosin Reservoir Campaign*, 319.

47. Russ, *Breakout*, 406–11; Montross and Canzona, *Chosin Reservoir Campaign*, 314–16.

48. Marguerite Higgins, *War in Korea*, 195–96; Montross and Canzona, *Chosin Reservoir Campaign*, 305–32; Simons, *Frozen Chosin*, 106; Russ *Breakout*, 398.

49. Marguerite Higgins, *War in Korea*, 197; Montross and Canzona, *Chosin Reservoir Campaign*, 333; *Time*, December 18, 1950, pp. 18–19.

50. Quoted in Joseph H. Alexander, *Fellowship of Valor*, 300.

51. *Clinton News*, July 13, 1951, p. 1.

52. Demoney, interview; *Clinton News*, December 29, 1950, p. 1.

53. *Jackson Clarion-Ledger*, March 4, 1951, pp. 3–13; *Clinton News*, January 5, 1951, p. 3.

54. Russ, *Breakout*, 343–46; Patch, "Blue Star Turned to Gold."

Chapter 6: An Entirely New War, December 1950–April 1951

1. *Time*, December 11, 1950, p. 17; *Newsweek*, December 11, 1950, p. 11.

2. Bevin Alexander, *Korea*, 375–76.

3. Tucker, *Encyclopedia*, 2:495, 657.

4. *Life*, December 11, 1950, p. 46.

5. Montross, Kuokka, and Hicks, *East-Central Front*, 5–6.

6. *Time*, January 1, 1951, pp. 16–23.

7. Blair, *Forgotten War*, 566–68.

8. Leckie, *Conflict*, 237–38.

9. Ridgway, *Korean War*, 85–86, 264–65.

10. Quoted in Blair, *Forgotten War*, 570–71.

11. Blair, *Forgotten War*, 574.

12. Leckie, *Conflict*, 240.

13. Blair, *Forgotten War*, 572.

14. Montrose, Kuokka, and Hicks, *East-Central Front*, 42–44; Blair, *Forgotten War*, 579.

15. Montrose, Kuokka, and Hicks, *East-Central Front*, 48, 51–53.

16. Blair, *Forgotten War*, 687–96.

17. Montross, Kuokka, and Hicks, *East-Central Front*, 163.

18. Bevin Alexander, *Korea*, 396.

19. Blair, *Forgotten War*, 718.

20. Blair, *Forgotten War*, 731–32; Montross, Kuokka, and Hicks, *East-Central Front*, 82, 95.

21. Montross, Kuokka, and Hicks, *East-Central Front*, 94–95.

22. Leckie, *Conflict*, 250–52.

23. Leckie, *Conflict*, 253–55; Tucker, *Encyclopedia*, 3:949–50.

24. Blair, *Forgotten War*, 758–61; Tucker, *Encyclopedia*, 3:957; Spanier, *Truman-MacArthur Controversy*, 199–203.

25. Collins, *War in Peacetime*, 269–70; Blair, *Forgotten War*, 766–68; Tucker, *Encyclopedia*, 3:957–58.

26. Collins, *War in Peacetime*, 270–71.

27. Blair, *Forgotten War*, 768; Tucker, *Encyclopedia*, 3:957.

28. Blair, *Forgotten War*, 783; Tucker, *Encyclopedia*, 3:957.

29. Blair, *Forgotten War*, 785–86.

30. Blair, *Forgotten War*, 784–87; Spanier, *Truman-MacArthur Controversy*, 205–7.

31. Blair, *Forgotten War*, 787–88.

32. Collins, *War in Peacetime*, 285.

33. Blair, *Forgotten War*, 788.

34. Blair, *Forgotten War*, 789, 794–95.

35. Blair, *Forgotten War*, 794–95.

36. McCullough, *Truman*, 843–56; Whelan, *Drawing the Line*, 301–2.

37. Blair, *Forgotten War*, 796–97.

38. Blair, *Forgotten War*, 788–89, 794–97.

39. Reischauer, *Japanese Today*, 104–5; Blair, *Forgotten War*, 809.

40. Blair, *Forgotten War*, 905–7.

41. Spanier, *Truman-MacArthur Controversy*, 213–15.

42. McCullough, *Truman*, 851–52.

43. Spanier, *Truman-MacArthur Controversy*, 221–22.

44. Spanier, *Truman-MacArthur Controversy*, 248–56.

45. Spanier, *Truman-MacArthur Controversy*, 275.

46. Maihafer, *From the Hudson to the Yalu*, 229.

Chapter 7: Fallen Comrade, April–June 1951

1. Homer Ainsworth to Ralph Marston, February 7, 1951, copy in possession of author.

2. Homer Ainsworth to Ralph Marston, February 7, 1951, copy in possession of author; *Clinton News*, February 2, 1951, p. 1, February 9, 1951, p. 1.

3. *Clinton News*, February 16, 1951, p. 1.

4. George Waller King to John King, n.d., copy in possession of author.

5. *Clinton News*, July 3, 2008, pp. 1, 6, March 23, 1951, p. 3.

6. Demoney, interview.

7. Waller King, "Marines in Korea," 1–3.

8. Nicholson, *George-3-7th Marines*, 145.

9. Headquarters and Services Company, 1st Marine Regiment, Muster Roll, April 1951, Marine Corps Muster Rolls, 1798–1958, RG 127: Records of the US Marine Corps, National Archives and Records Administration, College Park, MD.

10. Waller King, "Marines in Korea," 6–8.

11. Nicholson, *George-3-7th Marines*, 143.

12. Blair, *Forgotten War*, 822–31; Montross, Kuokka, and Hicks, *East-Central Front*, 104–7.

13. Montross, Kuokka, and Hicks, *East-Central Front*, 108–12.

14. Montross, Kuokka, and Hicks, *East-Central Front*, 113–15.

15. Blair, *Forgotten War*, 851–52.

16. Montross, Kuokka, and Hicks, *East-Central Front*, 119

17. *Clinton News*, May 25, 1951, p. 2.

18. Nicholson, *George-3-7th Marines*, 143–45; Nicholson, interview.

19. Montross, Kuokka, and Hicks, *East-Central Front*, 114–15.

20. *Clinton News*, May 25, 1951, p. 2. See also *Jackson Clarion-Ledger*, May 21, 1951, pp. 1, 10.

21. Nicholson, *George-3-7th Marines*, 173–74.

22. Waller King, "Marines in Korea," 10–12.

23. Waller King, "Marines in Korea," 10–12; George Waller King interview.

24. Blair, *Forgotten War*, 842.

25. Blair, *Forgotten War*, 842.

26. 3/7 Daily Action Report, Historical Diary, May 4, 1951, RG 127: Records of the US Marine Corps, National Archives and Records Administration, College Park, MD.

27. Montross, Kuokka, and Hicks, *East-Central Front*, 123–25.

28. 3/7 Daily Action Report, Historical Diary, May 17, 1951, RG 127: Records of the US Marine Corps, National Archives and Records Administration, College Park, MD.

29. Montross, Kuokka, and Hicks, *East-Central Front*, 126; 3/7 Daily Action Report, Historical Diary, May 1951, RG 127: Records of the US Marine Corps, National Archives and Records Administration, College Park, MD; Nicholson, *George-3-7th Marines*, 195–96.

30. 3/7 Daily Action Report, Historical Diary, May 24, 26, 1951, RG 127: Records of the US Marine Corps, National Archives and Records Administration, College Park, MD.

31. Montross, Kuokka, and Hicks, *East-Central Front*, 133.

32. 3/7 Daily Action Report, Historical Diary, May 1951, RG 127: Records of the US Marine Corps, National Archives and Records Administration, College Park, MD.

33. Ridgway, *Korean War*, 188; Blair, *Forgotten War*, 899–900.

34. Blair, *Forgotten War*, 916–17.

35. George Waller King, interview; *Clinton News*, June 29, 1951, p. 1.

36. Montross, Kuokka, and Hicks, *East-Central Front*, 146–47.

37. Montross, Kuokka, and Hicks, *East-Central Front*, 148–50.

38. Montross, Kuokka, and Hicks, *East-Central Front*, 151.

39. 3/7 Daily Action Report, Historical Diary, June 1951, RG 127: Records of the US Marine Corps, National Archives and Records Administration, College Park, MD; Montross, Kuokka, and Hicks, *East-Central Front*, 151; Nicholson, *George-3-7th Marines*, 222.

40. 3/7 Daily Action Report, Historical Diary, June 1951, RG 127: Records of the US Marine Corps, National Archives and Records Administration, College Park, MD; Nicholson, *George-3-7th Marines*, 222–24.

41. Nicholson, *George-3-7th Marines*, 224; Nicholson, interview.

42. *Clinton News*, July 20, 1951, p. 1.

43. *Clinton News*, June 29, 1951, p. 3.

44. G/3/7 Unit Diary, April 17, 1951, Marine Corps Muster Rolls, 1798–1958, RG 127: Records of the U. S. Marine Corps, National Archives and Records Administration,

College Park, MD; *Clinton News*, July 20, 1951, p 1; *Jackson Clarion-Ledger*, March 31, 1955, p. 2.

45. *Clinton News*, July 20, 1951, p. 1

46. *Clinton News*, November 9, 1951, p. 1; *Jackson Clarion-Ledger*, November 8, 1951, p. 3.

Chapter 8: The Fight for Hill 749, June–November 1951

1. Montross, Kuokka, and Hicks, *East-Central Front*, 153.

2. Bevin Alexander, *Korea*, 427.

3. Blair, *Forgotten War*, 925–27.

4. Blair, *Forgotten War*, 925–40.

5. Waller King, "Marines in Korea," 14.

6. Waller King, "Marines in Korea," 15.

7. Waller King, "Marines in Korea," 16–17.

8. Montross, Kuokka, and Hicks, *East-Central Front*, 158–60; Millett, *Drive North*, 24–28.

9. Ridgway, *Korean War*, 198–99; Blair, *Forgotten War*, 941–43.

10. Blair, *Forgotten War*, 942–43.

11. Waller King, "Marines in Korea," 18.

12. Waller King, "Marines in Korea," 19.

13. George Waller King to John King July 7, 1951 copy in possession of author.

14. George Waller King, interview; Headquarters and Service Company, 1st Marine Division, Muster Roll, April 30, 1951, Weapons Company, 1st Marine Division, Muster Roll, July 1951; Headquarters and Service Company, 1st Marine Division, Unit Diary, August 12, 1951; Marine Corps Muster Rolls, 1798–1958, RG 127: Records of the US Marine Corps, National Archives and Records Administration, College Park, MD.

15. Headquarters and Service Company, 3rd Batallion,7th Marine Division, Unit Diaries, September 15, December 31, 1951, Marine Corps Muster Rolls, 1798–1958, RG 127: Records of the US Marine Corps, National Archives and Records Administration, College Park, MD.

16. Montross, Kuokka, and Hicks, *East-Central Front*, 161–62.

17. Montross, Kuokka, and Hicks, *East-Central Front*, 163–64.

18. Blair, *Forgotten War*, 944–46.

19. Bevin Alexander, *Korea*, 440–42.

20. Bevin Alexander, *Korea*, 440–47.

21. Montross, Kuokka, and Hicks, *East-Central Front*, 162, 171–75.

22. 3/7 Daily Action Report, Historical Diary, August 31, 1951, RG 127: Records of the US Marine Corps, National Archives and Records Administration, College Park, MD; Montross, Kuokka, and Hicks, *East-Central Front*, 175–81; Nicholson, *George-3-7th Marines*, 267, 271.

23. 3/7 Daily Action Report, Historical Diary, September 12, 1951, RG 127: Records of the US Marine Corps, National Archives and Records Administration, College Park, MD.

24. Cerasini, *Heroes*, 310–11; 3/7 Daily Action Report, Historical Diary, September 1951, RG 127: Records of the US Marine Corps, National Archives and Records Administration, College Park, MD; Montross, Kuokka, and Hicks, *East-Central Front*, 184.

25. Waller King, "Marines in Korea," 20–22.

26. Montross, Kuokka, and Hicks, *East-Central Front*, 186–90.

27. Waller King, "Marines in Korea," 22–23; Cerasini, *Heroes*, 287.

28. Montross, Kuokka, and Hicks, *East-Central Front*, 193.

29. Montross, Kuokka, and Hicks, *East-Central Front*, 193–94.

30. Montross, Kuokka, and Hicks, *East-Central Front*, 190–94.

31. *Clinton News*, November 23, 1951, p. 1.

32. 2/5 Daily Action Report, Historical Diary, September 16, 17, 1951, RG 127: Records of the US Marine Corps, National Archives and Records Administration, College Park, MD.

33. *Clinton News*, November 23, 1951, p. 1.

34. 2/5 Daily Action Report, Historical Diary, September 18, 1951, RG 127: Records of the US Marine Corps, National Archives and Records Administration, College Park, MD.

35. Montross, Kuokka, and Hicks, *East-Central Front*, 196–98; 3/7 Daily Action Report, Historical Diary, November 1951, RG 127: Records of the US Marine Corps, National Archives and Records Administration, College Park, MD; Nicholson, *George-3-7th Marines*, 317–24.

36. Montross, Kuokka, and Hicks, *East-Central Front*, 178–80

37. Montross, Kuokka, and Hicks, *East-Central Front*, 199–203.

38. Montross, Kuokka, and Hicks, *East-Central Front*, 206–8.

39. Montross, Kuokka, and Hicks, *East-Central Front*, 208

40. Montross, Kuokka, and Hicks, *East-Central Front*, 210–12,

41. Waller King, "Marines in Korea," 21-b.

42. Blair, *Forgotten War*, 951.

43. Blair, *Forgotten War*, 955–60.

44. Toland, *In Mortal Combat*, 488–89.

45. Montross, Kuokka, and Hicks, *East-Central Front*, 220–21.

46. Maihafer, *From the Hudson to the Yalu*, 248.

47. 1st Marine Division Historical Diary, October 1951, RG 127: Records of the US Marine Corps, National Archives and Records Administration, College Park, MD.

48. Montross, Kuokka, and Hicks, *East-Central Front*, 212–13.

49. Montross, Kuokka, and Hicks, *East-Central Front*, 214.

50. Montross, Kuokka, and Hicks, *East-Central Front*, 214–15.

51. Waller King, "Marines in Korea," 24–25.

52. 3/7 Daily Action Report, Historical Diary, October 1951, RG 127: Records of the US Marine Corps, National Archives and Records Administration, College Park, MD.

53. 2/5 Daily Action Report, Historical Diary, October 1951, RG 127: Records of the US Marine Corps, National Archives and Records Administration, College Park, MD.

54. Montross, Kuokka, and Hicks, *East-Central Front*, 217–18

55. Montross, Kuokka and Hicks, *East-Central Front*, 219.

56 Nolan, *Run-Up to the Punchbowl*, 209.

57. 2/5 Daily Action Report, Historical Diary, November 11, 1951, RG 127: Records of the US Marine Corps, National Archives and Records Administration, College Park, MD. D/2/5 Unit Diary, October 11, November 11, November 17, 1951, Marine Corps Muster Rolls, 1798–1958, RG 127: Records of the US Marine Corps, National Archives and Records Administration, College Park, MD.

58. Nicholson, *George-3-7th Marines*, xix; Nicholson, interview.

59. *Jackson Clarion-Ledger*, December 11, 1955, sec. 4, pp. 1, 10.

Chapter 9: The Armistice, December 1951–July 1953

1. Waller King, "Marines in Korea," 60.

2. Montross, Kuokka, and Hicks, *East-Central Front*, 224–25.

3. George Sharp to D. O. Ellis, February 6, 1952, copy in possession of author; Headquarters Company, Headquarters Battalion, 1st Marine Division, Unit Diary, November 19, 1951, Marine Corps Muster Rolls, 1798–1958, RG 127: Records of the US Marine Corps, National Archives and Records Administration, College Park, MD.

4. Waller King, "Marines in Korea," 25.

5. Waller King, "Marines in Korea," 26.

6. Montross, Kuokka, and Hicks, *East-Central Front*, 237.

7. Blair, *Forgotten War*, 962–64.

8. Bevin Alexander, *Korea*, 457; Collins, *War in Peacetime*, 344.

9. Doyle, *Enemy in Our Hands*, 255–62; Bevin Alexander, *Korea*, 458–63; Collins, *War in Peacetime*, 344–47.

10. Clark, *From the Danube to the Yalu*, 70–73.

11. Clark, *From the Danube to the Yalu*, 105–9.

12. Montross, Kuokka, and Hicks, *East-Central Front*, 251–57.

13. Meid and Yingling, *Operations in West Korea*, 114–43; 1st Marine Division Command Diary, August 1952, RG 127: Records of the US Marine Corps, National Archives and Records Administration, College Park, MD.

14. Meid and Yingling, *Operations in West Korea*, 203–11.

15. Meid and Yingling, *Operations in West Korea*, 211–12, 230–31.

16. Blair, *Forgotten War*, 970–71.

17. Collins, *War in Peacetime*, 324–25; Clark, *From the Danube to the Yalu*, 233–39.

18. Tucker, *Encyclopedia*, 3:987–88; Bevin Alexander, *Korea*, 472–73.

19. Meid and Yingling, *Operations in West Korea*, 317–18.

20. Bevin Alexander, *Korea*, 475.

21. Clark, *From the Danube to the Yalu*, 268–69.

22. Clark, *From the Danube to the Yalu*, 263–64.

23. Bevin Alexander, *Korea*, 478–81.

24. Armistice agreement in Tucker, *Encyclopedia*, 3:1026–39.

25. Bevin Alexander, *Korea*, 482–83.

26. Bevin Alexander, *Korea*, 483; James Stueck, *Korean War*, 360–61.

Afterword

1. Waller King, "Marines in Korea," 12.

2. US Census Bureau, "Quick Facts: Clinton City, Mississippi," https://www.census.gov/quickfacts/fact/table/clintoncitymississippi,MS/RHI225222 (accessed October 22, 2023).

3. *Clinton News*, May 23, 1952, p. 3.

4. Nicholson, interview.

5. *Florida Times-Union*, September 11, 2011.

6. Elwood Franklin Ratliff Jr., *Find a Grave*, https://www.findagrave.com/memorial/214618933/elwood-franklin-ratliff (accessed October 22, 2023).

7. Measels, *Branch Baptist Church*, 31.

8. *Clinton News*, May 1, 2003, 1A, 4A.

9. Warren, *American Spartans*, 181.

10. *Memphis Commercial Appeal*, August 19, 2003, pp. DS3, DS5.

11. Tharp, *For Those Who Served*, 13.

12. Gore's original sketch for the monument is dated 2009; Jacque Tharp, email to author, May 11, 2020.

13. Tharp, *For Those Who Served*, 14; Henry Lackey, email to Waller King, October 2, 2014, copy in possession of author.

BIBLIOGRAPHY

Not all details in this book are specifically cited. Readers may find the bibliography useful for further study.

General Histories of the Korean War

Alexander, Bevin. *Korea: The First War We Lost*. New York: Hippocrene, 1986.

Berger, Carl. *The Korean Knot: A Military-Political History*. Philadelphia: University of Pennsylvania Press, 1957.

Blair, Clay. *The Forgotten War: America in Korea, 1950–1953*. New York: Times Books, 1987.

Brady, James. *The Coldest War: A Memoir of Korea*. New York: Dunne, 1990.

Cumings, Bruce. *The Korean War: A History*. New York: Modern Library, 2010.

Fehrenbach, T. R. *The Fight for Korea: From the War of 1950 to the Pueblo Incident*. New York: Grosset & Dunlap, 1969

Fehrenbach, T. R. *This Kind of War: The Classic Korean War History*. Washington, DC: Brassey's, 1994.

Goulden, Joseph C. *Korea, the Untold Story of the War*. New York: Times Books, 1982.

Hastings, Max. *The Korean War*. New York: Simon and Schuster, 2015.

Hoyt, Edwin P. *The Bloody Road to Panmunjom*. New York: Stein and Day, 1985.

Jackson, Robert. *Air War over Korea*. New York: Scribner's, 1973.

Langley, Michael. *Inchon Landing: MacArthur's Last Triumph*. New York: Times Books, 1979.

Leckie, Robert. *Conflict: The History of the Korean War, 1950–53*. New York: Putnam's, 1962.

Lee, Steven Hugh. *The Korean War*. New York: Longman, 2001.

Merrill, John. *Korea: The Peninsular Origins of the War*. Newark: University of Delaware Press, 1989.

Middleton, Harry J. *The Compact History of the Korean War*. New York: Hawthorn, 1965.

Rees, David, consultant ed. *Korea: The Limited War*. New York: St. Martin's, 1964.

Rees, David, consultant ed. *The Korean War: History and Tactics*. New York: Crescent, 1984.

Sandler, Stanley. *The Korean War: No Victors, No Vanquished*. Lexington: University
    Press of Kentucky, 1999.
Stokesbury, James L. *A Short History of the Korean War*. New York: Morrow, 1988.
Stone, I. F. *The Hidden History of the Korean War*. New York: Monthly Review Press, 1952.
Stueck, William. *The Korean War: An International History*. Princeton: Princeton
    University Press, 1995.
Toland, John. *In Mortal Combat: Korea, 1950–1953*. New York: Morrow, 1991.
Tomedi, Rudy. *An Oral History of the Korean War*. New York: Wiley, 1993.
Tucker, Spencer C., ed. *Encyclopedia of the Korean War*. Santa Barbara, CA: ABC-
    CLIO, 2000.

US Marine Corps in the Korean War

Alexander, Joseph H. *A Fellowship of Valor: The Battle History of the United States
    Marines*. New York: Harper-Collins, 1997.
Alexander, Joseph H. *Battle of the Barricades: U.S. Marines in the Recapture of Seoul*.
    Washington, DC: History and Museum Division, U.S. Marine Corps, 2000.
Ballenger, Lee. *The Outpost War: U.S. Marines in Korea, 1952*. Washington, DC:
    Potomac, 2005.
Bartlett, Merrill, and Jack Sweetman. *Leathernecks: An Illustrated History of the United
    States Marine Corps*. Annapolis, MD: Naval Institute Press. 2008.
Berry, Henry. *Hey Mac, Where Ya Been? A Collection of Memories of Marines from the
    Korean War*. New York: St. Martin's, 1988
Brown, Ronald J. *A Few Good Men: The Story of the Fighting Fifth Marines*. Novato, CA:
    Presidio, 2001.
Cerasini, Marc. *Heroes: U.S. Marine Corps Medal of Honor Winners*. New York:
    Berkley, 2002.
Chapin, John C. *Fire Brigade: U.S. Marines in the Pusan Perimeter*. Washington, DC:
    History and Museum Division, US Marine Corps, 2000.
Clark, Johnnie M. *Gunner's Glory: Untold Stories of Marine Machine Gunners*. New
    York: Ballantine, 2004.
Drury, Bob, and Tom Clavin. *The Last Stand of Fox Company*. New York: Atlantic
    Monthly Press, 2009.
Krulak, Victor H. *First to Fight: An Insider View of the U.S. Marine Corps*. Annapolis,
    MD: Naval Institute Press, 1984.
Meid, Pat, and James Yingling. *Operations in West Korea*. Vol. 4 of *U.S. Marine
    Operations in Korea, 1950–1953*. Washington, DC: US Marine Corps Historical
    Branch, 1972.
Millett, Allan R. *Drive North: U.S. Marines at the Punchbowl*. Washington, DC: US
    Marine Corps Historical Center, 2014.
Montross, Lynn, and Nicholas Canzona. *The Chosin Reservoir Campaign*. Vol. 3 of
    U.S. Marine Operations in Korea, 1950–1953. Washington, DC: US Marine Corps
    Historical Branch, 1957.

Montross, Lynn, and Nicholas Canzona. *The Inchon-Seoul Operation.* Vol. 2 of *U.S. Marine Operations in Korea, 1950–1953.* Washington, DC: US Marine Corps Historical Branch, 1955.

Montross, Lynn, and Nicholas Canzona. *The Pusan Perimeter.* Vol. 1 of *U.S. Marine Operations in Korea, 1950–1953.* Washington, DC: US Marine Corps Historical Branch, 1954.

Montross, Lynn, Hubard D. Kuokka, and Norman Hicks. *The East-Central Front.* Vol. 4 of *U.S. Marine Operations in Korea, 1950–1953.* Washington, DC: US Marine Corps Historical Branch, 1962.

Nalty, Bernard. *Outpost War: U.S. Marines from the Nevada Battles to the Armistice.* Washington, DC: US Marine Corps Historical Center, 2002.

Nolan, John. *The Run-Up to the Punchbowl: A Memoir of the Korean War, 1951.* Bloomington, IN: Xlibris, 2006.

Russ, Martin. *Breakout: The Chosin Reservoir Campaign, Korea 1950.* New York: Penguin, 2000.

Simmons, Edwin Howard. *Frozen Chosin: U.S. Marines at the Changjin Reservoir.* Washington, DC: US Marine Corps Historical Center, 2002.

Sides, Hampton. *On Desperate Ground: The Marines at the Reservoir, the Korean War's Greatest Battle.* New York: Doubleday, 2018.

Warren, James. *American Spartans—The U.S. Marines: A Combat History from Iwo Jima to Iraq.* New York: Free Press, 2005.

Biographies, Special Studies, and Personal Accounts of the Korean War

Acheson, Dean. *Present at the Creation: My Years in the State Department.* New York: Norton, 1969.

Acheson, Dean. *The Korean War.* New York: Norton, 1971.

Clark, Mark W. *From the Danube to the Yalu.* New York: Harper, 1954.

Collins, J. Lawton. *War in Peacetime: The History and Lessons of Korea.* New York: Houghton Mifflin, 1969.

Dean, William F. *General Dean's Story.* New York: Viking, 1954.

Halberstam, David. *The Coldest Winter: America and the Korean War.* Westport, CT: Hyperion, 2007.

Halberstam, David. *The Fifties.* New York: Villard, 1993.

Hamby, Alonzo L. *Man of the People: The Life of Harry S. Truman.* New York: Oxford University Press, 1995.

Higgins, Marguerite. *War in Korea: The Report of a Woman Combat Correspondent.* New York: Doubleday, 1951.

Higgins, Trumbull. *Korea and the Fall of MacArthur.* New York: Oxford University Press, 1966.

James, D. Clayton. *The Years of MacArthur.* Vol. 3, *Triumph and Disaster, 1945–1964.* Boston: Houghton Mifflin, 1985.

MacArthur, Douglas. *Reminiscences.* New York: McGraw-Hill, 1964.

Maihafer, Harry James. *From the Hudson to the Yalu: West Point '49 in the Korean War.*
     College Station: Texas A&M University Press, 1993.

Marshall, S. L. A. *The River and the Gauntlet.* Alexandria, VA: Time-Life Books, 1953.

McCullough, David. *Truman.* New York: Simon & Schuster, 1992.

Miller, Merle. *Plain Speaking: An Oral Biography of Harry S. Truman.* New York:
     Berkley, 1974.

Nicholson, Jim. *George-3-7th Marines: A Brief Glimpse through Time of a Group of
     Young Marines.* 2nd ed. Dallas, TX: Brown Books, 2015.

Oliver, Robert T. *A History of the Korean People in Modern Times: 1800 to the Present.*
     Newark: University of Delaware Press, 1993.

Patch, Nathanial. "Blue Star Turned to Gold: The Loss of Ens. Jesse L. Brown."
     Rediscovering Black History, March 23, 2023. https://rediscovering-black-history
     .blogs.archives.gov/2023/03/23/blue-star-turned-to-gold-the-loss-of-ens-jesse-l
     -brown/.

Pierpaoli, Paul G., Jr. *Truman and Korea: The Political Culture of the Early Cold War.*
     Columbia: University of Missouri Press, 1999.

Ridgway, Matthew W. *The Korean War.* Garden City, NY: Doubleday, 1967.

Rishell, Lyle. *With a Black Platoon in Combat: A Year in Korea.* College Station: Texas
     A&M University Press, 1993.

Roskey, William. *Koje Island: The 1952 Korean Hostage Crisis.* Arlington, VA: Institute of
     Land Warfare, Association of the US Army, 1994.

Spanier, John W. *The Truman-MacArthur Controversy and the Korean War.* New York:
     Norton, 1965.

Truman, Harry S. *Memoirs.* 2 vols. Garden City, NY: Doubleday, 1958.

Truman, Harry S. *Off the Record: The Private Papers of Harry S. Truman.* Edited by
     Robert H. Ferrell. New York: Harper & Row, 1980.

Whelan, Richard. *Drawing the Line: The Korean War, 1950–1953.* Boston: Little,
     Brown, 1990.

Weintraub, Stanley. *War in the Wards: Korea's Unknown Battle in a Prisoner-of-War
     Hospital Group.* San Rafael, CA: Presidio, 1976.

Other Works

Doyle, Robert C. *The Enemy in Our Hands: America's Treatment of Enemy Prisoners
     of War, from the Revolution to the War on Terror.* Lexington: University Press of
     Kentucky, 2010.

Howell, Walter. *Town and Gown: The Saga of Clinton and Mississippi College.* Saline, MI:
     McNaughton & Gunn, 2014.

Kurzman, Dan. *Kishi and Japan: The Search for the Sun.* New York: Obolensky, 1960.

Lange, Alan, and Tom Dawson. *Kings of Tort.* Battle Ground, WA: Pediment, 2009.

Measels, Sandra. *Branch Baptist Church: Celebrating the First One Hundred Years
     in Scott County, Mississippi, 1909–2009.* Morton, MS: Branch Baptist Church
     Publishing, 2015.

Oberdorfer, Don. *The Two Koreas: A Contemporary History*. Reading, MA: Addison-Wesley, 1997.

Reischauer, Edwin. *The Japanese Today: Change and Continuity*. Cambridge: Belknap Press of Harvard University Press, 1988.

Sullivan, Charles L., and Bourbon Hughes. *Valor Remembered: War Dead of the State of Mississippi*. Perkinston: Mississippi Gulf Coast Community College Press, 1996.

Tharp, Jacque, ed. *For Those Who Served: Clintonians in the U.S. Military*. Clinton, MS: Clinton Visitors Center, 2012.

Interviews by Author

Bradley, Laura Lipsey, 2010.

Demoney, Betty Jo Connolly Smith, May–July 2018.

King, Bettye Shores, January 15, 2018.

King, George Waller, January 2018–April 2019.

McMahon, Tom, 2018.

Nicholson, Jim, 2023.

Ratliff, Elwood, January 20, 2018.

INDEX

References to illustrations appear in **bold**.

ABOUT THE AUTHOR

Walter Howell is a former mayor of Clinton, Mississippi, and he was appointed city historian in 2013. He is a former professor of history at Mississippi College and author of *Town and Gown: The Saga of Clinton and Mississippi College* and *Preachers and the People Called Methodists in Clinton, Mississippi Since 1831.*